DIVINE HUMILITY

DIVINE HUMILITY
God's Morally Perfect Being

MATTHEW A. WILCOXEN

BAYLOR UNIVERSITY PRESS

Cover Design by Savanah N. Landerholm
Book Design by Scribe Inc.

The Library of Congress has cataloged this book under ISBN
978-1-4813-0998-1.

Printed in the United States of America on acid-free paper with a minimum
of thirty percent recycled content.

For Annie
quia respexit humilitatem ancillae suae

CONTENTS

ACKNOWLEDGMENTS

However small a contribution the present work might make to the discipline of Christian theology, it is a significant achievement for me personally. As such, it manifests the humility of God displayed toward me through so many other people.

I want to express my gratitude in particular to Mickey Klink, Thomas Swanton, Bob Covolo, Steve Wright, Janice McRandal, Ian Packer, Jeff Aernie, Paul Yeates, David Sandifer, Dan Anderson, Bruce Pollard, Dan Claire, and Lou Huesmann. In one way or another, each of them has contributed significant levels of companionship, encouragement, and personal support over the past several years.

Among those who interacted with this book directly, Benjamin Myers stands above the rest. This book started as a doctoral thesis under his supervision, and he pushed me to become a more rigorous theologian, a more charitable reader, and a much better writer. I am also thankful for the critical feedback of Oliver Crisp, Michael Allen, Katherine Sonderegger, and Matthew Levering. I know I have not addressed their concerns to their complete satisfaction, but the work is better nonetheless for their help.

I am profoundly thankful to Carey Newman, the director of Baylor University Press, for his enthusiastic and cheerful support for this project. Editing the manuscript under the patient tutelage of Carey and assistant editor Cade Jarrell was one of the most instructive writing experiences I have ever had.

Throughout every stage of research, I was involved in vibrant Christian communities: Grace Brethren Church in Long Beach, California; Trinity Chapel at Macquarie University and All Saints' Anglican Church, both in Sydney, Australia; and the Church of the Resurrection in Washington, D.C. These communities taught me the practices of faith that respond, and correspond, to the humility of God.

I have dedicated this work to my wife, Annie. She embodies, more than anyone I know, the greatness that is humility. This book would not have been possible without her many cheerful sacrifices on my behalf.

MAW
Washington, D.C.
Advent, 2018

INTRODUCTION

The doctrine of God should go beyond merely collecting and categorizing those things that are attributed to God in the pages of Scripture. It ought to do more than merely rehearse the deliverances of the great theologians of times past. These are necessary undertakings for all who would think and write about God, no doubt, but the goal of systematic theology is to build constructively on the biblical and theological foundations that have been laid. As John Webster writes, the vocation of Christian dogmatics is to worship God "by crafting concepts to turn the mind to the divine splendor."[1] Since they aim to be communicative tools of the knowledge of God, such concepts in Christian theology must be crafted carefully and evaluated as to their coherence with holy writ, their place within the matrix of creedal dogma, their basic logical consistency, and their ability to solve or ameliorate existing conceptual difficulties within the theological tradition or some substratum thereof. To the degree that they fulfill these criteria, theological concepts can be offered to the Christian community as what Webster calls "instruments for spiritual apprehension," instruments that are to be used in Christian thought, speech, and prayer.[2] Of course, the relation between concepts and prayer is not unidirectional; theologians have long recognized the fact that what they are engaged in is a conceptual development of an apprehension that is already embedded in the spiritual life of the Christian faith: *lex orandi, lex credendi.*

1

The words that stayed with me as I wrote this book are from Thomas Cranmer's famous "Prayer of Humble Access": "We are not worthy so much as to gather up the crumbs under thy table. But thou art the same Lord whose property is always to have mercy." How serious is one to take the words of this Anglican prayer? Does it encapsulate some metaphysical truth of the gospel, or is it mere rhetorical flourish? In the Australian prayer book from which I first prayed these words, the term "nature" is substituted for "property." Is it God's "nature," his very being, to condescend to creatures who, being both finite and sinful, are doubly unworthy? Is this God's nature "always"—that is, from all eternity? Is it possible to attribute "mercy" to the eternal being of God while preserving the non-negotiable self-existence of God? If the answer to this cluster of questions is yes, then the next question is how this might be accomplished conceptually. This book argues that it is possible to answer these questions in the affirmative and attempts to show just how one might give this answer, namely by taking the ethical concept of humility to be an attribute of God, a divine perfection.

A doctrine of divine humility will strike some as novel, and for good reason. The concept of humility does not make its way into, for example, Thomas Aquinas' catalogue of divine attributes. Nor is it found explicitly in any of the handbooks of dogmatics produced in the Middle Ages or in the wake of the Reformation. Put simply: stating that God, in his eternal being, is humble has not been the majority viewpoint. However, many of the most influential theological movements of the past century could rightly be seen as efforts to articulate an account of divine humility. One thinks here of kenotic theologians, the radical ontological Christocentrism awakened by Karl Barth, open theism, and even process theology. Motivated in various ways by a concern about a cleavage between who God is in himself and who he is for us, these various movements have proposed metaphysical revisions, some of them quite radical.

The account of divine humility offered in this book straddles the divide between the classical conceptions of the divine being and some of the modern theological movements noted in the previous paragraph. On the one hand, the argument that proceeds through the book attempts to develop an account of divine humility out of the resources of the doctrines of, for instance, simplicity, aseity, and eternality, as well

as by way of traditional distinctions made in trinitarian and christological theology. At the same time, divine humility is developed from
within these classical resources as an attempt to answer at least some
concerns that are distinct to modern theologians. The resultant doctrine of divine humility is not novel, properly speaking. Instead, it is
the fresh discovery of something that has lain beneath the surface all
along. Just as the foundation of a building is usually only considered
when the structure is challenged in some way, so, too, divine humility
is uncovered in response to a philosophical and theological crisis.

Part of the context into which systematic theology speaks today is
the thought-world bequeathed by Enlightenment philosophy and its
progeny, postmodernism. In this intellectual milieu, the very possibility
of a conceptual representation of God is called into question. Speaking
of God's being is met with the allegation of projection. For this reason,
chapter 1 of this book takes up the question of whether, and in what
manner, one can speak of God's being at all. The chapter approaches
this question by way of what Alasdair MacIntyre calls a "conflict
of traditions," examining Martin Heidegger's influential and representative critique of ontotheology, and concluding that the critique is
questionable in relation to its own rationalist Enlightenment tradition,
let alone for the tradition of inquiry that is Christian theology. Therefore, Christian attempts to conceive of God on these terms—that is,
without being—are, the chapter argues, fundamentally flawed. Jean-
Luc Marion is a representative case. What is required to envision a
different theological possibility is a better grasp of how concepts work.
Kevin Hector is helpful here. Hector reminds us that concepts are not
fixed containers projected on to objects but, rather, open-ended ways
of naming generated in the context of sociolinguistic communities in
their interactions with concrete realities in the world. And since God
is known only through his works *pro nobis*, it is to these that we must
look for knowledge of his eternal life *in se*. With this, Hector gestures toward the fact that it is impossible to develop concepts of God's
"perfect being" that are not already personal and moral—outwardly
oriented—through and through.

Divine humility is the concept I propose for expressing the fact
that God's perfect being is always and already oriented toward his
creature. Humility serves to express the interrelation between the

attributes of God's intrinsic being and his actions *ad extra*. Chapter 2, therefore, seeks to define humility. Humility comes down to modern Christian theology with two millennia worth of accretions. The concept is polythetic, open to a range of possible meanings, some of which may be morally objectionable, or simply unsuitable for application to God. The chapter begins, therefore, with a set of analytic definitions of humility and proceeds to use this as a lens with which to view the concept's history through the moral and intellectual traditions in which it lives. In Aristotle's virtue ethics, if humility means mere lowliness and servility, it has no place and would, in fact, be morally objectionable. The chief virtue in Aristotle is that of greatness—magnanimity. Versions of this rejected definition of humility are assumed in the protests of various modern thinkers such as Nietzsche, Hume, and even the theologian Valerie Saiving Goldstein. However, these objections fail to take adequate stock of the way humility is defined by significant strands of the Christian tradition. Taking their cue from the incarnation of Christ, influential Christian voices like Athanasius, Augustine, and Basil portray humility as itself a species of magnanimity; humility is true greatness, "the virtue of virtues." The essence of humility here is the use of one's strength—and not the loss thereof—for the sake of the true *polis*, the city of God. One's greatness increases as it is used to elevate others. In this way, humility brings with it implications of authority and greatness. I argue that only when the concept of humility is cut off from this native soil can the concept be written off as mere lowliness. Defined within this social vision, however, humility is a concept that is eligible for application not only to Christ in his human nature, but even more so to Christ in his divine nature.

It is widely known that humility is a central concept in Augustine's soteriology and in his moral theory, but Augustine goes even further than this, at points attributing humility to God himself. Augustine has a nascent doctrine of divine humility, which I explore in chapter 3. For Augustine, the doctrine of divine humility is generated by a recurring theological tension that emerges from scriptural exegesis—the tension between God *in se* and God *pro nobis*. This is seen specifically in the treatment of three touchstone passages that manifest this tension in different ways. In Exodus 3:14-15 Augustine finds this tension in the interplay of the "name of being" and the "name of mercy"; the link between the two is the mystery of God's humility. He sees the tension again in John 5:19-30 as he considers the unified action of the Holy Trinity in relation to the appropriation of operations to the persons in the economy. Sound theological reasoning about the Johannine text causes him to conclude that the demonstration of humility in Christ is a manifestation of the unified agency of God, rather than something that can be predicated either of the Son alone or of the human nature of Christ alone. In his exegesis of Philippians 2:6-7, Augustine attempts to make sense of how God communicates his divine nature through the human nature of Christ, with each nature retaining its integrity. The question here is how to affirm the immutable God's presence in the mutable world of creation. Augustine answers by offering a christological formulation (the *forma dei/forma servi* schema) wherein God communicates his ontological perfection by way of his moral blessedness. Thus, whether Augustine is engaged in an analysis of the divine names, a discussion of the trinitarian processions, or the parsing of christological dogma, he finds himself grappling with the tension between God's life *in se* and the manifestation of that life *pro nobis*. At every stop along the way, Augustine refuses to resolve this tension, but instead resorts to the concept of humility. Nonetheless, he does not spell out with precision what it would mean doctrinally to attribute humility to God.

In chapter 4 I turn to a theologian who is far from ambiguous in articulating a version of divine humility. In the fourth volume of his *Church Dogmatics*, Karl Barth makes the claim that the humility shown by Christ in the work of redemption is an eternal attribute of the divine being. Specifically, Barth concludes that obedience itself is an eternal, inter-trinitarian reality. The Father commands, the Son obeys, and the Spirit acts in mutual affirmation. Barth recognizes the rather stunning novelty of this formulation. There are two theological procedures that lead Barth to this point, and both are closely linked to Barth's ontology, which subordinates the concept of being to that of act. First, Barth employs a particular mode of transcendentalism in his theology, wherein the economic works have a structure sufficient to mirror the immanent being of God without conceptual qualification from outside the event of revelation itself. God is act—the same act in eternity that he is in the economy. Second, Barth sees the act that is

God in fundamentally voluntaristic terms; God is his eternal decision to be the God of the gospel, Jesus Christ. When divine humility is conceived on these grounds, serious doctrinal problems emerge. The relation of command and obedience requires two volitional centers, and Barth's transcendentalist approach leads him to posit something akin to two wills in God's eternal being. Barth knows this is heresy if taken straightforwardly and so explains this feature by reference to the trinitarian relations; he takes the will as a feature of the hypostasis rather than a feature of God's being. This move is problematic not only for the doctrine of the Trinity, but in that it would result inevitably in a monothelite Christology. Thus, while Barth, by linking God's divine being with his redemptive work, offers a model for what it means to attribute humility to God, the theological price to pay for this achievement is simply too high. Another way forward must be sought if a doctrine of divine humility is to be viable.

Katherine Sonderegger's recently published doctrine of God is a morally perfect being theology. Her stated aim therein is to "ethicize" the doctrine of God's being. She wants to conceptualize the intrinsically moral nature of God's being, and she does this specifically through a doctrine of divine humility. Sonderegger analyzes the canonically foundational act of God's revelation at Horeb and posits what she calls "theological compatibilism." This is a descriptive epistemology wherein God himself, in his very ineffable self-existence, dwells in creaturely reality and yet remains unknowable not because he is distant, but because he is humbly present to the creature as all-surpassing light. The dogmatic, ontological basis of God's nearness to creation is God's holy humility, Sonderegger's gloss for the traditional perfection of omnipotence. In reframing divine omnipotence in terms of humility, Sonderegger undertakes to consider the power that God is as neither that of sheer willing nor in terms of absolute cause. Instead, she develops the concept of energy as most helpful for capturing the fact that, in the personal, moral power that is God in divine humility, the objective and subjective, the divine being and the divine will, are compatibly intertwined. However, this version of divine humility only serves to intensify, and not to solve, the question of whether God could have done otherwise than create and redeem his creatures. Sonderegger responds by saying that the antinomy of counterfactual questions like this is itself a communication of divine humility to the creature. The questions correspond to something fundamental in God himself, something that cannot be penetrated behind or solved; they bring us to the high point of theological mystery. For Sonderegger, the only possible answer to the question of how God's eternal being relates to his turning toward creatures—the only answer to *Cur Deus Homo*—is that it is "fitting" to God to do this because he simply is this morally perfect being that is divine humility. This is a considerable advance beyond some of the more problematic aspects of Barth's account.

In sum, by examining the role of metaphysical concepts in theology, by exploring the concept of humility as a candidate for application to God's being, and by engaging in an extended dialogue with three theologians who have, in various ways, employed the concept of humility in their understanding of God, I make the central contention that humility not only can, but should, serve an important function in the Christian doctrine of God, because humility is a divine attribute. Humility, properly understood, suffices as a theological answer to the conceptual problem of the relation between the immanent and economic realities of the triune God. This is not to say that humility is an answer in the sense of an "explanation." Instead, with the statement of divine humility, a theological, dogmatic statement is made. By giving the name of divine humility at the point where no explanation is possible, even the high point of mystery is understood in a way that accords with the gospel.

This book is first and foremost a contribution to theology in general, and to the doctrine of God specifically. Its questions are narrowly focused on the concepts that are applied to the divine being. These concepts are important in their own right—it matters that what we predicate of God is theologically accurate, consistent, illuminating, and even beautiful. A doctrine of divine humility certainly has the potential to live up to those high expectations and to provoke the worship that is due the divine name. Whether this articulation of the doctrine of divine humility achieves all of this will only become known over time, as fellow enquirers test its arguments. My hope is that others will find what is written in this book such they would desire to extend and to improve upon it.

This work of "morally perfect being theology" is not only a study in the doctrine of God but will also prove useful in some way for Christian moral theology. The language of Christian communities is shot through with references to the need for humility, but what is meant by that term is often a truncated, internalized, and intellectualized version of the true humility that is displayed first and foremost by the God who is revealed in Christian Scripture. While there can be, of course, no straightforward transfer of a divine attribute into discussions of human virtue, perhaps a thoroughgoing doctrine of divine humility might help to rehabilitate a more empowering and transformative version of the human virtue that goes by that name.

1

MORALLY PERFECT BEING THEOLOGY

From the self-consciously trinitarian renaissance to postmodern theologies to feminist theologies to the burgeoning movement of Radical Orthodoxy, the question of whether one can speak of God's being—and, if so, how and on what basis—is a key point of contention in contemporary theology. In one sense this is to be expected. Ever since there has been something we can call "Christian theology" there have been debates about both the *who* and the *what* of God. These questions were at the heart of the christological and trinitarian debates that played out in the early centuries of the faith. Yet there are certain factors unique to the contemporary situation—certain intellectual events, arguments, theories, and thinkers that have come to exercise power over large realms of theological discourse, rendering talk of the being of God problematic. While there is no strict requirement that one run this gauntlet before speaking of God, this chapter enters the fray with the ambition of clearing the ground so that this book's positive contribution to the doctrine of God might be heard by the widest audience of contemporary Christian theologians. What is pursued in subsequent chapters is the construction of a "morally perfect being theology."

Proposing to elaborate God's life through the concept of being is already an endorsement of the claim that it is possible and, indeed, necessary, to speak of God in terms that are robustly metaphysical. Yet this claim itself has been in dispute in certain theological circles for some time. As Matthew Levering writes:

> The gauntlet thrown down by [William] James in the United States, and by Kant and Schleiermacher in Europe, has greatly influenced how Christian theologians understand theology and in particular how they understand the place of metaphysical arguments within theology. Most contemporary theologies of the triune God shy away from metaphysics as overly abstract and instead seek practical, rather than contemplative ends.[1]

What Levering has in view here is a specific, widespread strand of anti-metaphysical trinitarianism that eschews the concept of being as problematically abstract and coldly speculative, instead favoring those that are relational and practical—moral, one might say—in nature. Levering rightly notes that this anti-metaphysical trend in the doctrine of God developed under the pervasive influence of Kantian idealist epistemologies and the varieties of romanticism that run alongside them.

Indeed, the doctrine of God in the modern period unfolds in the midst of what MacIntyre calls a "conflict of traditions." This should be understood as follows. Christian theology is a tradition-constituted inquiry, an interpretive schemata that begins from its own first principles and progresses incrementally through ongoing debate and clarification. At any stage in the process, epistemic justification consists of a narration of the argument thus far, a narration that results in a restatement that more consistently follows from the tradition's first principles, and is less vulnerable to objection, than previous iterations.[2] If at some point the methods of inquiry employed by the tradition cease to enable progress and, in fact, begin only to erode previous certitudes, the tradition is thrown into "epistemological crisis." This crisis can be precipitated by the emergence of an incoherence or an unresolved question from within the tradition itself, by a substantive conflict with a rival tradition of inquiry, or by some combination of both. In any case, the crisis is an opportunity for the tradition in question to reconstitute itself by drawing upon its own resources in a conflictual, "argumentative retelling" that attempts to show its own rationality and to demonstrate the superiority of its truth-claims over against its rival.[3] If the tradition fails this test, its adherents should acknowledge the superiority of the rival tradition.[4] What is least desirable is that a tradition avoid conflict by constructing "a set of epistemological defenses which enable it to avoid being put in question or at least to avoid recognizing that it is being put in question by rival traditions."[5] In that case, the challenged tradition will be unable to vindicate either its own superiority or that of any rival.[6]

Christian theology has been grappling with an epistemological crisis since the time of the Enlightenment. It has been challenged from without by successive species of philosophical rationalism that challenge the possibility of its most fundamental claims about the nature of God and knowledge thereof. This external challenge has, in turn, led to the internal splintering of theological inquiry as theologians have sought the best way to respond. Far too often, the strategies employed have in fact been those of avoidance: whether efforts to construct a bulwark that isolates the doctrine of God from this questioning or efforts to make its theological claims fit within the rival tradition. Neither of these approaches can overcome the crisis. According to MacIntyre, what any tradition of inquiry requires in this situation is "the invention or discovery of new concepts and the framing of some new type or types of theory" that are able (1) to articulate the systematic coherence of the tradition's central beliefs, resolving to some degree problems that have otherwise seemed intractable; (2) to explain what it was that precipitated the crisis and required new resources in the first place; and (3) to demonstrate a fundamental continuity between the new conceptual structures and the tradition of inquiry thus far.[7]

The overall task of this chapter is to contribute something toward the achievement of the first criterion on behalf of the Christian doctrine of God. This is done by bringing together in the concept of divine humility two things that have largely been separated in modern theology: God as an object available to human knowledge (the question of "what," of God's being) and God as a free person who radically transcends all creaturely categories (the question of "who," of God's moral character). The third criterion is met in that this conceptual elaboration of divine humility takes place in the form of an "argumentative retelling" of, and is shown to be an immanent development from within, the tradition of Christian thought. But first, it is the task of this chapter to meet the second criterion by offering an explanation as to why the doctrine of God requires such reframing in the first place. The first section of this chapter takes up the philosophical narrative as told by Martin Heidegger. Heidegger is chosen as an exemplar of the challenge put to the doctrine of God for several reasons. First, Heidegger is situated between the most influential modern philosophers of the eighteenth and nineteenth centuries and the postmodernists of the twentieth century, representing in important ways how the latter developed in response to the ambiguities and incoherencies of the former. Second, Heidegger self-consciously sees his own thought as part of a distinctly Enlightenment tradition of inquiry in conflict with other traditions of Western thought, including Christian theology. Most importantly, Heidegger argues against the use of the concept of being in respect to God in his critique of "ontotheology," an argument that has had an outsized influence on Christian theology since the mid-twentieth century. For many, Heidegger has created an epoch, establishing the challenge to traditional metaphysics that theology must face.[8] Heidegger thus brings to light a genuine conflict of traditions. Taking MacIntyre's cue, then, the way to proceed is to articulate Heidegger's argument so that one can, first, make explicit the way this is compatible with one's own tradition of inquiry and, second, determine whether, if at all, this rival tradition can point out and explain inadequacies within one's own tradition.[9]

HEIDEGGER'S CRITIQUE OF ONTOTHEOLOGY

Martin Heidegger has been decisive in defining the terms "being" and "metaphysics" for a significant strand of contemporary theology. Of course, Heidegger's thought is not only influential in contemporary systematic theology, but his understanding of being as a temporally dynamic construct is an idea that has been taken for granted in poststructuralist, postmodernist, and deconstructionist philosophies. Yet nowhere in the vast bodies of literature dedicated to the criticism of metaphysics can one find a "careful reconstruction of the idiosyncratic understanding of metaphysics upon which Heideggerian historicity is based."[10] Ironically, Heidegger's critique of ontotheology is often presupposed but seldom deconstructed.

The term "ontotheology" was coined first by Immanuel Kant in the *Critique of Pure Reason*. Whereas "cosmotheology" attempts to prove the existence of an original being from the need for a first cause to end the infinite regress of causation, ontotheology is the attempt to prove or think this supreme being's existence through the use of concepts alone, without any aid from experience.[11] These two proofs exist alongside a third: the "physico-theological," which attempts to ground certainty regarding the existence of God in one's experience of the design of the present world. According to Kant, all three of these proofs in the end can be reduced to the *ontological*—the attempt to reason from the actuality of thought to its possibility in a supreme being.[12] For Kant, ontotheology is the epitome of all theology that proceeds as "transcendental theology." Though Kant thinks this endeavor ultimately fails in its stated aim, it is nonetheless ineradicable and does have a practical utility: by its concept of a first cause possessing freedom and intelligence, it frees reason from both theological and naturalistic fatalism.[13] Further, he says that the theological proofs can even serve the negative theological use of purifying, but only after the supreme being's existence is established on some grounds other than that of pure reason.[14]

Kant's neologism becomes for Heidegger a more expansive program. For this reason, ontotheology is almost always associated with Heidegger, though he himself stands in a tradition of critics of this so-called ontotheology, including Feuerbach, Nietzsche, Marx, Freud, and Derrida. These philosophers speak of God as a projection of human ideas and values. Their criticisms have some affinity to Kant's criticism of the proofs of God's existence; Feuerbach even invokes the term "ontotheology" in describing projection.[15] However, whereas for Kant ontotheology was one mode of thinking of God, one that belongs to dogmatic scholastic metaphysics, for Feuerbach it describes theology *simpliciter*.[16] Kant says he "had to deny knowledge in order to make room for faith."[17] For Feuerbach and the masters of suspicion, if faith has any content, then it, too, is projection.

Heidegger is aware of this wider context of ontotheological critique and sees himself as having brought it to perfection. It is not that Heidegger thinks Kant or Nietzsche did not see what he sees, but just that he sees more clearly what they "had wanted to say."[18] While Kant finds a practical utility and possibly a purifying theological function of ontotheological arguments, Heidegger sees these as the epitome and culmination of Western philosophy. For Heidegger ontotheology is equated with metaphysics, and metaphysics is grounded in a primordial, accidental error. Heidegger's narrative of ontotheology proceeds partly as a taking-apart of the history of Western philosophy and partly as a phenomenology of human existence. For Heidegger, the question that animates this history is "what is a being?" This question focuses not on the word "being" but on the copulative verb "is"; the question itself implies an attempt to come to a unified theory of things that can serve as the basis of successful predication. However, the question is ambiguous and yields a dual answer: one about a thing's *essence* and another about a thing's *existence*.[19] The former seeks to find something common to all acts of predication and corresponds to ontology. The latter looks for the conditions of possibility of predication and corresponds to theology.[20] Metaphysics is the attempt to come up with an ultimate principle that can unite both aspects of theology and ontology in one.[21]

Heidegger says the attempt by Western metaphysics to find its basis in an uncaused cause has been exposed definitively by Kant; Nietzsche has pointed out what Kant has accomplished: the God of ontotheology is dead.[22] Heidegger, however, sees Nietzsche as merely replacing one form of nihilism with another.[23] In fact, Heidegger thinks that Nietzsche does not escape from "thinking the same"— something that has been present in Western thought since at least Aristotle.[24] "The same" refers to a relation of with-ness, a synthesis of two things into a unity in which the difference does not disappear.[25] In other words, from Aristotle to Nietzsche, all of Western metaphysics retains its ontotheological character. Heidegger's claim here is either an indefensible a priori structure of thinking, or else it is something that must be accounted for historically. Heidegger needs to account for how these two ways of asking about being—the questions of essence and existence—were intertwined, and whether such an intertwining was necessary.[26] The answer to this question of intertwining begins, for Heidegger, with Thales and Anaximander, who split something primordial and unified into the two questions of essence and existence, ontology and theology.[27] This split was then, beginning with Aristotle, unified in an ontotheological formulation. It was with

Aristotle's formulation of *prōte* and *deutera ousia* that Western metaphysics becomes inscribed with the essence and existence distinction Heidegger thinks is so fateful.[28]

As for the question of whether or not this primordial split, located historically in Thales and Anaximander, was necessary, Heidegger says no. He does so on the basis of a primordial speculation, reasoning that the problem occurs when the dynamic emergence (or temporality) of being—the coming into being and passing away—is conceptually frozen into a notion of permanent presence.[29] Being mistakenly comes to be seen as a substance and the wild goose chase of Western metaphysics ensues. Throughout his work, Heidegger seeks to remove this distraction of substance and refocus human thinking on the phenomenon of temporal dynamism. "What is being?" is ultimately a question about the essence of the one asking; the real question, underneath it, is "who am I?" Heidegger's philosophy turns this question back at the questioner and poses it in the future tense—"who will you be?"

Heidegger tells the story of Western human thought falling into an unnecessary primordial error that led to a long history of philosophy as ontotheology. This philosophical narrative is not read off the surface of the history of Western philosophy, but rather comes as the outworking of Heidegger's own phenomenology of human existence that he spelled out in *Being and Time* and that he attempted to substantiate through his subsequent reading of Kant.[30] This analysis of Heidegger's argument will take these two works in reverse order.

Heidegger's Reading of Kant

Heidegger's *Kantbuch* is a careful, though uniquely Heideggerian, reading of *The Critique of Pure Reason*. Heidegger sees Kant raising the fact that metaphysics names not a solution, but a problem.[31] By focusing on the possibility of synthetic a priori judgments, Kant shows himself to be engaging not in epistemology proper, but in the human ontology that must necessarily ground epistemology.[32] According to Heidegger, Kant's work places knowledge at the level of "intuition," with "thinking" something that comes along afterward, in the service of intuition, and that is necessary only because intuition is finite.[33] Intuition is immediate, but knowledge is mediate; knowledge requires conceptual representations of the thing that produces the intuition.[34] It is here that Heidegger finds the reason for the split between the *noumena* and the *phenomena*. The fact that all our representations are *phenomena* points up the fact that all finite knowledge is mediate.[35] There is a promising, unexplored ambiguity in Kant that Heidegger will exploit: the notion that intuition and knowledge, which come from sensibility and understanding, may "spring forth from a common, but to us unknown root." Heidegger says that Kant's project therefore functions as a pointer to this root that remains unknown for Kant.[36] This unknown root is what Heidegger calls "fundamental ontology"— the primordial unity of human beings.

According to Heidegger, the gesture toward a fundamental ontology occurs in stages throughout *The Critique of Pure Reason*. First is the isolation of space and time as "pure intuitions." Kant is especially insightful, Heidegger says, in that he provides some indication of the preeminence of time over space; time is an "essential bit of pure ontological knowledge." Heidegger thinks this is the attainment of ontology in incipient form, though he sees Kant as quickly losing track of the insight.[37] Kant's analysis of "pure thinking," Heidegger says, only confirms that all conceptual representation is rooted in the intuition.[38] In the second stage, Heidegger sees Kant demonstrating the essential unity of pure knowledge. Kant locates the power of unification or synthesis in the "imagination."[39] Thus synthesis is not something that comes about ex post facto or as a second moment; rather, the unity of knowledge is primordial. In the third stage, Heidegger's own agenda starts shining through even more as he breaks from step-by-step analysis when it comes to Kant's "Transcendental Deduction" (sections 16–18). His aim is to show how, in the first edition of *The Critique of Pure Reason* anyway, that what is primarily at issue is the knowing subject being turned toward an object. More specifically, this section asks about the possibility of this turning-toward (or what Heidegger calls "transcendence").[40] Heidegger's point revolves around the idea that the unifying tendencies Kant finds in the operations of reason must themselves presuppose some fundamental unity that is held in advance. Heidegger sees this pointing back to the grounding of all intuition and knowledge in the "transcendental power of imagination."[41] As Heidegger has it, the fourth stage of Kant's ground-laying is the development of the "transcendental schematism." All conceptual representation is schematism, Kant says: the movement from a particular thing perceived (e.g., a house) to the feeling that there must be a general category (e.g., house-ness). Heidegger reasons that if such schematizing is the essence of finite knowledge, and if finitude is necessarily a structure of transcendence, then there must be a transcendental schematism—a possibility of conceptual schematism in the knower's own structure of transcendence.[42] Heidegger argues that this transcendental schematism has, in the end, one pure image in which it is rooted—time.[43] Even the category of "substance" is dependent upon time.[44] In the fifth and final section, Heidegger reads Kant as locating all possible experience and knowledge in the ecstatic-horizontal structure of transcendence.[45] This is true "ontological knowledge" to the extent that it is seen that this structure of transcendence is the "original truth." If only Kant's ontology will grasp itself as providing such ontological knowledge "then the expression 'ontology' will have been given its true essence for the first time."[46]

Heidegger's aim is not necessarily to bring out of *The Critique of Pure Reason* "what is said in uttered propositions" but rather what lies "before our eyes as still unsaid, in and through what has been said."[47] Again, Heidegger is after what Kant "had wanted to say." Heidegger can sum up "the concealed inner passion" of *The Critique of Pure Reason* in this way:

> Kant's laying of the ground for metaphysics leads to the transcendental power of imagination. This is the root of both stems, sensibility and understanding. As such, it makes possible the original unity of ontological synthesis. This root, however, is rooted in original time. The original ground which becomes manifest in the ground-laying is time.[48]

The Critique of Pure Reason has raised the problem of the ground-laying of metaphysics. Heidegger sees himself as going one further step backward in his own *Being and Time*, asking the grounding question only pointed to by Kant's grounding question.[49] By retrieving hidden possibilities, Heidegger picks up the baton of the transformation of *Metaphysica Generalis* (ontology). When this "ground upon which traditional metaphysics is built is shaken . . . the edifice of *Metaphysica*

Specialis [which has its highest end in natural theology] begins to totter."[50]

Ultimately, Heidegger's transformation of the traditional ontology is not destruction from within—as if the ideas of Western philosophical history deconstruct themselves—but rather the discovery of a primordial unity in the phenomenological analysis of the human subject. Here the meaning of "being in general" is already comprehended in the attempt at a "fundamental ontology" through the analysis of the temporal structure of the human being. To see the way the *metaphysica generalis* of *Dasein* limits the possibilities of a *metaphysica specialis*, we turn to the movement of the two divisions of *Being and Time*.

Heidegger's Being and Time

In the first division of *Being and Time*, which Heidegger calls "preparatory," he argues that the way *Dasein* comports itself toward the world reveals its fundamental descriptive characteristic to be "care" (*Sorge*). This is the basic determination that founds all other ways in which *Dasein* is revealed: "such as will, wish, addiction, and urge." This analytic of *Dasein* as care lays the ground for the "problematic of fundamental ontology—*the question of the meaning of Being in general*."[51] Even in the preparatory work, Heidegger says, the answer to this greater question is already comprehended. This is the hermeneutical circle of ontology. "The 'circle' in understanding belongs to the structure of meaning, and the latter phenomenon is already rooted in the existential constitution of Dasein."[52] This existential constitution of care—and the clue to the answer of our question about the meaning of being—is disclosed by the anxiety of *Dasein*.[53]

Heidegger says that anxiety is essentially definable as *Dasein's* attempt to "flee in the face of itself."[54] This is ascertainable through the way *Dasein* falls into the "they" and allows itself to be absorbed into objects of its concern.[55] When *Dasein* is denied these possibilities of absorption it enters a state of anxiety. Anxiety is different from fear, which is always fear of a definite thing. "That in the face of which one is anxious is completely indefinite. . . . What oppresses us is not this or that, nor is it the summation of everything present-at-hand . . . it is the world itself." After the anxiety has subsided we can say "it was nothing."[56] Thus Heidegger infers that, when stripped from all our absorptions, the world is "nothing" to us. In this, our most primordial state, we feel our "homelessness" (*Befindlichkeit*).[57] Far from an alien intrusion upon one's felicity, anxiety reveals the possibility of authentic existence.[58]

What anxiety reveals is the nature of *Dasein* as temporality; this was confirmed in Heidegger's reading of Kant in which the a priori of *time* points to the basis of fundamental ontology. *Dasein* is temporality: always "beyond itself," concerned with the potential for what it might be. It is a *being-ahead-of-itself*.[59] For Heidegger, the fundamental ontology that will be the basis for all other knowledge of the world and all other statements of predication is this, the temporal constitution of the human person.

In the first division, Heidegger discusses the phenomenologically ascertained concern of *Dasein* for its own being; being is itself a question the subject anxiously asks. In the second division ("Dasein and Temporality") he turns to answer the question. What *Dasein* longs for is its own being. By Heidegger's lights, this must mean that it already has access to this being in some fashion. Something quite like the classic paradox of inquiry is at play here.[60] So while the being of *Dasein* in its care has been called "potentiality-for-being," this potentiality is rooted in *Dasein's* "being-a-whole." Heidegger seeks a way to make this wholeness of being appear.[61] The problem at this point is that *Dasein* has been defined essentially by "care" in the sense of a "being-ahead-of-itself." *Per definitionem*, therefore, "there is *constantly something still to be settled.*"[62] The moment that a human person reaches the point of wholeness, there is nothing still outstanding, nothing still to be settled. At this point it is simply no-longer-*Dasein*. This point is, of course, death.

Despite the fact that one cannot experience death as an event, it represents the possibility of wholeness. "Death is the possibility of the absolute impossibility of Dasein."[63] The absolute impossibility of *Dasein* is the "being-a-whole." It is an absolute impossibility because it is something that we cannot actually possess. Death, however, as the concept of the subject's end, reveals this in fact to be a possibility.[64] Death is a certainty, a possibility that is "not to be outstripped," and as such allows for being to be taken as a whole in advance.[65] It is only against this background of "being-as-a-whole" that one can comport oneself toward anything at all; one's existence as the subject of possibilities is predicated on the prior basis of finitude.[66] Essentially, the possibility of wholeness, which is grasped proleptically in the certainty of death, is the ground of existence as care. As one anticipates the possibility of the wholeness of being, one "temporalizes," or becomes "futural." The existential movement toward this possibility is what creates time. The connection between temporality and care is finally drawn: "*Temporality reveals itself as the meaning of authentic care.*"[67] But this should not be taken to mean that care is the basis for temporality, for in the next breath Heidegger says that "*the primordial unity of the structure of care lies in temporality.*"[68] The relation between the two is equiprimordial.

Heidegger puts forward this work as an uncovering of the true structure of being. The traditional attempts to ask and answer the question of being by locating a substratum (a "substance") or by finding the ground of being in something like "being itself" are merely evasions; these distract from the real question—the subject's self-concern. Genuine existential questions are thus what really lie at the bottom of our quest for essences. By destroying the distraction of essence, Heidegger believes he has made space to once again discover authentic existence.

Evaluation

Heidegger's thought is argumentative narration within the Enlightenment tradition. The first principle of this tradition is the absolute autonomy of an individual's faculty of reason. Within this tradition, the problem of skepticism quickly emerges, as Hume demonstrates the inherent uncertainty of universal concepts such as causation, founded as they are in our finite experience of empirical correlations. Kant proposes a solution to Hume's skepticism: the attempt to show that reason itself comes already equipped with certain synthetic concepts by which it organizes the raw material of sense impressions. But this solution, in turn, generates a problem of its own: that of the relation between one's conceptual representation of things (*phenomena*) and the nature of things in themselves (*noumena*). In other words, the potential for skepticism is transferred to a new register: now, the question is whether one's rational knowledge has any take on external reality—whether one can know the essences of things. Heidegger's response is to draw on Kant's own philosophy to claim that one can know and, in fact, determine, the essence of the one thing that matters most—one's own existence. The question of essences of other things is an evasion of one's fundamental responsibility—a moral ought—to enact authentic existence. The question of the essence of God is, then, this moral evasion writ large.

Using the rubric provided by MacIntyre, it is possible to provide a summary evaluation of Heidegger's response to the epistemological crisis of the Enlightenment. First, Heidegger (1) addresses the threat to the systematic coherence of the Enlightenment tradition. This threat is an intractable skepticism that seems only to be transferred from one location to another in the tradition of inquiry. Heidegger's procedure, for all its complexity, amounts simply to denying the validity of the problem. He contends that the real question that reason is concerned with is not the essence of things (metaphysics), but one's own existence. Next, Heidegger (2) purports to explain how the problem of seeking metaphysical knowledge arose in the first place. Here he reaches all the way back to the beginning of recorded philosophy, to Thales and Anaximander, and says that these thinkers broke the question of authentic existence into two separate questions: essence and existence. Heidegger's interpretation begs the question, merely assuming his own account of fundamental ontology. Finally, Heidegger (3) shows the continuity of his own solution with the Enlightenment tradition and the older metaphysical tradition by drawing his ontological concepts from thinkers ranging from Aristotle to Augustine to Kant. Yet, as Heidegger himself sometimes lets on, this exegesis of the tradition is principally concerned with finding within it what can be wrested out of context for his own purposes. Thus, while Heidegger correctly identifies a problem within the Enlightenment tradition, his solution (1) is to deny the validity of the problem and shift the discussion. His explanation for how the problem arose (2) is historically dubious and begs the question. Finally, Heidegger's implicit claim that his solution is in substantial continuity with the tradition of inquiry (3) is at best highly debatable.

The Heideggerian critique of ontotheology is an important part of the Enlightenment's tradition of inquiry. Yet, as the analysis above shows, Heidegger is unable to resolve in any meaningful way the basic problem generated by the tradition's central commitment to the autonomy of the individual's faculty of reason. Thus, Heidegger's position that metaphysics is problematic, and that it is a category error to speak of God's being, is ultimately unconvincing, especially for one outside this tradition of inquiry. Nonetheless, there are those who have attempted to do Christian theology within the anti-metaphysical boundaries set by Heidegger. One influential exemplar warrants particular consideration.

LOVE OVER BEING: JEAN-LUC MARION

Jean-Luc Marion represents one of the most influential attempts to do Christian theology in the wake of Heidegger. Marion is not uncritical of Heidegger's philosophy, but the critiques he makes are largely immanent critiques; he works within a framework that is basically Heideggerian. Given his assumption that describing God as a being (even a supreme being) is to fit God into an anthropological category, Marion writes that his goal is "to render problematic that which seems obvious about which the philosophers descending from metaphysics agree with the theologians descending from Neo-Thomism: God, before all else, has to be."[69] On the constructive side, Marion wants to understand God under the rubric of "charity": "And what if God did not have first to be, since he loved us first, when we were not? And what if, to envisage him, we did not have to wait from within the horizon of Being, but rather transgress ourselves in risking to love love."[70] God does not dwell "within the domain of Being" and so "comes to us and in us as a gift."[71] It will be helpful to tarry for a while both with what Marion is rejecting (theologies of "being") and what Marion is proposing (a certain theology of self-giving).

From Metaphysical Idols to Moral Icons

For Marion, there are two ways that one can comport oneself toward reality. The first is represented in the phenomenon of idolatry and the latter in the phenomenon of iconography. While Western people lack the aesthetic imagination for physical idols, the same proclivity is seen in the use of metaphysical concepts. Any concept thought to apply to

God displays the same phenomenon as the idol: "the measure of the concept comes not from God but from the aim of the gaze."[72] But this is not the only possibility—one can comport oneself toward ultimate reality by way of an icon. The icon renders visible the invisible but without ceasing to refer beyond itself. The one gazing on an icon gazes *through* the icon. The gaze here is infinite.[73] In contrast to the idol-making gaze, in an icon the gaze gets lost in "the invisible gaze that invisibly envisages him."[74] Iconography, too, employs concepts—but in a different way. What is necessary is a set of concepts that (1) maintains both a differentiation and union between the visible and the invisible, (2) derives its normativity from Christology, and (3) is able itself to undo the idolatrous gaze in the same way "as one opens a body with a knife."[75]

As Marion has it, it is not just that idols give an untrue image of the divine, but rather that they are, invoking Heidegger, "a real, limited and indefinitely variable function of *Dasein* considered in its aiming at the divine." The idol is a frozen image of "an always-real experience of *Dasein*." The idol is a sort of crystallization of the human quest for God.[76] This is essentially a repetition of Feuerbach. Marion turns Feuerbach against Nietzsche, showing that Nietzsche's "death of God" is as dependent upon the idolatrous projection of a "moral God" as are the proofs for God's existence in Kant, Thomas, and Aristotle.[77] This means that all conceptual discourse about God—even atheism—is idolatrous. Does this disallow any knowledge of God whatsoever? No, the critique applies only to "metaphysics," defined essentially as "the thought of Being" that "keeps ontological difference unthought as such."[78] Here metaphysics is the attempt to derive a category—being—that encompasses a variety of beings in one whole. According to Marion, in metaphysics so defined, God is allowed entry only on philosophy's terms, rather than from an impulse in God.

Marion rightly points out that God transcends all thought. On this basis, he says that even negative concepts that employ ontological difference cannot not do justice to divine unknowability.[79] Yet God can still enter the field of thought—the unknown can be known. "What name, what concept, and what sign nevertheless remain feasible?"[80] The answer: love, or *agape*. Marion says that love is a term that can free the thought of the self-revealing God from the second idolatry of ontological difference. This is because agape remains "unthought" and so can be developed and unleashed as a tremendously speculative power. This development of the concept is an "immense and, in a sense, still untouched" task—one that Marion will not undertake in full. In lieu of it, he points to two features of love and hints at their "speculative promise." These are (1) the fact that love is self-giving and thus, if God is love, then God is not constrained by some prior condition; and (2) the fact that love's self-giving cannot freeze the gaze like an idol; the nature of love as self-abandonment is an overflow of the self, a transcendence that critiques attempts to represent it.[81]

The argument thus goes, it is necessary to liberate our thought about God from the question of being, but this liberation is against every possibility of our thought. Heidegger tries to think of the possibility of God without being, but Marion finds this attempt deeply flawed, for the following reasons. Heidegger proceeds by cutting off theology from philosophy entirely. He says that theology must regard philosophy and the question of being as foolishness, an alien logic that theology can have nothing to do with. This will not work, Marion says, because such an account contradicts itself in that philosophy here already dictates a rule theology must follow—the avoidance of the question of being. It also fails in that it has philosophy demanding that theology redefine itself: since some thoughts about "God" are off limits for theology, theology cannot claim to have God for its formal exclusive object. Instead, theology's object becomes human faith.[82] Defining theology in this way, however, places it as just one of the many sciences operating within the overarching realm of *Dasein*. For Heidegger, when theology tries to say anything about being it is intruding into a sphere that is far beyond its capabilities.[83] Here, the backdrop of all knowledge has been defined in advance and, if God is to appear at all, God will have to appear as a being in *Dasein's* field of vision.[84] Even when Heidegger tries to describe the God of Christian theology, the God revealed on the cross, the concept of the *ens supremum* predominates.[85]

Marion rejects the traditional attempts to describe God in terms of being on the basis of Exodus 3:14. He contends that the passage aims to describe God in terms of God's action, and even if it did describe God as being, why should such a description control the other divine names, such as love? He faults Aquinas for making this move, subordinating the *ens* to the *bonum*. There are alternatives, Marion says, in Bonaventure and Pseudo-Dionysius, who submit "all of [their] concepts, not excepting the *ens*, to a 'destruction' by the doctrine of divine names."[86] Despite this possibility, Marion wants to rethink the relation between God and being even more radically.

Having already excluded the attempt to conceive of God in terms of being, as well as Heidegger's failed attempts to make space for a God without being, Marion says that if God is to be free from being this can only occur in an act of self-liberation. Here, the rules of ontological difference are turned against their own game and God is revealed in a difference that is indifferent to ontological difference. The game of being is "outwitted."[87] Marion says: "Incontestably, biblical revelation is unaware of ontological difference, the science of Being/beings as such, and hence of the question of Being. But nothing is less accurate than to pretend that it does not speak a word on being, nonbeing, and beingness."[88] Marion sees biblical revelation as the revelation of a God whose difference transcends ontological difference precisely in that this God is *indifferent to* the limits marked out by ontological difference. The manner of this indifference is concretized for Marion in certain biblical texts.

Predication Yielding to Praise

In Romans 4:17 Paul discusses Abraham's calling: "as it is written, 'I have made you the father of many nations'—in the presence of the God in whom he believed, who gives life to the dead *and calls into existence the things that do not exist*." Marion is interested in the final, italicized clause in that it discusses a transition from nonbeing to being. He sees here philosophy's distinction between being and nonbeing confirmed, but in such a manner that God is entirely indifferent toward it.[89] When it comes to 1 Corinthians 1:28, Marion is of course interested in the meaning found in God's use of "the things that are not" to "bring to nothing the things that are." While the Romans text showed only one direction of God's indifference to ontological difference, here we see that the directionality goes both ways: God can also bring to nothing the things that are.[90] Here we see that this bringing-into-existence and making-nothing are not acts concerning metaphysical being, but rather judgments or callings.[91] To explore what this means, Marion turns to a third passage, the parable of the prodigal son.

In the Lukan parable, the prodigal son asks for his share of the *ousia*, which he then wastes in the far country (Luke 15:11-13).[92] The word, normally translated as "being," here refers to disposable goods. While Marion knows *ousia* is not being used in the parable in any technical philosophical sense, he points out that even in philosophy the word has the notion of "present disposability." According to Marion, what occurs in the parable is that the son, who already enjoys the father's *ousia*, wants it as a possession rather than a gift. "He asks for the *ousia* without the concession, the *ousia* less the gift, the *ousia* without concession—without having to concede that it comes to him by a gracious concession."[93] In seeking this possession, the son gives up the gift of "filiation"; he freezes the dynamic and "admirable exchange of aims" into an idol.[94] But *ousia* is only improperly a possession. Rightly, *ousia* is an "admirable exchange": a dynamic of "donation, abandon, and [in light of the son's folly] pardon."[95]

On the basis of these texts, Marion claims that there is a strand of biblical revelation that shows an indifference toward the question of being, privileging rather "the gift."[96] The gift crosses, opens, and distracts being.[97] What Marion is arguing for, in other words, is the sublimation of the question of metaphysics (the question of being) to a dynamic process of exchange. This giving is prior to being/Being, such that the question of being is an artificial isolation: idolatry. The dynamic process of giving referred to here is God's *crossing* of being. If the objection is raised that this act of the gift implies a prior being who does the giving, then this self-giving is either (1) a self-giving in which the gift results in a total collapse of distance between the giver and the recipient; or (2) it is not a self-giving at all, and the giver stands behind the gift as an "indeterminate power."[98] On the other hand, if we start with the gift, conceived of as the self-giving of *agape*, we see a crossing of being that does not collapse all distance. In other words, we see a self-giving that does not exhaust the gift nor obliterate the recipient.[99]

The theological import of this conception of God without being is a certain type of *silence*. Marion goes out of his way to say that this is not the silence of agnosticism, a silence derived from metaphysical considerations—that is, the idolatrous silence of Heidegger. Rather, "The silence that is suitable to the God who reveals himself as agape in Christ consists in remaining silent through and for agape: to conceive that if God gives, [then] to say God requires receiving the gift and—since the gift occurs only in distance—returning it."[100] Marion's silence is the silence of listening to the divine names, which always serves the purpose of manifesting God's ineffability—the impossibility that we might ever grasp God with our words and concepts.[101] Silence is the entry into God's own crossing of being, wherein "predication must yield to praise."[102]

Evaluation

Marion works within the basic structures of Heidegger's critique of ontotheology: he sees the traditional metaphysical concepts as inevitably projectionist. And since concepts of being have to do with any type of copulative verb, there can be no predicative statements made of God that have the power within themselves to refer. There is no conceptual knowledge of God. This is ruled out ipso facto not because all conceptual knowledge is mediated by the knowing subject's categories (as in Kant), but rather because it is produced by the knowing subject's imagination (as in Heidegger's reading of Kant). As a way forward, Marion draws from certain biblical passages and the threads of theological apophaticism to fund an account of God that will not be subject to the critique of ontotheology. He proposes to do this by sublimating the concepts of being into the moral concept of self-giving love. This results less in a doctrine of God proper than a phenomenology of God, whereby God is encountered in the "saturated phenomena" of the Eucharist. For Marion the archetypal example of this encounter is that experienced by the disciples on the Emmaus road in Luke 24. The moment of revelation is the same moment Christ disappears from the disciples' perception.[103] Revelation is the overrunning of all concepts.

Evaluating this effort at anti-metaphysical theology requires asking, first, (1) whether Marion has been able to articulate the systematic coherence of the tradition of inquiry in such a way that pressing tensions or incoherences within the tradition have been resolved. With respect to Christian theology's doctrine of God, the problem Marion addresses is that of idolatry. To solve this issue, Marion rejects for use in the doctrine of God the concepts derived from being, emphasizing instead an event in which one encounters God not as being, but as self-giving love. The second evaluative question to be asked is (2) whether it has been explained how this problem arose in the first place—how an epistemological crisis arose with respect to the doctrine of God. It must be noted that Marion simply assumes the critique of ontotheology as establishing a binding problem for Christian theology. Within this framework, concepts are inherently projectionist. Finally, it needs to be asked whether (3) Marion's new conceptual structures can demonstrate a fundamental continuity with the shared beliefs of the tradition thus far. It seems the question must ultimately be answered in the negative. For, while Marion draws on genuine apophatic threads of the tradition and emphasizes that God's nature is identical to love (1 John 4:8), he does so in the context of rejecting entirely the conceptuality of being that, among other things, is essential to the ecumenical creeds.

In the end, Marion's project falters at multiple points. The problem he purports to deal with is that the concept of being—which encompasses all acts of predication—is inherently projectionist and therefore, when used in relation to God, idolatrous. There are at least two reasons why this problem is not a legitimate burden for the Christian doctrine of God. First, it assumes the Heideggerian critique of ontotheology, an argument that, as argued above, begs the question and ultimately requires assent to its own "fundamental ontology." Second, Marion's project is theologically problematic in that it takes idolatry to be an inherent function of the human knowing itself, rather than a moral and spiritual perversion thereof. Even if one were to overlook the highly questionable nature of the purported problem Marion raises, the restatement he offers in response has a dubious claim to continuity with the church's doctrine of God. In fact, Marion's project is a radical rejection of central components of the Christian tradition.

Despite this negative assessment, Marion's project nonetheless gestures toward a central question for constructive work in the doctrine of God. That is, Marion pits the encounter of divine love against the concepts of perfect being, sublimating the latter to the former as if the use of metaphysical predicates were a superfluous aberration. Such an approach underscores the ambiguity of the relation between metaphysical attributes and moral attributes in the doctrine of God throughout the modern period. Unless these two sides are shown to cohere organically within the doctrine of God, the tendency will be toward either abstract conceptions of deity on the one side, or phenomenologies of religious encounter on the other. What is needed—if the doctrine of God is to overcome this impasse—is an understanding of concept formation as something that occurs through personal, moral encounter and that, in turn, mediates that encounter. Kevin Hector's theological epistemology is of great value in this regard.

THERAPY FOR METAPHYSICAL MALAISE: KEVIN HECTOR

In *Theology without Metaphysics*, Hector rejects the idea that language itself presents us with a difficulty in regard to knowing and naming God. He makes no direct argument against Heidegger's notion of metaphysics as "the attempt to secure human knowledge by identifying the fundamental reality of objects with our ideas about them."[104] Instead, he offers a Wittgensteinian, indirect, or "therapeutic" approach. He paints another picture about how language works in practice, one that will allow for the development of concepts, meaning, reference, and truth—and that will do so without falling under the Heideggerian critique of ontotheology. The Heideggerian critique simply is not the way things actually work, according to Hector. Thus, while a work attempting to chart the course for "theology without metaphysics" may sound at first blush like it belongs in the same vein as those by, for example, Marion and John Caputo, it is in fact an attempt to respond to these projects by subverting them entirely.

With respect to the constructive proposals of his anti-metaphysical colleagues, Hector questions their fundamental reliance on the notion of distance: "Why would one assume that God must stand at a remove from that which one experiences (or could experience)?"[105] Hector poses an apparent dilemma which he wants to lead us beyond: that we must choose either a correspondentist way of knowing and naming that sees a gap between our experience and that which transcends our experience, or the particular type of apophaticism of Marion and

Caputo in which we embrace silence with regard to God.[106] Hector's way out of the dilemma is to rehabilitate the possibility of an *experience* of God—an experience of God just as God is in Godself. He finds resources for this project in the Rahnerian and Barthian rejection of an "immanent" and "economic" split with regard to God's trinitarian life. Such moves have the point, he says, of telling us that God's appearance in the realm of creaturely experience is not a *mere* appearance.[107] God's work in the world is God's eternally willed repetition *ad extra* of God's own life. There is therefore no possible contradiction between God and God-for-us.[108]

Hector realizes that even if God does not stand at a distance from our experience of God ("God-for-us"), there is still the issue of how language about God is not distant from God.[109] He wants to account for how it is that Christian language names and describes God, without resorting to an account that implies that the concepts are already present as containers within the human knower. This is important because if the concepts by which we describe God are resident within the human knower, then there appears to be no escaping the argument that our knowing is just some form of projection. For this reason, Hector's project focuses not on the development of any concepts about God, but rather on an account of theological language that shows how such concepts about God can come about in the first place.[110]

The way to avoid a metaphysical account of concepts as containers forcibly imposed upon realities, according to Hector, is to ground concepts in everyday social practices of recognition.[111] To do this Hector adopts Kant's understanding of a concept as a rule by which one orders one's experience, setting a thing in relation to other things. However, Hector will modify the use of a concept as "rule following" rather drastically. Here, to adopt a concept "is to undertake a commitment which is susceptible to normative assessment, and to use it correctly is to contribute to the norm by which other uses may be assessed."[112] The first step in naming a particular reality, therefore, is to adopt intentionally a precedent set by others, and in doing so to render oneself responsible to the judgment of others as to whether or not one is using the concept appropriately.[113] Hector calls this kind of concept use "going on in the same way."

This "going on in the same way" implies that one is embedded in a community, and concept use is the conferral of authority on other people as norm setters, but also the seeking of authority for oneself through participation in the authoritative (normative) trajectory established by the practically derived concept use.[114] This is not a mindless process of norms such that the status quo is invincibly defended. The concept-adopter's recognition of an authoritative use to be imitated is prior in one sense to the community's recognition that the adopter's use goes on in the same way.[115] Further, since the concept is built through contact with realities, from the ground up, there is no way to fix in advance what constitutes a correct usage. The process of recognition in community is ongoing.[116]

In order to turn this general account of language use into one that is specifically theological, Hector gives an account of how "the normative Spirit of Christ" enters into the everyday process of naming and applies ordinary concepts to God.[117] The jumping-off point for this procedure is through Schleiermacher's notion of *Gefühl* as an immediate, pre-reflective attunement to one's environment. Within this model

> a person's outward expression manifests his or her disposition toward some circumstance; this expression is perceived by another as how "we" respond to such circumstances; the latter thus imitates that expression in similar circumstances until he or she has become reliably disposed to respond in this way, at which point the response is an expression of his or her own disposition; others may then perceive his or her outward expression as how "we" respond, and so on.[118]

In other words, the non-inferential attunement toward one's environment is circulated through custom. Here Christian doctrine is a custom of speech by which the common piety (attunement) of the Christian church is circulated. Theological claims are put forward in the church and judged as to whether they are within the trajectory of precedent claims and whether they should be normative for subsequent theological claims.[119] For Schleiermacher, "the Spirit of Christ" enters into this natural chain of recognition that stretches back through Christ's followers to Christ himself. As Hector summarizes: "[W]hat is carried forward through this chain just is the normative Spirit of Christ."[120] This is offered as an account of the mechanics of the Spirit's operation to lead believers into all truth.[121] Hector glosses this specific chain of recognition as "'apostolic succession' (with a small 'a,' as it were)."[122]

Since, in Hector's account, concepts are norms that are derived from the bottom up, the meaning of a concept is a normative trajectory of precedent use; meaning cannot be fixed in advance.[123] So meaning itself, as a function of the concept, implies a similarity to precedent uses and provides a case that carries on the use in such a way that it norms subsequent uses.[124] There simply is no "literal meaning" of a word, if by this we mean a fixed, essence-like concept that the word is thought to denote.[125] If this is the way concepts work in everyday speech, this opens up the possibility for how it is that concepts are said to apply to God. Here Hector employs Karl Barth's account of how it is that our knowledge of God is true.[126]

For Barth, our concepts do not have any immanent ability to denote God's reality, yet God takes them up and causes them to refer in the event of revelation. It is not, Hector says, that human concepts are applied to God arbitrarily, but rather that human concepts come to their fulfillment in God's use of them—a fulfillment that makes sense retrospectively but never could have been ascertained prior to the event of fulfillment.[127] For example, the words "father" or "son" could never yield knowledge of God, but in retrospect—after God applies them to God—we can see how the application brings to perfection the trajectory of our creaturely concept.[128] What Hector has done is to supplement Barth's account of theological meaning by showing Barth's account to be a special instance of the regular way meaning works.

With this understanding of concepts and meaning in tow, Hector raises two further issues relevant to freeing us from the dilemma of metaphysical theology and anti-metaphysical apophaticism: reference and truth. In Hector's account, reference does not occur by a word conveying a fixed description to the human knower, such that language precedes acquaintance with an object. Rather, one becomes acquainted with an object more immediately, and one uses concepts to refer to the object via a process of triangulation.[129] Reference is explained in terms of "what one does with words rather than in terms of words themselves."[130] This is really another way of describing the process of mutual recognition discussed above, except here Hector gives an account of how such a chain of reference might be initiated in anaphora.[131] To explain how this anaphoric chain works in theology, Hector turns to the way the ancient Israelites named God with reference to a specific event in the past but in such a way that the name was open to further fulfillments and referents—ultimately coming to completion in Jesus Christ.[132]

As the final lynchpin of his therapeutic account, Hector gives an alternative to correspondentist theories of truth. This cuts to the core of the anti-metaphysical attempts to remove concepts from theology. If truth is an isomorphism between our mind or our propositions and the objects referred to, then it is hard to know how any of our statements could be true of God.[133] This type of correspondentism generally uses a theory to explain the practice of taking-true, but Hector proposes to explain truth by inverting that order; he wants to develop a concept of "truth" from our everyday practices of taking-true.[134] The question is, how do we evaluate whether one of our beliefs is correct or not? Hector offers a definition of truth that is neither narrowly "realist" nor "coherentist," but rather contains elements of both.[135]

Truth is a judgment made about a referential assertion: Does this assertion get its subject matter right? Can it be a true belief? We have to make this judgment on the basis of other beliefs we take to be true. We accept this candidate belief as carrying on the trajectory of other beliefs. In taking the candidate belief to be true, we thereby set it up as a potential norm by which we may judge other beliefs.[136] We then make assertions about this belief, putting them forward as suggested norms for others to receive as authoritative claims.[137] With this account of truth in hand, Hector goes on to the special case of theological truth. Following Bruce Marshall, Hector claims that whereas there are two truth conditions for an ordinary belief—(1) what the statement refers to and (2) how things are with the world—a theological belief adds a third: (3) the believer's correspondence to Christ.[138] Jesus Christ is the truth in the sense that he gets the Father right, and in the sense that one accepts him as the normative authority for theological claims.[139] Conformity to Christ, then, is internalizing the norms that are passed on by Christ—that is, in Hectorian terms, receiving the Spirit. These norms are beliefs by which we judge other claims, and we in turn can pass along these norms in our own claims.[140] This special type of belief or taking-as-true, which is self-involving and requires a transformation of our other beliefs, is called "faith."[141]

Evaluation

When Hector says he endeavors to do theology without metaphysics, he is not after a theology without concepts, nor is he against concepts that name the divine nature. He is, instead, seeking to persuade that concepts do not serve as barriers between God's being and human knowledge. Hector shows how concepts can be rooted in social practices and how this does not require one to give up on realism. In essence, Hector has provided a model in which concepts are not pernicious in the way Heidegger, or Marion after him, says they are. Furthermore, Hector's account represents a correction against a trend within modern theology as influenced by Schleiermacher.

When Schleiermacher discusses the relation between knowing and doing in the opening salvo of *The Christian Faith*, he says that these two aspects of the religious life come about as a third (*Gefühl*), which "sometimes comes to rest in a thinking which fixes it, sometimes discharges itself in an action which expresses it." *Gefühl* is immediate and receptive, while knowing and doing arise, rather spontaneously, out of this receptivity. Piety is the state in which these three are united without subordination in a non-abstracted "living moment."[142] While for Schleiermacher piety always contains knowing (and doing), as it pertains to God knowing is ultimately reducible to *Gefühl*, as is evident in the way Schleiermacher reinterprets all of the divine attributes in terms of the one relation between God and the world (that of absolute dependence).[143] This is also perhaps seen in the way that the Trinity is seen as a synthesis of separate expressions of the Christian self-consciousness. Thus, while in one sense the doctrine of the Trinity is the "coping-stone of Christian doctrine," in the very next breath Schleiermacher denounces the idea that we could proceed from encountering God in Christ to positing any eternal distinction in the divine nature.[144] The feeling of absolute dependence becomes, in a sense, our immediate access to the thing-in-itself, of which all other concepts are secondary grammatical expositions. In other words, for Schleiermacher—and a whole tradition of modern theology—the content of knowledge becomes separated from, and subordinated to, the fundamental intuition. By contrast, Hector's therapeutic rehabilitation of concepts shows how the content of knowledge and the intuition of it are dialectically related. The knowledge of God comes only through language—in the sense of words and concepts—and yet what those words and concepts convey is a fundamental attunement to reality. Knowledge goes far beyond—but is never without—conceptual representation.

THE NECESSITY OF "PERFECT BEING THEOLOGY"

Thus far we have examined the influential critique of ontotheology, looking at the way Heidegger's understanding of "fundamental ontology" asserts that conceptual representations of God and/or being itself are distractions in our quest for authentic existence. Heidegger finds the impetus for this discovery in Kant's *Critique of Pure Reason*, but he goes far beyond Kant in turning an analysis of the operations and sphere of reason into an encompassing ontology. We then turned to Jean-Luc Marion's *God without Being*, illustrating a representative way theology might progress if Heidegger's critique is compelling. For Marion, God commandeers not language (as in Barth) but particular phenomena. God appears to us in the Eucharist and overruns all conceptual representations. Marion thinks we can describe this event conceptually, and that we can respond with praise, but that we cannot make predications of God, as these would require a common realm of being to ground the copulative verb. In the immediately preceding section, Kevin Hector's theological epistemology helped to chart a third way between the conceptual isomorphism critiqued by Heidegger and the postmodern apophaticism that Marion develops as a response. Hector's account makes sense of the Christian tradition's use of theological concepts and shows how such concepts are used to convey an attunement to God without thereby containing or limiting God to said concepts.

Now, if one is to go on in the same way as Hector, is it necessary to use "being" as a concept in regard to God? Arguably, it is. As Augustine indicates, an understanding of God in terms of "being" actually serves to safeguard our thinking from projectionist fancy. His opening salvo in *De Trinitate* states that the entire work is a correction to those who would allow reason to take the lead role in defining God. He gives a comprehensive summary of how this error occurs. Some project the characteristics of material creation onto God. Others project characteristics of spiritual creation onto God. The worst off are those whose vanity convinces them that they can ascend beyond all created concepts to see God as he really is.[145] By contrast, Augustine reads Exodus 3:14 ("*I am who I am*") to mean that God's being cannot be defined by anything other than God himself and is therefore not ascertainable by any method other than simply thinking (and acting) along the lines provided by the divinely ordained created realities presented to us in biblical revelation—culminating in the humanity of Jesus Christ.[146] The tautologous nature of the divine name—God as "being" itself—can discipline the mind so that it stays trained on this biblical and christological path, rather than falling into idolatrous projection.[147]

Karl Barth makes a similar point as he begins his treatment of the doctrine of God with a section on the meaning of "being." In a section titled "The Being of God in Act," he states:

> If the Word of God forbids the question of God's being as a particular question or leaves us in doubt about this particular question, it means that it gives us no real revelation of God. It does, of course, reveal to us perhaps a very significant and effective action and working, but it keeps from us, and therefore does not reveal, the fact that it is, and how far it is, the action and the working of God.[148]

Barth's point here is simple yet profound: to discuss the being of God is most simply to say what God is *like*. If we refuse the concept of God's being, then we disallow the copulative verb that allows all speech—and therefore thought—to get off the ground in the first place. The statement "God is" is important because it allows us to know the parameters within which we can speak of God at all. We may place a full stop at the end of that sentence, making the verb intransitive, so long as we follow it up with another sentence in which "is" becomes transitive. God is only "the one he is in his works."[149] Barth's mature theology is the attempt to hold these two things together—that God is, and that God is *for us*. For Barth God's being is truly and wholly expressed in God's temporal, personal manifestation in Christ, but in such a way that this action is God's free choice.

Like Augustine, Barth also sees the concept of God's being—in the precise sense that God is what God is—as safeguarding our thoughts about God, rather than leading them into error. It is worth hearing him at length again:

> The validity of every further statement about God, as a statement about the living God, depends on the avoidance of this confusion, or this comparison and contrast, between His life and ours. But this will happen automatically if the positive content of the rule which has emerged [that God is who God is] is clear to us, if every further statement what and how God is is always linked with the fact that God is He who is not only to be found alone in his act, but is to be found alone in His act because alone in His act He is who He is. If we keep this clearly in mind, if all our thoughts are always grasped by God's action, because in it we have to do with God's being, we may be sure that they cannot err, and become either openly or secretly thoughts about ourselves.[150]

In other words, an understanding of God in terms of purely actualized being, derived from Exodus 3:14, is for Barth the qualification by which predications of God can avoid the error of projection. In order that the concept of "being" itself not be a projection, it must function in this way as a grammatical rule rather than as something with its own content; it is necessary but not sufficient.

Both Augustine and Barth, at decisive moments in their doctrines of God, note the danger of metaphysical projection. They have seen it at work in other theologies. Yet their response to this danger is not to avoid the concept of being, but to take it more seriously. God is being itself, the perfection and foundation of being. It is right, and indeed necessary, for the doctrine of God to be "perfect being theology," though this term must be understood correctly.

Philosopher of religion Brian Leftow describes a type of "perfect being theology" (PBT) that originates in the ancient Greco-Roman philosophical context and that is at odds with what is sought here. This is the method, pioneered by Plato, Aristotle, Zeno, and others, which tries to conceive God a priori. Within this schema, "perfect" has the sense of "complete." Because these arguments take as supremely perfect the totality of all being ("the cosmos"), God can be called the most perfect possible being only in a more limited sense. The options this type of reasoning presents to us are either (1) God is the most perfect possible being and creation has a zero or even negative value, or (2) God is only the most perfect non-composite being, though not *the* most perfect (read: complete) being qua being, since he indwells a larger totality.[151]

Leftow goes on, however, to advocate another type of perfect being theology, to which he provides the prefix "scriptural" (S-PBT). S-PBT does not require "such notions as *perfection of being*, perfection simpliciter or greatness simpliciter."[152] This is because, Leftow says, S-PBT starts with authoritative statements about God's perfection in Scripture and seeks only to work out the entailments of these statements.[153] S-PBT starts with "thick" biblical descriptions of God and therefore does not need to resort to "these allegedly more fundamental notions" (such as being).[154] This more limited, more precise version of perfect being theology is said to have "no implications about the overall structure of value." That is, it asks not about God's greatness in relation to everything else that is, but only about God's relation to other possible members of God's own kind.[155]

Leftow's project is promising. It recognizes a fatal problem of any form of a priori perfect being theology. His alternative, beginning with "thick" descriptions that are established by authority rather than pure reason, is something of great pedigree. Yet there is a place where Leftow is uncharacteristically ambiguous. For though he attempts to sideline the concept of being qua being in favor of "thick" descriptions, he appears to see the need for being after all. As he lays out a summary biblical depiction of God he reasons from God's eternality to the concept of "'intrinsic being' for lack of a better phrase," by which he means that God is immutably what God is.[156] Leftow's S-PBT thus rejects any general concept of being as something by which we can describe God, and yet he is moved to reintroduce it to create a complete contrast between God and creation. "Intrinsic being" is not a content-filled concept revealed directly in Scripture, but it forms part of what we might call the grammar of God's perfections. The concept of being, and the suite of concepts that comes with it, are necessary, but not sufficient. The concept of being must be attended by moral concepts—the what by the whom. The successful holding together and relating of these two types of concepts is what we will call "morally perfect being theology."

A MORE EXCELLENT WAY: MORALLY PERFECT BEING THEOLOGY

The nineteenth-century Lutheran theologian I. A. Dorner takes a step in the direction of a morally perfect being theology. In fact, he takes a step too far. Dorner offers a reappraisal of one specific doctrine of one attribute of God's being—the doctrine of divine immutability. Though his focus appears narrow, his book, *Divine Immutability: A Critical Reconsideration*, is in fact a bold attempt to reconceive the doctrine of God altogether. With the alluring elegance of Hegelian dialectic, Dorner sets up a number of tensions in the tradition that his own doctrine of God is meant to take up into a higher synthesis, thus restoring the doctrine of God to cultural relevance. Dorner finds Christianity to stand between the anthropomorphism of paganism and the "Jewish" emphasis on God's immutability.[157] It is the latter emphasis—on immutability—that has held pride of place throughout the Christian tradition. To this overemphasis, his Lutheran contemporaries' various forms of kenotic theology were "a necessary reaction."[158] In other words, Dorner sees the traditional doctrine of God as having two components—a set of concepts relating to God's being and a set of concepts relating to God's personal or ethical qualities. He contends that these two sets of concepts have not been brought together adequately.

The problem in the doctrine of God is illustrated, according to Dorner, by the emergence of the doctrine of divine simplicity within the tradition. Divine simplicity occurs when one takes the biblical emphasis on God's personal and ethical immutability and extends it to the divine knowledge and the divine will, making these into things rigid, inflexible, and, therefore, impersonal. This means that neither God nor the world any longer have freedom in any meaningful sense, a repugnant conclusion.[159] As divine simplicity allegedly crystallizes in the Thomist tradition and all "plurality, process, change, [and] contingency" are denied of God, Dorner says they must also be excluded of the world. This is because in Thomism, for example, Dorner thinks, "whatever the world has of being, it has necessarily from God, in whose being it participates in varying degrees."[160] This would mean that creation is a divinely willed good, but one that exists necessarily and eternally. Creation has no real ontological existence, and it cannot be the result of God's personal good pleasure, since it would simply be included with the being of God. Scotist simplicity, on the other hand, wins freedom for both God and the world by conceiving the relation between the two as one of cause and effect. However, the price for this is high: God is himself absolute, unfettered freedom, and the world itself is the result of his entirely arbitrary will.[161] The moral law God ordains for the world has no connection with God's nature.[162] In short, Christian theology's move away from the personal but mutable and fate-bound gods of paganism leads to a doctrine of God's simplicity in which the only two options are pantheism or deism.[163]

For Dorner, the crowning failure of the doctrine of divine simplicity, and yet also the pointer beyond it, is found in Schleiermacher's theology. Schleiermacher, along with the tradition, continues to insist on the ontological immutability of God and therefore the simplicity of God.[164] Yet Dorner believes that Schleiermacher's denial of all contrast and opposition in God is retrograde and does not properly support the basis of Schleiermacher's theology: the feeling of utter dependence. This is because, Dorner says, the feeling of utter dependence depends for its basis on a real contrast between the world and God, a real contrast that makes sense of the religious experience.[165] While divine simplicity provides a dependable God, it denies freedom and therefore must be rejected. In its place he proposes a reformulated doctrine of divine immutability without metaphysical simplicity. This is really nothing less than the nucleus of a reformulated *doctrine of God*.

In recasting the doctrine of God, Dorner proposes what he sees as a new method, one that is rooted in the Reformation's emphasis on salvation through a vital, personal disposition toward God—*faith*. This was an emphasis that, in the Reformation, was acutely felt on the backend of the dogmatic system—in the soteriological loci—but failed to penetrate the church's doctrine of God.[166]

To right this wrong, Dorner insists that the moral relatedness of God and humanity must be given pride of place and read back into the doctrine of God. What this means methodologically is that one must treat the so-called incommunicable attributes of God within the wider context of God's ethical attributes. Dorner asserts "the independence of theology" as the philosophical categories of being are subordinated to the particularity of the Christian God—the God who is love.[167]

Dorner's fears about what takes place when concepts of being are allowed to predominate over concepts of the ethical—that theology would disintegrate into either deism or pantheism—brings him, in a roundabout way, into common cause with Jean-Luc Marion. Yet because Dorner does not share with Marion the Heideggerian dis-avowal of ontotheology, so he does not have to share the burden of escaping from concept of being altogether. Whereas Marion's concept-less project curiously requires him to develop an alternative con-ceptuality of God as self-giving love, Dorner points forward to the possibility of a doctrine of God that fully integrates what are tradi-tionally called the metaphysical concepts with the moral concepts. This integration is achieved by subordinating the former to the latter.

Dorner's effort to subordinate the concepts of being to the ethical concepts of God derived from the gospel has been highly influen-tial in a certain strand of theology in the twentieth century, largely because of the way that Karl Barth picks up this baton and carries it forward. As Barth says at one point in his doctrine of the divine attri-butes: "Those who know the essay will recognise . . . how much I owe to Dorner's inspiration."[168] What is helpful about Dorner's approach is that it mediates between two potential pitfalls for the doctrine of God, one belonging to the classical doctrine of God, the other belong-ing to modern concerns represented by "process" theologians. On the one hand, Dorner emphasizes the centrality of the biblical portrayal of God's character (i.e., the moral concepts) in the believer's faith, warding off the dangers of deism. On the other hand, Dorner resists the pantheistic danger of collapsing God's being into creaturely being by emphasizing God's own identity.[169]

While Dorner is correct to want to hold together the concepts of being and the moral concepts, this book will make the case that seeing the two in conflict so that one must be subordinated to the other is a mistake. Instead, what is needed is a morally perfect being theology that respects the integrity of both types of concept and shows how they exist in a harmonious relationship. This morally perfect being theology is charted by the development of a doctrine of divine humility.

Conclusion: Toward a Doctrine of Divine Humility

This chapter has sought to uncover the reasons why so much of modern theology has demonstrated an aversion to the concept of being. Heidegger's critique of ontotheology was seen to be the culmination of a development of thought that treats concepts as fixed within the human knower and projected onto the objects of knowledge, including and especially, God. Jean-Luc Marion represented an attempt to work largely within the Heideggerian framework, deepening it so that it critiques itself. Marion negated the Heideggerian strictures on God but offered no positive vision for speaking or thinking of God. God can only be encountered eucharistically in a punctiliar fashion. Kevin Hector's full-orbed epistemology that is rooted in social practices successfully puts the lie to this framework, freeing theology to speak of God without necessarily committing the sin of idolatrous projection. In fact, with Augustine and Barth, it is only by speaking of God's perfect being that one avoids this danger. Yet "perfect being theology," while necessary, is not sufficient. One must successfully hold together the concepts of the divine being (the "what") with the moral concepts (the "who").

As indicated above, the Dornerian solution to uniting the doctrine of concepts of God's being with moral concepts—subordinating the former to the latter—is ultimately undesirable. An implicit burden of what follows will be to show why this is the case and to propose a plausible alternative that has more to commend itself, while avoiding some of the worst problems with the Dornerian approach. Dorner himself will not serve as a major interlocutor in this task. Instead, we will take up the matter with his more influential theological progeny, Karl Barth, situating him between both ancient and contemporary pioneers in divine humility: St. Augustine and Katherine Sonderegger. However, it is first necessary to come to terms with the concept of humility.

2

DEFINITIONS OF HUMILITY

The present work depends heavily on a concept of "humility" and will treat this moral concept not merely as a human virtue, but as a divine attribute. Unfortunately, it is not possible to speak of *the* concept of humility, since the term has proven notoriously difficult to define with precision and general agreement. What is more, some of the definitions that have gained common coinage have been met with open scorn—accused of being antithetical to all moral goodness. It is necessary, therefore, to engage in a sustained coming-to-terms, explicating the range of meanings which the concept of humility carries in our intellectual and moral traditions. This will enable me to avoid misunderstanding and equivocation in the use of this term. More substantially, it will show how and why the moral concept of humility, if understood aright, is fit for attribution to the omnipotent God of Christian faith.

Analytic Definitions of Humility

Whether one concludes that humility is a virtue—a moral quality that is to be lauded and fostered for its ability to lead us to the good life—will depend largely on how one defines humility. Many authors throughout history who employ the concept work with implicit rather than explicit definitions. It is therefore helpful to start with a measure of analytic rigor and conceptual clarity. The definitional clarity achieved here will hopefully provide a lens for what follows.

In an article entitled simply "Humility," the analytic philosopher James Kellenberger lays out a set of features inherent in the common, day-to-day uses of the term humility:

(1) Having a low opinion of oneself, especially when others have a higher opinion of one . . .
(2) Having a low estimate of one's merit . . .
(3) Having a modest opinion of one's importance or rank, so that when reasonable judgments can vary, one's judgment is on the low side . . .
(4) Absence of self-assertion . . .
(5) Claiming little as one's desert . . .
(6) Having or showing a consciousness of one's defects . . .
(7) Not being proud, haughty, or arrogant . . .[1]

Kellenberger points out that while these definitions have some overlap, they are all distinct ways of being humble. Humility, he says, is a "polythetic" concept—defined by these family resemblances, rather than a statement of necessary and sufficient conditions. "This polythetic classification stems from the notion that humility is what J. L. Austin calls a "trouser-word," a word that gets its meaning only in context-specific contrasts with its negation (in this instance, pride).[2]

Having recognized the polythetic ways humility is used generally, Kellenberger locates something more profound at work in humility. As a polythetic concept, humility gets meaning from contrast. Superficially, this is a contrast with pride. More accurately, though, humility functions around a core contrast with the pride–shame axis (also a polythetic concept). Pride and shame are reactions based on how well one measures up to a standard or ideal. (The ideal in question can be public and objective, or internal and idiosyncratic.) In Kellenberger's account, humility, then, is a certain type of freedom from self-concern; it is "deeply opposed to engaging life in terms of the self-concerned states of pride and shame at all."[3]

Though his account of humility has hitherto been nonreligious, Kellenberger turns to Christian sources and sees there the same abiding characteristics of humility (with some exceptions that tend toward conceptions that rule out healthy self-respect). Religious humility in the Christian tradition (and, Kellenberger assumes, all Judeo-Christian-Islamic traditions) involves (1) an essential turn away from the "pride–shame axis of self-concern"; (2) a corresponding turning toward God; (3) and an encompassing "experiential or cognitive element"[4] that itself has three subcomponents: (a) a recognition of oneself as one is, (b) a recognition of God, and (c) a recognition of one's relation to God.[5] (A nonreligious version of humility could perhaps retain (1) and a modified version of (2), conceived perhaps as a turn toward the transcendent or toward "the other.") So Kellenberger sees religious humility as essentially a turning away from self-concern that is the engine of the pride–shame axis and a corresponding turn toward something else. In the case of religious humility, one turns toward God.

J. L. A. Garcia classifies accounts of humility as either being "inwardly directed" or "outwardly directed." The former versions focus on mental states and the latter focus on actions.[6] Examples he gives of inwardly directed accounts of humility are Julia Driver's definition of it as underestimating one's good features, Owen Flanagan's definition of humility as an accurate (but not overinflated) sense of one's self, which is similar to Norvin Richard's definition of it as having a true view of oneself, particularly when one is tempted to err by overexaggeration.[7] Richard Roberts and Jay Wood offer a rather different, inwardly directed account of humility as being unconcerned with being regarded well by others.[8] Garcia's own definition of humility as being "unimpressed with their own admired or envied features" is essentially an inwardly directed account that attempts to take up and improve upon what is right in these other accounts.[9] As for outwardly directed accounts of humility, Garcia notes A. T. Nuyen's definition of humility as a desire to apportion credit for one's achievements to all those who contributed to the circumstances of said success.[10] Also placed in this outwardly focused category is Thomas Aquinas' definition of humility as "a praiseworthy self-abasement to the lowest place."[11] We will return to Thomas' account in more detail later.

Of these various definitions of humility, Kellenberger's seems the most promising and the most profound. If humility is, as Kellenberger has defined it, one's tendency not to engage life in terms of the pride–shame axis of self-concern, then it is not only "inwardly directed" in the sense of being unimpressed with one's own best features (Garcia)—though it is that. It also inherently carries with it the notion that one is inwardly disposed in order to be "outwardly directed" toward some other person, be it God or another human being. This means that, unlike definitions (1)–(3) above, Kellenberger's version does not require that the humble person have an inaccurate, low view of oneself. Unlike (4)–(5), this humility does not necessarily exclude self-assertion or rightful claims. In contrast to (6), this definition of humility does not require that one be morally (or otherwise) flawed to possess this virtue. Like (7), this version of humility *is* defined by the contrast between humility and pride. However, unlike many versions of (7) it does not make humility an opposite of pride. Humility thus conceived is not on the continuum of self-concern that runs from pride to shame, but is rather a different way of one being oriented toward (or perhaps, away from) the self altogether.

MAGNANIMITY AND NOT HUMILITY: ARISTOTLE

If some version of humility as a virtuous quality has, for much of our past, been taken for granted, one need only to look to the ancient philosopher Aristotle to realize what an intrusion this value is from the moral trajectory he canonically established in his *Nicomachean Ethics*.[12] What one finds there is the complete absence of the concept. As Alasdair MacIntyre writes in *After Virtue*: "[O]ne is to note that humility, thrift, and conscientiousness could appear in *no* Greek list of the virtues."[13] Of Aristotle specifically he later writes: "[I]n the only place where anything resembling humility is mentioned, it is as a vice."[14] So how does Aristotle think of virtue and why does this lead to such a negative valuation of anything like humility?

According to Aristotle, everything necessarily aims at some good, and the good is simply whatever things aim at by their nature.[15] The highest concrete *telos*, which gives meaning to all other aims, is the well-being of the *polis*.[16] Yet the flourishing society aims at something beyond itself—*eudaemonia*.[17] This is, MacIntyre interprets it, "the state of being well and doing well in being well, of a man's being well-favoured himself and in relation to the divine."[18] Eudaemonia is a state in which the human person is complete; she requires nothing more, she is self-sufficient—not in isolation, but in the sphere of the community.[19] This state of eudaemonia will be attained, Aristotle assumes, as she lives out a complete life in conformity with her rational nature.[20]

Virtues are the characteristics that underwrite the concrete actualization of a human being's rational nature and therefore enable her to achieve eudaemonia. Without the virtues, she will fail to reach her *telos* and so be ultimately unhappy.[21] Since virtue is essentially the proper function of the rational human nature, it is always the mean between two types of errors—excess or deficiency.[22] The virtue related most clearly to our discussion of humility is what Aristotle calls magnanimity or high-mindedness (Gk. *megalopsychia*). Magnanimity is the virtue; the error of deficiency is pusillanimity or small-mindedness, and the error of excess is vanity.

Aristotle defines magnanimity as thinking one deserves great things and being correct in that evaluation.[23] This is not simply saying that one's claims correspond to one's deserts. For the one who strives after very little, deserves very little, and acknowledges that fact, is not magnanimous. It is also important to note the content of the great things after which one strives: "A high-minded man is, then, primarily concerned with honor and dishonor."[24] Magnanimity, then, is the characteristic of a person who seeks the highest honor, attains it, and is aware of attaining it. It is important to understand what Aristotle means by "honor" in this context. To modern ears it may sound as trite as an attribution of worth that depends on the subjective recognition of others. In an ancient society, however, honor as an act of recognition points beyond itself to one's objective worth. This is why in ancient societies, an insult is criminal—it steals from a person what he is objectively due.[25] With this in mind, it seems that magnanimity is a striving for and achieving a deserved (because genuinely virtuous) greatness within the patronage system and the attendant personal satisfaction that comes with that attainment.[26] The magnanimous person is precisely not motivated like some by the mere appearance of superiority, but instead simply *is* superior. This is why, Aristotle says, magnanimity is actually the "crown" of the virtues, a virtue that connects, and even infuses, all the rest.[27]

The errors on either side of the mean of magnanimity are, as stated above, vanity and pusillanimity. Aristotle does not have much time for these two mistaken mind-sets. The vain person is the person who overreaches, thinking himself worthy of more honorable undertakings than he really is. He puts his focus on external shows of honor. He thinks that mere good fortune or wealth, rather than the true greatness of virtue, constitutes his being deserving of honor. Aristotle does not see vanity as a pressing problem in the way that pusillanimity is, though, saying that "small-mindedness is more opposed to high-mindedness than vanity is, for it occurs more frequently and is worse."[28] The pusillanimous person is not bad, but merely mistaken and deficient. His problem is that he deprives himself of whatever good he deserves, thinking that he does not deserve it at all. This person will not be seen as foolish in the way a vain person will be, but rather as passive. "For while any given kind of man strives to get what he deserves, these people keep aloof even from noble actions and pursuits and from external goods as well, because they consider themselves undeserving."[29]

Now to plot Aristotle's magnanimity, vanity, and pusillanimity in terms of the definitions of humility given above. Magnanimity is diametrically opposed to some of the definitions of humility given in the previous section. Magnanimity allows no possibility of (1) having a low opinion of oneself, (2) having a low estimate of one's merit, (4) absence of self-assertion, and (5) claiming little as one's desert. (3) Erring on the low side on one's opinion of oneself when reasonable judgments might vary is also ruled out, since true magnanimity requires self-awareness. If, with (6), one is conscious of one's defects, then one is conscious of not being magnanimous (among other things). And as far as (7)—not being proud—is concerned, magnanimity, like humility, is in a certain type of contrast to pride. But this is only true of magnanimity if pride is defined with the precision of Aristotle's "vanity": having an overinflated view of oneself. If pride is defined, with Kellenberger, as a manifestation of self-concern, then magnanimity itself appears to be a species of pride—the self-concern of the person who is indeed superior to others.

As alluded to above, Aristotle's depiction of the virtues is intimately bound up with the patronage system of his Greek context.[30] For this reason, Aristotle's outlook is radically different from a modern Western view that has been significantly, though not entirely, shaped by Christianity. For instance, Aristotle does not believe that all human beings are of equal moral worth, and, more profoundly, he does not think they even can be of equal moral worth, since their moral worth will depend on their natural endowment of reason and how they choose to employ it.[31] Aristotle has built into the good a certain "worldliness" that is alien to his predecessor, Plato. To be virtuous one must assert oneself in greatness.[32] This greatness is always a socially embedded greatness—being great in stature within (and for the sake of) the *polis*, and deservedly so.

Ultimately, Aristotle's concept of magnanimity is a socially relative concept of greatness. This does *not* mean that Aristotle's ethics are egoistic in the modern sense, it is important to note. This is so for Aristotle, because a person's honor or greatness is something that is essentially a function of the greatness attaching to the city.[33] While this shields Aristotle from the misguided criticism that his virtue theory advocates a form of obsessive self-concern, it also further serves to underscore the notion that virtue itself is essentially the fact of being located on one side of a worldly continuum—through both fortune and wise choices. While magnanimity operates between the two extremes of vanity and pusillanimity, it still depends for its existence on the assumed shame–honor (shame–pride) scale that humility, as Kellenberger defines it, so radically subverts. On that account, the humble person, whatever else we might say about her, does not concern herself with her status in the *polis*. Such a notion is outside of the social imaginary of Aristotle or other ancient writers. For them "humility" (Gk. *tapeinos* and Lat. *humiles*) refers to one's objective social status at the bottom of the continuum. The terms imply "lowly" and "pressed down." In the ancient social world, "the humble are condemned to flattery, trod upon like slaves, utterly without public honour and incapable of higher thought."[34] The polythetic versions of humility listed in the first section of this chapter might apply to these people, but only the subjective acceptance of one's objective humility, and certainly not as virtues worthy of imitation.

While Aristotle does not have a place in his moral vision for humility as a virtue, his discussion of magnanimity is deeply resonant with the Christian account of humility that this chapter aims to reclaim. To understand why this is the case it is necessary to turn first to some influential modern critiques of Christian humility.

AGAINST HUMILITY: HUME, NIETZSCHE, AND GOLDSTEIN

David Hume

The eighteenth-century Scottish philosopher David Hume says that it is "impossible we can ever, by a multitude of words, give a just definition" of either pride or humility. This is not a recognition that the terms are polythetic in the way discussed above, but rather because, within Hume's anti-rationalist understanding of human nature, pride and humility are impressions made upon the soul at a prerational level. As he famously writes in *A Treatise of Human Nature*: "Reason is, and ought only to be the slave of the passions, and can never pretend to any other office than to serve and obey them."[35] Pride and humility are violent emotions, or proper "passions."[36] Reasoned description is only a secondary and somewhat artificial effort at capturing these passions in words. Nonetheless, these two terms are said to represent something common to all—everyone knows experientially what they are.[37]

Hume's analysis of pride and humility has the following features. They are direct contraries. They share the same object: one's view of oneself. Pride is a sense of elation with oneself, and humility is a sense of dejection.[38] The cause of these two passions is not the same as its object; the cause is not the self. There are two types of causes for these passions: what we might call a material cause (e.g., one's house or one's spouse) and what we might call a formal cause (e.g., the beauty of one's house or the ugliness of one's spouse).[39] These causes direct and inform the self's feeling about the self and can engender the passions of pride or humility. Hume takes it as obvious that power, possessions, and pulchritude are the perpetual formal causes of pride. However, this does not explain the origin or the efficient cause of pride and humility.[40] Yet

Hume takes it as axiomatic that there is a natural explanation for these passions. Hume's explanation depends upon three principles he takes for granted: (1) the mind does not fix on one idea, but moves from idea to idea by a process of associated resemblance, continuity, or cause; (2) a similar chain of impressions results, with the caveat that the relation between the impressions is the much more vague process of association; (3) the chain of associated impressions, which sets in motion chains of ideas, sets off a sort of domino effect in which one dominant impression comes to color other impressions and other ideas.[41] One's natural self-relatedness becomes tinted by the pleasurable or unpleasurable impressions one is experiencing: "[P]ride is a pleasant sensation, and humility a painful."[42]

In Hume's account the idea that one would intentionally cultivate humility is absurd, given its association with disagreeable and painful impressions. In *An Enquiry Concerning the Principles of Morals*, he writes:

> Celibacy, fasting, penance, mortification, self-denial, humility, silence, and solitude, and the whole train of monkish virtues; for what reason are they everywhere rejected by men of sense, but because they serve to no manner of purpose, neither advance a man's fortune in the world, nor render him a more valuable member of society; neither qualify him for the entertainment of company, nor increase his power of self-enjoyment? We observe, on the contrary, that they cross all these desirable ends; stupify the understanding and harden the heart, obscure the fancy and sour the temper.[43]

On the basis of its association with aesthetically displeasing and painful sensations, then, Hume transfers humility from the catalogue of virtues to the catalogue of vices. Though it does not receive as acute or colorful a treatment, Hume also regards magnanimity—or the desire thereof—as indispensable to the good life. While a certain bias toward modesty (without denying one's good qualities) is to be favored, this is essentially because it will help one not to tread on the inherent ambitions of the other people with whom one interacts. This will allow one, theoretically, to be more successful in one's own pursuits to gain something vaguely akin to Aristotle's "honor." "A desire of fame, reputation, or a character with others, is so far from being blameable, that it seems inseparable from virtue, genius, capacity, and a generous or noble disposition."[44]

Hume thus has no place for humility in the sense of most of the definitions given above. However, his "modesty" is a pragmatic species of humility that has a close resemblance to (3)—having a modest opinion of one's importance and rank, with a bias toward low estimation. It is pragmatic because what is important to Hume is not one's internal valuation of oneself, but rather one's appearance to others. This species of humility or "modesty" is thus a means to attaining the pleasurable end of a greater status among one's fellows.

Friedrich Nietzsche

Friedrich Nietzsche shares Hume's disdain for humility, but for very different reasons. In *Beyond Good and Evil* Nietzsche understands the morality of European civilization as a fall away from what is noble, high-minded, and individualistic and into the mediocrity of a herd instinct driven entirely by fear. It is the fear of the neighbor that gives rise to the morality of the "love of the neighbor."[45] The progenitor of this morality is most directly the Christian religion—"a religion which indulged and flattered the most sublime herd-animal desires."[46] Thus, Western society becomes, in a sense, a 2000-year inversion of morals. That which is high is called base, and that which is lowly is exalted. Christian society is the culmination of a "slave rebellion in morals" that began even earlier with the Jewish people.[47]

The supposedly true origin of "good" and "evil" is laid out in Nietzsche's *Genealogy of Morals*. In contrast to the "English psychologists," who anachronistically took it for granted that virtue referred to altruistic actions, Nietzsche says that the more ancient definition of "the good" was whatever the powerful and noble defined as that which set them apart from "all the low, low-minded, common and plebeian."[48] The great reversal of values is principally brought about through religion—and the ultimate representation of religion is the Jewish people.

> All that has been done on earth against "the noble," "the power-ful," "the masters," "the rulers," fades into nothing compared with what the Jews have done against them; the Jews, that priestly people,

who in opposing their enemies and conquerors were ultimately satisfied with nothing less than a radical revaluation of their enemies' values, that is to say, an act of the most spiritual revenge. . . . It was the Jews who, with awe-inspiring consistency, dared to invert the aristocratic value-equation (good = noble = beautiful = happy = beloved of God) and to hang on to this inversion with their teeth, the teeth of the most abysmal hatred (the hatred of impotence), saying "the wretched alone are the good; the poor, the impotent, lowly alone are the good; the suffering, deprived, sick, ugly alone are pious, alone are blessed by God, blessedness is for them alone—and you, the powerful and noble, are on the contrary the evil, the cruel, the lustful, the insatiable, the godless to all eternity.[49]

This slave people's hatred plots its revenge against all that is strong and powerful, and triumphs through a seductive new notion of selfless "love." This revenge-masked-as-love achieves its victory over the non-Jewish world (over European society) through the religion of Jesus of Nazareth. "The 'redemption' of the human race (from 'the masters' that is) is going forward; everything is visibly becoming Judaized, Christianized, mob-ized (what do the words matter!)."[50]

The central virtue in this inverted schema is humility. For Nietzsche humility is defined as a demand laid upon strength that it should not be expressed as strength. Strength here is "a desire to overcome, a desire to throw down, a desire to become master, a thirst for enemies and resistances and triumphs."[51] The proponents of humility insist that the strong person is free to be weak. Those deceived by this fail to recognize that to be impotent is to give up all strength; there is no such thing as a strong "soul" with impotence in actions—one is simply as one acts.[52] This slave morality is thus primarily verbal sleight of hand: it takes something base—"anxious lowliness"—and gives it a meritorious sounding name: "humility."[53] This virtue results in what is, to Nietzsche, a disastrous situation in which all difference of rank is abolished and the highest possibilities of the strongest humans are never realized.[54]

Superficially, Nietzsche's critique of humility is predicated on a revival of something like the ideal of Aristotle's magnanimous person—the one whose virtue depends on their place in a social hierarchy. There is a radical difference, however. Absent in Nietzsche's philosophy is the notion of the greater good of the *polis* for which one is virtuous; his is an unabashedly egoistic conception of virtue. Any attempt to set up an ideal that one must strive for is viewed cynically as the attempt to constrain the free expression of the nonrational will to power.[55]

In relation to the seven common definitions of humility laid out by Kellenberger above, Nietzsche's philosophy would clearly reject all seven as being part and parcel with the oppressive project of morality *per se*. As for Kellenberger's own definition—that humility be seen as a freedom from self-concern, a freedom to engage life without regard for the pride–shame axis—one surmises that Nietzsche would regard this as merely a subtler form of the slave morality he ridicules. In practice, it would be yet another form of suicide by morality. For even if powerful individuals were to form an aristocratic society within which they treat one another as equals, collectively their union would require weaker people to exploit. To attempt to establish a nonexploitative society is the height of decay, "because life simply *is* the will to power."[56]

Valerie Saiving Goldstein

It is all too easy for the theologian to find in Nietzsche the perfect foil for his or her own reading of history—a reductio ad absurdum of sorts. Reinhold Niebuhr, for instance, writes: "Nietzsche is quite right. Christianity does transvalue historical values. In human history wealth, fame and immortality are given to the wise, the mighty and the noble. . . . Their bodies are fed by the toil of their fellows and the pride of their souls is sustained by the adulation, respect, fear and even resentment of those whom they bestride."[57] Niebuhr continues the same line of thought as both the Bible and the predominant history of the church when he says that pride is the root of all sin.[58] Here, pride is the effort of the self to deny its own finitude and inherent weakness, and to secure itself against the threat posed by others. Pride is fundamentally self-assertion. This pride infects every part of humanity's life—its willing, its knowing, and its worship. Anders Nygren famously identifies pride with the self-love of human *eros*. The polar opposite, antidotal love, is the divine *agape*—a self-giving, nonacquisitive love.[59] Yet not every theologian is content with this analysis.

Valerie Saiving Goldstein writes in a seminal (though now perhaps somewhat dated) essay, "The Human Situation: A Feminine View," about the shortsightedness of allowing pride as self-assertion to be the primary lens through which sin is viewed. This is insensitive, Goldstein writes, to the way women experience the world. Goldstein recognizes a great amount of gender fluidity ("the tremendous plasticity of human nature") beyond what can be seen at the purely physiological level. Yet she sees it as an error to overlook or underestimate the way that physiology shapes the respective experiences of men and women.[60] Following the earlier work of Margaret Mead, she examines the way sexual difference shapes the human experience of the world from the time of infancy forward. Both male and female children must differentiate themselves from their primary attachment to their mother, but they do so in very different ways. The female's differentiation is the realization that she, too, is already a female, and that by waiting she will grow into her full femininity. By contrast, the male must differentiate himself in a more radical way. He realizes that he is not a female, but that he is also not yet a man. Neither is his achievement of his full masculinity a given that he can merely wait for; instead, it is a challenge he must meet. This makes the male subject to a more intense experience of anxiety, which in turn often engenders a greater creative drive.[61] This sexually differentiated experience—though culturally shaped in a multitude of ways—is basic.

Against the background of this basic difference, Goldstein critiques the doctrine of sin in terms of pride, and the corresponding antidote of self-giving love as being doctrines formulated in the context of masculinity.[62] This doctrine of sin was not wrong; in fact, Goldstein says, it was "profoundly responsive and relevant" to men in the hypermasculine modern world. It is an inadequate teaching for contemporary women, however.[63] For the feminine temptation, as structured by sexual difference and experience in childbearing and childrearing, makes a woman susceptible to "give too much of herself, so that nothing remains of her own uniqueness; she can become merely an emptiness, almost a zero, without value to herself, to her fellow men, or, perhaps, even to God."[64] Terms like "pride" and "will-to-power" do not generally address the form sin takes in regard to "the basic feminine character structure." A more pervasive sin in this context is "underdevelopment or negation of the self."[65] Emphasizing sin as pride, and self-giving love as its antidote, may lead women to further descend into their own form of sin: the failure to actualize their own identities. According to Goldstein, this one-sided emphasis on pride is not only irrelevant to women, but also to men. This is true, she suspects, because she sees Western culture moving out of the hypermasculinity of modernity and into a new era in which "the character traits inherent in femininity are being increasingly emphasized, encouraged, and absolutized."[66]

The influence of this analysis on feminist theology can be seen in the comment of Daphne Hampson, who echoes Goldstein when she writes that the emphasis on sin as self-assertion and the subsequent focus on Christ's self-emptying (*kenosis*) "may well be a model which men need to appropriate and which may helpfully be built into the male understanding of God. But . . . for women, the theme of self-emptying and self-abnegation is far from helpful as a paradigm."[67] And this "feminine view" is a warning that needs to be heard, as Goldstein's analysis illuminates how humility may be seen as a vice rather than a virtue. All the common definitions of humility, listed at the beginning of this chapter, operate as negations of harmful, prideful self-assertion. None of them explicate sufficiently what constitutes proper self-assertion. This leaves each of them open to being interpreted simply as self-abnegation.

Kellenberger's account of humility as being "deeply opposed to engaging life in terms of the self-concerned states of pride and shame at all" holds more promise in relation to the feminist concern raised by Goldstein.[68] If humility involves the wholesale rejection of the pride–shame axis, then a new vista of freedom is opened to the humble person. In turning from self-concern toward others and toward God, conceivably she would comport herself toward others in a way that makes her neither oppressively assertive toward them, nor submissive in a way that denies her personhood in any manner. Humility would mean she could escape, at least in her own psyche, being either master or slave.

This feminine concern brings out the incomplete nature of Kellenberger's otherwise helpful analytic definition of humility. While he speaks of humility as a turning away from self-concern with the pride–shame axis, and a turning toward God and toward others, his definition does not give concretion either to the manner or the purpose of one's turning toward. One assumes that this "turning toward" is a movement of interest in, or concern for, the other person or even God. One also assumes that this "turning toward" is not merely cognitive, nor merely emotional, but a more robust relational concept. In other words, we are now faced with the question of the *telos* of humility—what is the good and desirable state of affairs one hopes to achieve by being humble?

Humility as Magnanimity: The Classical Christian Context

It is clear now that the concept of humility is difficult to define with precision. As stated in analytic terms at the outset: humility is a "polythetic" concept, encapsulating multiple definitions united by family resemblances rather than necessary and sufficient conditions. This is true, of course, but there is a deeper reason that contributes not only to the difficulty of definition, but also to the moral ambiguities that arise in response to the various definitions. As MacIntyre puts it, "Every particular view of the virtues is linked to some particular notion of the narrative structure or structures of human life."[69] Philosophers and theologians can operate with different and conflicting lists of virtues, as well as different variations of a virtue that is called by the same name, because (1) virtues are best identified by experiencing them in the concrete context of a MacIntyrean "practice"[70] and (2) these various "practices" are hierarchically arranged within a unified vision of the human *telos*.[71] In other words, a virtue concept is situated within a moral tradition and has its meaning therein. In this section we therefore turn our attention with greater specificity to the concept of humility as it comes to expression in the classical Christian tradition.

The roots of the virtue of humility within the Christian tradition are to be found within the sacred Scriptures of Israel and the church. The canonical narratives provide the dogmatic framework within which moral concepts have their meaning. Because we are interested in the Christian moral tradition to which these texts gave rise, we will not focus here on biblical exegesis per se, but rather on select patristic and medieval accounts of humility that arose in response to these texts. The tradition is shot through with humility and so we cannot hope to attain anything like an exhaustive treatment. Instead, texts are prioritized under the discipline of two basic criteria: (1) those in which humility is embedded within a discernible, broader moral vision; and (2) those that have had an outsized influence on the subsequent Christian moral tradition.

Athanasius' The Life of St. Anthony

In his *Confessions* Augustine relays the story of two acquaintances—also rhetors—who skip the city's morning gladiatorial affair to take a walk around the city. They chance upon a monastery into which they are invited. Inside they find a book that contains Athanasius' account of the life of St. Anthony the Great. Reading the book aloud has a visceral effect on one of the young men, inspiring him to interrogate his friend reflectively: "Tell me: where do we hope all our efforts are going to get us? What are we looking for? In whose cause are we striving? Does life at court promise anything better than promotion to being Friends of the Emperor?" And, as he continued to read, a new possibility for life dawned upon him suddenly. He remarked to his friend: "I have already torn myself away from the ambitions we cherished, and have made up my mind to serve God." His friend, Augustine tells us, also determined to join "both in the noble reward and in the glorious combat."[72] These two men gave up on one stadium to embrace another. *The Life of St. Anthony* had that effect on people in the fourth century; it inspired many people to take up the mantles of monasticism and virginity.[73] Beyond this, it was a source of moral inspiration even to those who did not or could not follow Anthony's way of life. The scene Augustine recounts is in keeping with Athanasius's intent to present fourth-century Christians with an alternative moral vision articulated through the lens of Anthony.

The arena presented by the life of St. Anthony, and monasticism more broadly, was one of "training in the way of virtue."[74] Athanasius emphasizes from the beginning that Anthony's life was one of renunciation. He came from good stock and serious wealth, but he was willing to give up his societal position for the pursuit of Christ.[75]

Viewed from the lens of late antiquity this was moral suicide—the giving up of advantage to pursue the good, seemingly for no reward. Yet from the standpoint of Athanasius and his readers, Anthony was thereby availing himself of a far superior opportunity to win glory. Anthony comes off not as a weakling, but as a hero. Time and time again his ambition for virtue is emphasized; it is even said that he made sure that others did not surpass him in this regard.[76] Echoing the Pauline epistles, the language of agonistic competition is frequently used, and Anthony is even referred to as an "athlete."[77] The *telos* for which Anthony goes to battle is not earthly glory, but perfection in the love of Christ. The enemies, as well as the weapons used against them, are not earthly weapons, but spiritual and moral. "[T]he great weapon against [evil spirits] is a virtuous life and confidence in God." The evil spirits are powerless before those who live under the sign of the cross—to those who are formed by ascetical practices into Christlike virtues like meekness, humility, gentleness, and selfless charity ("love for the poor").[78] Since these virtues are won in battle with a fierce opponent, they are not exclusive of virtues of courage, zeal, and especially single-mindedness—indeed, within the narrative of Anthony's life it is quite the opposite. These virtues are on colorful display in Anthony's keen willingness to face martyrdom for his Christian practice.[79] In conflict with idolaters, Anthony is quoted as saying that confessing the cross is "proof of manliness, a token of our contempt of death."[80]

The Life of St. Anthony is more than biography; it gives insight into what was perhaps the dominant moral vision of late antiquity. As Peter Brown's analysis of Syrian asceticism has shown, it was during the period when the stable institutions of the classical period were evaporating, while those of the Middle Ages had yet to materialize, that "the holy man" emerged as a new locus of societal power.[81] Through a long, drawn-out process of asceticism, these powerful figures had dissociated themselves from the normal ties of family, economic, and even ecclesial interest.[82] By living in a way that may appear to us to be subhuman, the ascetics became the arbiters of divine power, able to mediate between the warring interests that had been unleashed as social and economic power became more widely diffused throughout society. Brown's analysis helps to make sense of how humility and power were two sides of the same coin in late antiquity. By ascetically proven extrication from the competitive desires that threatened to upend every aspect of daily life, these individuals could save people from their own desires and those of others. Those who made the most extreme and consistent renunciations of power were invested in turn with the greatest power. As Brown writes: "[B]oth Emperor and patriarch ended up, stretched full length, at the feet of the holy man."[83]

Humility as defined and modeled in asceticism seems at different times to comport straightforwardly with all of the common usage definitions offered at the outset: (1) "having a low opinion of oneself," (2) "having a low estimate of one's merit," (3) "having a modest opinion of one's importance or rank," (4) "absence of self-assertion," (5) "claiming little as one's desert," (6) "having or showing a consciousness of one's defects," and (7) "not being proud, haughty, or arrogant." For example, when the fourth-century Gazan holy man, Barsanuphius, is asked in his letters to define humility, he writes: "Humility means regarding oneself as 'earth and ashes' [see Job 42:6], in deeds and not just in words, and saying: 'Who am I? Who counts me as anything? I have nothing to do with anyone.'"[84] Yet in this context, as in *The Life of St. Anthony*, one can see the more profound dynamic of humility at work. For it was only as holy men like Barsanuphius won glory for their ascetic humility—their resistance to engaging life on the pride–shame axis (Kellenberger)—that they could assume the powerful role of providing spiritual, moral, and practical guidance to their community.

Augustine's The City of God

In a letter (132) dated sometime during 411 or 412, Augustine offered himself as a dialogue partner to an eminent pagan intellectual, Volusian, as the latter examined the teachings of the Christian faith.[85] Volusian did not let the opportunity pass, but wrote a letter back (135) to Augustine asking for an explanation of the doctrine of the incarnation.[86] It came to Augustine's attention from a mutual friend, Marcellinus, that Volusian was also raising a serious political question about whether Christ's commandments to meekness and gentleness were not in fact deleterious to the life of the state.[87] This was no idle speculation in the face of the sack of Rome by Alaric in 410. Augustine responded to Volusian via two further letters (137–38), but within a year this question spurred him to begin his magnum opus, *The City of God*, designed ultimately "to persuade the proud how great the power of humility is."[88]

In the first seven books of *The City of God* Augustine provides his nuanced diagnosis of the downfall of the Roman Empire: an immanent critique of the moral and political life of the empire from its founding to the present day. The massive growth of Christianity, to the detriment of the traditional gods, was said to be the cause of Rome's descent. On the contrary, Augustine argues that Rome's convoluted history with her gods was one of "domination of prideful demons," but now through Christ she had received truly "divine teaching . . . which moves human affections in humble piety to the pursuit of the heavenly—or more than heavenly."[89]

Prior to the neglect and cessation of the sacrifices to the gods, prior to the coming of Christ, Rome had been subject to various historical disasters. Augustine lays these disasters at the feet of Roman immorality and consequent societal discord. He contends that the worship of the gods did not help them to become better morally, but worse.[90] From Greek times, obscene theatrical performances had been an integral part of the worship of the gods. This tradition was also instituted early on by the pontiffs at Rome.[91] However, Romans, unlike the Greeks, recognized that the actions attributed to the gods in the plays were not things fit for a moral society, and so denied that the actors were to be celebrated.[92] Augustine chides them for not drawing the logical conclusion that if the human beings who imitated the gods were not worthy of being celebrated, then such gods were not worthy of worship.[93] They are similarly inconsistent, he writes, in making laws that portray the rulers in debased fashion, all the while allowing the poets to compose these plays about the gods. He thus reasons: "[I]n their own laws they already outdo and indict the gods."[94] Furthermore, whatever just laws were present in Roman society from its founding did not have a lasting impact. Augustine argues, following the Roman historian Sallust, that "oppression by the more powerful, leading to the alienation of the people from the patricians and to other discords in the city, was present right from the beginning." This struggle for power and the desire of the more powerful to subjugate the less powerful is, to Augustine's mind, what constitutes "the worst dregs of immorality."[95] It was this fundamental root of injustice that the gods were powerless to stop and even gave implicit license to through their dramatized power struggles.

The "domination of prideful demons" produced an empire built on society-destroying, self-aggrandizing domination. As an early example of this dynamic, Augustine points to the rise and reign of a man who was rewarded with the kingdom for his murder of his own father-in-law—Tarquin the Proud.[96] Augustine takes the pride of Tarquin to be paradigmatic for the long history that followed; in Livy's words: "[W]hoever was the wealthiest and had the most power to do harm was counted as good."[97] The same dynamic of prideful self-aggrandizement was not only evident in the internal life of Rome, but also in its lust to build an empire—to extend rather than defend its boundaries.[98] And success in this domineering endeavor, Augustine contends, is by no means its justification. In the most approximately just of situations, the extension of boundaries and the acquisition of wealth is only a necessary evil—it certainly does not bring felicity, as the Romans thought.[99] Nonetheless, Augustine recognizes a certain providential, relative good mixed in with the Roman lust for empire. The Roman vice of "the love of praise" was used to "counteract the terrible evils of many other peoples."[100] Augustine contends that this love of praise is precisely opposite to the character of the true God— "for each person is more like God the more pure he is of this impurity."[101] Nevertheless, in keeping with the general understanding of evil as a malformed good, this vain ambition for mere human glory serves as an example for the saints to follow. For, as the Romans were willing to subordinate their other desires to seek the approbation of human beings, the Christians should be even more willing to despise human glory entirely to seek the approval of the eternal God. The beginning of true virtue, then, is to reject the whole system of earthly shame and glory to seek the true good of the heavenly city revealed in Christ.[102] Even those Christians who rule in the temporal realm are not to seek dominion to the exclusion of others, but rather are to act as servants to the heavenly kingdom "where they do not fear to have co-rulers." In contrast to the prideful amassing of power engendered by the worship of the gods of Rome, the offering the true God requires of a Christian emperor is "the sacrifice of humility and compassion and prayer."[103]

In book 7 of *The City of God*, Augustine completes his tour de force of the history of the Roman Empire and its religion. He turns to Varro, who attempted to demythologize the Roman gods and explain them as various forces of a "world-soul," which is the true God. Augustine argues that this attempt fails in that it is philosophically incoherent, and that it does nothing to ameliorate the deleterious moral sway that the civic theology exerts. In fact, it makes bare matter supreme, so that the highest apparent thing in the universe, the human soul, is led to bow down to what is manifestly lower than itself.[104] Varro's account of a senatorial cover-up of the true origin of the rites of the gods makes space for Augustine to hypothesize that the origin of the gods is not found in reflection upon nature, but rather in the lusts of demons and their attribution of deity to mere creatures.[105] The arrogant aspiration of these demons is unmasked when the one true God in Christ "who, to raise man up, offered an example of humility as great as the pride by which these demons fell." The content of this example of humility is that the Son "assumed flesh, was born, and suffered for our sake."[106] Rather than sowing discord or encouraging self-aggrandizement, the manifestation of God in the flesh was an act of self-sacrifice aimed at establishing a true republic—a just community founded on charity. Augustine encapsulates the driving force behind these two cities when he later writes: "Over against the pride of the demons, by which mankind has deservedly been held captive, there stands, in contrast, the humility of God, made known in Christ."[107]

The contrast between the earthly city and the heavenly is thus above all a contrast between competing moral visions—one that revolves around pride and one that revolves around humility. It is humility, Augustine says, that will ultimately exalt humankind, while pride is its downfall. This only *seems* paradoxical, since humility is defined as the turning away from self in submission to the one than whom there is no greater. Pride, by contrast, brings humanity down from this height, causing it to rise no higher than itself. Augustine makes this particularly explicit in book 14:

> For this reason, humility is especially commended in the city of God and to the city of God in the present, while it is on pilgrimage in this world; and humility is especially proclaimed in its king, who is Christ. At the same time, Sacred Scripture teaches that the opposite of this virtue, the vice of exaltation, is especially dominant in his adversary, who is the devil. Here, certainly, is the great difference that distinguishes the two cities of which we are speaking, one a company of the godly, the other a company of the godless, each including the angels that belong to it: in one the love of God comes before all else and in the other love of self.[108]

Humility, then, is for Augustine the moral virtue par excellence. It is defined by Augustine as the willing subjection of one's mind and affections to what is highest—the eternal God. It is important to see that this is not subjection in the abstract, nor subjection to any abstract God. Rather, humility is self-subjection to the God that is love, as defined concretely by God's self-giving in Jesus Christ. To subject oneself to his rule is not merely to subject oneself to a fiat distinct from the ruler, for the Word that comes forth is God's own self-giving. Subjection to Christ is moral participation in self-giving love—to God and, through God, to others. Pride, as the chief vice that stands behind all sin, is fundamentally a privation of the virtue of humility. It is a turning away from the divine orientation of self-giving love, to a self-aggrandizing lust.[109]

Augustine's use of humility is highly nuanced and subverts some of the commonplace definitions of humility laid out in the beginning of this chapter. The main emphasis within those definitions falls on one's opinion of oneself and one's deserts (1–3, 5), a sort of passivity (4), and a realization of one's own defects (6). Given Augustine's premise that the self-giving love of God exemplified concretely in Christ is the foundation of the eternal city, humility is not the embrace of what is lower, but what is higher. To be humble is not to be less, but to be *more*, because more like God. Therefore, humility is not the absence of self-assertion, but rather it is a more fitting self-assertion. Realizing the defects that stem from human pride is an important part of humility. However, this follows secondarily from humility as a primary recognition of the great things for which one is intended. Certainly, Augustine agrees that humility is "not being proud, haughty, or arrogant" (7), but this definition fails to encapsulate the fact that for Augustine, pride is dependent upon humility and not vice versa, just as evil is parasitic upon good.

When Kellenberger defines humility as an essential turn away from the "pride–shame axis of self-concern" and a corresponding turn toward God, he is expressing something that vaguely resembles the definition of humility embedded in Augustine's writings. However, the major differences are that this analytic definition of humility (1) does not give any specificity to the character of the "God" to whom it refers, and (2) does not include Augustine's premise that human beings are made in the image of God. Stated in this abstract theological form, and missing the anthropological premise, it is still susceptible to the criticism that humility is the turning toward another at the expense of oneself. To take it to the extreme, there is no reason why Kellenberger's definition might not in the end be seen as merely trading in all earthly tyrants for a heavenly one. In Kellenberger's account, the self and God might still exist in a zero-sum game of power. By contrast, Augustine's account of humility is designed very carefully to preclude any such notion. As such, Augustine's account appears well positioned to venture a response to the likes of Hume and Nietzsche.

What is perhaps most striking about Augustine's account of humility is that there is within it a partial resemblance to Aristotle's all-important virtue of magnanimity after all. Recall that magnanimity is the characteristic of a person who seeks the highest honor, an honor that she deserves. This is not the egoistic magnanimity Nietzsche takes it to be, but here one seeks to be great within and for the sake of the *polis*. Magnanimity is situated between the errors of wanting merely to *appear* great (vanity) and not seeking to live in accord with the great nature one has received (pusillanimity). Augustine's vision of a heavenly *polis* differs greatly from Aristotle's aristocratic vision and this gives rise to important differences. However, as Augustine has defined it, humility, like magnanimity, is the seeking of greatness. Augustine's understanding of pride attempts to encapsulate both vanity and pusillanimity in that it is at once an empty seeking for greatness (because it defines greatness wrongly) and a demeaning of one's own nature (since one does not rise to live in accordance with the divine image). For Augustine, the humble person is truly—and *not* paradoxically—the great person.

Basil the Great, The Rule of St. Benedict, *and the* Summa Theologica

Augustine's humility concept gets worked out in the context of his vision of the heavenly *polis*. He does not seek to define humility in general or abstract terms, but sees it as something in motion in the community God founds through Christ's humility. In keeping with this, he is not concerned with the practical management of an earthly community. He does not seek to lay down any concrete rules or behaviors that are to be deemed "humble"; instead, his ethical horizon is the ultimate. These factors explain the profundity and centrality of humility that emerged in the previous section. In the texts we turn to now, the focus is more directly on the spiritual formation of individuals, the specifics of regulating a monastic community, and, for Aquinas, in any case, on providing a system of doctrine replete with scholastic clarity. In these situations, the concepts that emerge are naturally more restrictive in their scope and application.

St. Basil of Caesarea was nearly a contemporary of Augustine, having died just seven years before the latter's conversion. Basil, too, lives in the shadow of the holy men of late antiquity. Basil's writings on the spiritual formation of monks in time established him as the father of Eastern monasticism. He also became influential in the West through an early Latin selection and translation by Rufinus of his works on the ascetical life. For Basil, the monastic life is not the exception to the normal Christian life of marriage and child-rearing, but rather vice versa.[110] Therefore, when Basil describes the life of virtue in the context of monastic instruction, what he says in this context is his teaching on virtue qua virtue.

According to Basil, the first step in the monastic contest is the renunciation of earthly goods so that one can be fully committed to fighting as one of Christ's spiritual soldiers. This is the step taken by those who "aspire to become a lover of the celestial polity" and is not to be taken lightly.[111] Once this commitment is made, the next front in the war is the actual living out of the monastic calling. This will involve the monk in the choice of and submission to a spiritual master, as well as the careful avoidance of sensual vices.[112] It will also involve him in various positive actions including prayer and physical labor for the sake of others. Together, these are the locus of the monk's spiritual formation: "The work of the ministry is an exalted work and leads to the kingdom of heaven. It is a dragnet of the virtues, comprising within itself all the commandments of God. It contains, first of all, the virtue of virtues, humility, which brings with itself a host of blessings."[113]

Humility is the virtue of virtues because, he writes, "[h]umility is the imitation of Christ; high-mindedness and boldness and shameless-ness, the imitation of the devil."[114] It is through humility, the attempt "to be the last of all and the servant of all," that one wins honor and glory.[115] Citing Matthew 18:3-4, Basil defines the childlike humility required by disciples as the abolition of hierarchy and competition in favor of a certain type of "equality."[116] Those who hold a position of power within the church should not use power in any abusive way, but do precisely the opposite: "[H]e should rather regard his position as a reason for showing humility toward them."[117] Those who come out of positions of worldly power and into the monastic community are correspondingly to be given the lowliest of tasks in order that they may imitate Christ.[118] Those in superior positions become "an exact copy of Him by practicing humility."[119] Of course, humility can also be used by those who find themselves as the less powerful within the community; these brethren are to obey their superiors voluntarily "in submissiveness and humility."[120] Among equals in rank, humility is the mutual service of one to another.[121] Later Basil instructs the monks that they are not to form special friendships or cliques, as these will fracture the community and make it so that "the reward of humility" is not available to everyone as a common good. The payoff of humility is a community of self-giving love.[122] And at the same time, life in com-munity is necessary so that one can excel in the virtue of humility.[123] Nearly all of Basil's practical advice revolves around how to be humble in various situations because through his commandments Christ "on all occasions habituates us to humility."[124]

Basil, like Augustine, takes his concept of humility from the model of Jesus Christ, specifically focusing on the incarnation as the act in which the one who made the earth deigns to take up residence in it. While in contrast to Augustine, Basil's vision of the polis at first seems temporally restricted to the earthly monastic community, he sees these specific communities as images of the "heavenly polis"—the city of God.[125] Therefore, the definitional discussion of Augustine's text above can be assumed to apply here. There is one particular feature of the concept of humility that, while implied in Augustine, shines forth more clearly in Basil. This is the explicitly two-way nature of humility. Humility is the virtue of virtues for both the powerful and the lowly, the superior and the subordinate. Because humility involves an orientation toward a community of self-giving love, it is incumbent upon all parties to pursue this virtue. It cannot be seen as merely the virtue of the lowly, nor is it exclusive to those who have power to put to use. Here, humility is not the loss of one's will to another's will, but a co-willing in which the will finds itself.

Rufinus' translated selection of Basil's ascetical works influenced *The Rule of St. Benedict* and the formation of a monastic tradition within Western Christianity in the early sixth century. In *The Rule of St. Benedict*, only one virtue is treated—*humility*. Benedict sets the stage for his rule by discussing the types of monks, the qualities one should find in an abbot, and the commitment of total obedience that is necessary on behalf of those who would be monks. Humility itself is conceived as a twelve-step ladder toward exaltation: "[W]e descend by exaltation and ascend by humility."[126] Renunciation of one's own will is "the first step of humility."[127] If the first step is turning away from oneself as free to do whatever one wills, the second step is loving to do the will of God.[128] The third rung on the ladder is seeing one's abbot as the concrete locus of submission to God.[129] Fourth on the way to humility is obedience in the case of "unfavorable, or even unjust conditions."[130] Fifth, humility is said to require total transparency with one's abbot. The sixth rung requires one to be content "with the lowest and most menial treatment."[131] The seventh step involves being internally convinced that one is inferior to all others.[132] The eighth step enjoins only behavior that is endorsed by the rule of the monastery.[133] The ninth, tenth, and eleventh rungs regulate quantity, frivolity, and volume in one's speech.[134] The twelfth and final step on the ascent is that all of one's outward behavior is to manifest the inward humility: "Whether he sits, walks or stands, his head must be bowed and his eyes cast down."[135] Having ascended through the descent of humility, the monk will be said to arrive at perfection in the love of God (as in 1 John 4:18).[136] The rest of St. Benedict's *Rule* is devoted to the very concrete ways in which one should embody humility within the context of the monastic community.

At the end of his *Rule*, Benedict indicates that it represents only a start toward the monastic life. It is a rule for beginners. He implores monks to go further in meditating on the meaning of monastic life; he commends them to study Scripture, the councils of the church, the writings and lives of the fathers, and "also the rule of our holy father Basil."[137] Thus, if we take him seriously as this point, Benedict himself expresses the inferiority of his rule to that of Basil. Nonetheless, he intends his account to be an apt introduction to the life of humility advocated in Basil's work. Upon analysis, though, there are some dramatic shifts in Benedict's concept of humility when compared to Basil's (and Augustine's). First, while Benedict, too, sees humility in terms of the imitation of Christ, he does not reference the act of incarnation as the paradigm of humility. Instead, as the second through fourth steps show, he sees the paradigmatic act of humility as Christ's suffering and crucifixion. Second, Benedict's concept of humility is not explicitly rooted in an eschatological vision of a "heavenly polis." The monastic life is here treated in terms of the individual's transformation rather than the creation of a community as itself "the common good" Basil was after. Third, Benedict's concept of humility starkly departs from Basil's in its demand for absolute obedience to the superior even in the case of injustice. Basil's ascetical writings include specific guidelines for a monk to challenge his superior if he believes that the superior's prescriptions are not in line with the teaching of Scripture.[138] What seems to underlie these three differences is that Benedict makes a direct equation between humility and obedience. At the beginning of the *Rule*, he advocates monasticism as "the labor of obedience" that is to bring one back from "the sloth of disobedience."[139] This is likely why in his section on the qualities of the abbot, the emphasis falls on just authority, but there is no mention made of the abbot being humble in relation to the monks. Humility and obedience to a superior have become synonymous.

Given the place humility occupies in Augustine, Basil, and Benedict, it is striking to turn to Thomas Aquinas' mature moral theology and find that humility has been relegated to the backwaters of his teaching on virtue. It is important to see where humility fits within Aquinas' overall treatment of the virtues in the *Summa Theologica*. For Aquinas, a virtue is the perfection of a power, and this perfection is measured with regard to the telos of that power.[140] The virtues are powers specifically of the soul[141]—especially the volitional or appetitive faculty of the soul, as opposed to simply the intellect.[142] The virtues are understood on two complementary levels: nature and grace. The virtues of nature are those powers that are perfected in a person's living in accordance with their human nature as such. The virtues of grace are those powers that surpass natural capabilities as such and so only come through participation in the divine nature.[143] The virtues of nature Aquinas places into four "cardinal virtues": prudence, justice, temperance, and fortitude. The virtues of grace are the "theological virtues": that Pauline triad of faith, hope, and love (in 1 Cor 13:13). Humility will be found deep within the drawer of the cardinal virtue of temperance.

The essence of temperance, for Aquinas, is the power of the soul to curb the passions that tend toward pleasures of bodily touch.[144] It is a virtue that is, more than any other, concerned with the good of the individual as opposed to the community, and therefore it is the least of all the virtues.[145] The necessary parts of temperance are shamefacedness (the fear of doing something disgraceful) and honesty (the spiritual clarity of reason).[146] The four species of temperance, which differ according to the objects of pleasure, are abstinence (food), drink (sobriety), chastity (sex), and purity (other types of bodily pleasures). In addition to these four species of temperance, Aquinas delineates a number of potential or "secondary virtues" within temperance. These are called secondary because they are not concerned with a "principal matter"—a direct moderation of the pleasures of bodily touch—but with "some other matter where moderation is not so difficult." However, because they moderate "the appetite in its impulse toward something, [they] may be reckoned a part of temperance, *as a virtue annexed thereto*."[147] Buried among these secondary, annexed virtues is humility.

In recent years, a number of articles and chapters, as well as one full-length work, have extolled the fecundity of Aquinas' treatment of humility within the context of the virtue ethics presented in the *Summa Theologica*.[148] Sheryl Overmyer argues, however, that these recent attempts overreach greatly: "The problem is this: Thomas did not have much to say about humility. Out of the 512 questions of his incomplete *Summa Theologica*, he devoted only one to the topic. Thomas gives short shrift to humility."[149] Overmyer contends that the reason for this is because, within the context of the *Summa*, Aquinas "relies too heavily on philosophical sources to organize the virtues," thus denying it the status it has in the Christian tradition—a status Aquinas knows full well.[150] To squeeze a more robust account of humility from within Aquinas' *Summa*, Overmyer makes two moves. First, she looks to the substance of his account of humility and finds that it is defined as "chiefly the subjection of man to God, for Whose sake he humbles himself by subjecting himself to others."[151] Second, on this basis she allies humility with two virtues within the cardinal virtue of justice—religion and truth, showing that humility "concerns" these virtues in that it is a sort of prerequisite for each of them.[152]

Aquinas says that the purpose of humility is to "temper and restrain the mind, lest it tend to high things immoderately" and there is a need for it to be complemented by one of the virtues of fortitude—magnanimity, which guards against despair and impels the moral agent to seek great things within the bounds of right reason.[153] Humility is defined by Aquinas as "praiseworthy self-abasement to the lowest place."[154] Humility should restrain a person from seeking by one's means to obtain things that are beyond one's means. In this way humility necessarily involves a knowledge of one's deficiency. At the same time, Aquinas says, humility does not preclude one from seeking what is beyond one's means by throwing oneself entirely upon God's help.[155] Since humility involves turning away from one's own means to God's help, humility can in one way be said to hold pride of place as a preparation for the influx of divine grace. In the next breath, however, Aquinas says that faith, as the first positive step toward God, "is the foundation in a more excellent way than humility."[156] Humility is a necessary ground-clearing virtue, but in and of itself it has no positive content or orientation. Aquinas calls humility a mere "disposition" and contrasts it with those greater virtues "whereby man approaches God directly."[157]

With respect to its sudden appearance within the realm of the cardinal virtues, Aquinas says that the reason Aristotle did not reckon humility as one of the virtues is that he was concerned only with those virtues that are "directed to civic life," whereas humility is primarily "the subjection of man to God."[158] This is not to say that humility has no bearing on one's relations with other human beings. For, within the subjection of oneself to God in consciousness of one's deficiency, one also can subject oneself to a fellow human being in respect of what is divine in the other. This means that one can esteem another as better than oneself in one respect, while at the same time recognizing one's own superiority in regard to what is divinely given in oneself.[159] In this way, Aquinas also strongly hints at a new, sacramental political reality opened by humility—a community of mutuality in which what is deficient in oneself is submitted to the divine gifts resident in others through the Holy Spirit.

Placing humility under the heading of the cardinal virtue of temperance elucidates the narrowing of the concept of humility found in Benedict's account. For Benedict, humility is equated with obedience to a superior, and this already represents a conceptual constriction in comparison to what is in Athanasius, Basil, and Augustine. Within the context of Benedict's *Rule* and Aquinas' *Summa*, humility becomes a propaedeutic. Humility removes the spiritual obstacle of pride, thus paving a smooth path of access to God.[160] Because of Aquinas' characteristic insistence that created things have their own creaturely goodness and integrity apart from grace, humility is essentially the acceptance of one's proper nature as a creature. At the same time, as a creature, one is inherently deficient in that one needs grace. To bring greater specificity to Overmyer's contention: it is this substantive theological nature–grace schema that accounts for the relegation of humility within the hierarchy of the virtues in the *Summa*, and not merely that Aquinas has been constrained by the philosophical organization of the virtues. It is for this reason that when Aquinas does mention Christ's humility in a subordinate discussion, he is unequivocal in saying that humility pertains "not as regards his divine nature, but only as regards his assumed nature."[161] While one finds a greater emphasis on humility in Thomas' biblical and creedal commentaries, there is no substantive change in the definition. Christ's teaching about humility, and his example of humility, show what it means to be a creature, subjecting oneself to God and what is God's in other creatures.[162] In light of this, Aquinas speaks inconsistently when he echoes the apostle Paul and says: "There never was humility so great as that of Christ, who, although He was God, yet wished to become man; and although he was the Lord, yet wished to take the form of a servant [Phil 2:8]."[163] Because humility is essentially creatureliness, it can only be attributed to the person of Christ in light of the incarnation, but it cannot, with Augustine and Basil, be the impetus for the incarnation. This is why Aquinas must also depart from the notion that humility *is* exaltation.

For Aquinas, humility is properly a term of creaturely restraint, a virtue of not reaching for things beyond one's natural or—in this life—fallen grasp, and of recognizing that all that one has is a gift from God. Meanwhile, the aspects of self-diffusion and desire for the good of others that mark divine humility in Augustine and Basil are accounted for by Aquinas under the rubric of God's "goodness."[164] In this way, Aquinas characteristically offers greater definitional clarity than his predecessors but, arguably, he does so at the cost of breaking apart what ought to be the organic unity, and thereby enabling the diminishment of the concept of humility.

Despite the fact that humility for Aquinas is a virtue of nature rather than grace, it is a decisively theological concept. It is not defined merely as (1) "having a low opinion of oneself," (2) "having a low estimate of one's merit," (3) erring on the low side concerning one's importance, (4) forgoing self-assertion, or (5) "claiming little as one's desert." It formally includes (6) "having or showing a consciousness of one's defects." However, it is important to see that the defect Aquinas speaks of is not, primarily, a defect of one's nature, but rather the acceptance that one's nature needs that which exceeds it. And while Aquinas' definition also includes (7)—"not being proud"—pride here has the specific theological content of turning away from creaturely dependence on God. While it seems consistent that the humble person would be "deeply opposed to engaging life in terms of the self-concerned states of pride and shame" (Kellenberger), for Aquinas this would be an effect of humility rather than its definition.

Conclusion: A Concept Fit for God

The concept of humility is "polythetic"— its multiple meanings are held together by various family resemblances. This chapter began with a set of concise, common-sense analytic definitions that revolve around a deeper reality: humility as the absence of some form of self-concern. Laid out as such, these uses have a possible, though not necessary, connection to one's relation to God. While these uses have taken on a life of their own, pressing deeper into the traditions of Western thought shows how dependent on religious notions these concepts are. For, in Aristotle's writings, there is nothing akin to humility in the way it is later conceived by influential Christian voices like Athanasius, Augustine, and Basil, who take their ethical cue from the reality of what God does in Christ in becoming incarnate for the sake of his *polis*. This alternative vision of a *polis* founded by Christ is the context in which humility is explicated as "the virtue of virtues." Christ founds his society by condescending in grace to what is beneath him by nature. For these authors, this is the archetype of humility: the divine self-giving.

Humility is the disposition to cross the boundary between grace and nature. Aquinas' commitment to analyzing the virtues as either virtues of nature or virtues of grace leaves no place for humility as "the virtue of virtues" (Basil). Rather, this place is taken for Aquinas by charity, or love. Aquinas' authority for this elevation is that irrefutable statement of holy Scripture: "[T]he greatest of these is love" (1 Cor 13:13).[165] This is in contrast not only to the way Augustine elevates humility to the highest place, but also to the way he uses the term "love." For Augustine, "love" is an ambivalent term: "Two loves, then, have made two cities. Love of self, even to the point of contempt for God, made the earthly city, and love of God, even to the point of contempt for self, made the heavenly city."[166] One manner of loving is equivalent to the vice of pride, the other manner of loving is equivalent to the virtue of humility. For Augustine to say consistently that love is a virtue (and he does at points call love a virtue) would seem to imply that it is a virtue that can be either a virtue or a vice. But is that a salvageable proposition?

The ambivalence in the term "love" and the ambiguity as to its status as a virtue is not unique to Augustine; it is found in the first of the Johannine epistles. On the one hand, John writes "do not love (*agapāte*) the world or the things in the world. The love (*agapē*) of the Father is not in those who love (*agapā*) the world" (2:15). By contrast, a wonderful love (*agapēn*) has been given to us (3:1), and the exemplar of love is simply stated: "[Christ] laid down his life for us" (3:16). And John goes so far as to say that "God is love (*agapē*)" (4:8). What it means for God to be love is spelled out in the next two verses: "God's love was revealed among us in this way: God sent his only Son into the world so that we might live through him. In this is love: not that we loved God but that he loved us and sent his Son to be the atoning sacrifice for our sins" (4:9-10). There is therefore a qualitative difference between the merely human loving that is possible by nature (2:15) and the love that *is* God and is *from* God. There is a form, or prototype, of love that belongs essentially to God alone, and there are human perversions of this love. Augustine illuminates the way humility is a conceptualization of the concrete act of God's love in Christ. Humility is the "greater love" of Christ's incarnation and crucifixion (John 15:13) that disciples are to receive with gladness and model analogically in their dealings with their fellows.[167] That is to say, humility has its creaturely correspondences. Human beings are "humble" insomuch as they receive God's act of condescension in Christ with gratitude. They are also said to be "humble" insofar as they willingly and joyfully embody this relationship of strength-serving-weakness in their lives—whether they are the giver or the receiver. This explains why humility in the literature can be predicated both of potentates and the impoverished. Humility is the concept that gives concrete definition to "love."

It is when the concept of humility is abstracted from its native embeddedness in the vision of a community founded by the incarnation and death of Christ that it begins to wither. The concept becomes deflated. This deflation is evident in the deficiency of Kellenberger's definition of humility as turning away from self-concern. Or when Benedict treats humility only in the specific application of how subordinates are to relate to their superiors. These attempts to define humility tend to remove from the concept the overwhelming sense of greatness that it has within its native ethical vision. They are only partial accounts of humility. When detached entirely from the framework of Christ's *polis*, humility becomes a passive-aggressive attempt to gain the upper hand (Nietzsche), or the "monkish virtue" of pain that it would be foolish to seek out (Hume). When Christianity tries to work with a deflated concept of humility, it can serve as a corrective in certain contexts (like that of hypermasculinity), but it is not a virtue in the true sense of the word (Saiving Goldstein).

Despite the tendency of philosophical analyses to deflate the concept of humility, a greater role for humility within the constellation of the virtues is portrayed beautifully in two examples from English literature. George Herbert's seventeenth-century poem "Humilitie" (63) portrays humility as the sine qua non of all the other virtues. As the personified "Verities" are seated on the heavenly throne, they receive tribute from the beasts of the earth (63.1–4). Humility has the role of receiving and distributing tribute to the other virtues for management (63.5–8). The lion's paw, representing physical strength, is given to gentleness (63.9–10). The cautious ears of the hare are given to fortitude (63.11–12). The turkey's wattle—symbolizing consumption—is given to temperance (63.13–14). Justice receives the fox's cunning mind (63.15–16). When it comes time to distribute the greatness of the peacock's plume, a fight breaks out between the virtues as to who should receive pride of place (63.17–20). As the other virtues quarrel the beasts begin to dethrone them (63.21–24). Only as humility's tears at this scene gain the attention of the other virtues do they realize that the self-seeking of greatness will undo them all (63.25–28). As they allow humility its rightful possession of the plume they are able to reassert themselves over the passionate beasts of the earth (63.28–32). Herbert makes the point that humility is identical to true greatness and power in that it seeks not its own, but the good of the community. Herbert thus understands, as evidenced in "The Church-Porch" that humility and magnanimity go hand-in-hand:

Pitch thy behaviour low, thy projects high;
So shalt thou humble and magnanimous be:
Sink not in spirit: who azimuth at the sky,
Shoots higher than much then he that means a tree.
   A grain of glory mixt with humblenesse
   Cures both fever and lethargicknesse. (17.331–336)[168]

A similar portrait of humility as true greatness is painted in Jane Austen's *Pride and Prejudice*. A most significant feature in the story is the development of the virtue of humility in Mr. Darcy. In a foreshadowing of things to come, he offers an important interrupting comment about Mr. Bingley's so-called humility of self-deprecation: "'Nothing is more deceitful,' said Darcy, 'than the appearance of humility. It is often only carelessness of opinion, and sometimes an indirect boast.'"[169] Humility is not, in other words, merely being unconcerned with the opinion of others. Humility is not at all about how one appears. For it is Mr. Collins who, though he embodied "great humility of manner," is nonetheless one of the most intransigently proud characters in the novel.[170] Yet this leaves open the question of what, precisely, is true humility? Furnished with every advantage of breeding, class, and wealth, Darcy possesses Aristotelian magnanimity. It is the introduction of love for Elizabeth that allows Austen to portray both true humility and press from Darcy's character a fuller expression of his greatness. Darcy embodies both as he decides to seek the good of Elizabeth (and for her sake, her shameful family's good) at his own expense. Rather than continue to live as a "selfish being . . . in pride and conceit," his love for Elizabeth leaves him "properly humbled" for the first time.[171] This does not mean that his wealth and status are lost through humility; on the contrary, the seeming inexhaustibility of his greatness is displayed in the way his condescension is able to lift up the object of his love to his own level without diminishing his own stature whatsoever.

The concepts of humility employed by theologians like Athanasius, Augustine, and Basil—and embodied by the writings of Herbert and Austen—do not contradict but rather refine and expand the notion of magnanimity that is so central to the Aristotelian vision. Unlike Aquinas, these authors do not need to develop a concept of magnanimity, because this would be largely superfluous in light of what they mean by humility. Where does this leave the critiques of humility discussed? As far as Hume goes, the concept of humility he critiques is at best badly truncated, at worst a complete misunderstanding. Humility has almost never been seen as an embrace of pain per se. If pain results for the one who possesses this virtue, it is only an accidental feature owing to the fact that one's fellows are not likewise humble. As for Nietzsche, his critique of humility penetrates more accurately to the roots of the concept of humility in the Jewish and Christian traditions. Yet his egoistic conception of greatness as domination rules out anything like humility. Whether one agrees with Nietzsche's assessment of humility will depend entirely on whether one has succumbed to the fundamental principle of the "will-to-power." As David Bentley Hart comments: "Nietzsche's disdain does not follow from the force of his reasoning; *it is that force.*"[172] The critique offered by Valerie Saiving Goldstein, and followed by some later feminist theologians, operates on the assumption that humility is defined essentially by lowliness—the diminishment of the self or the submission of the self to the power of another. This viewpoint serves to show why this central virtue of Jewish and Christian religions must be properly understood and explicated with great care. If humility is deflated, then it certainly may become an instrument of oppression; but this should be seen as a bug, not a feature, of this moral concept.

What follows is an exploration of the potential in taking the concept of humility-as-true-greatness as a candidate for application to the very being of God. Humility, as noted above, is universally predicated of Christ in Christian theology. When it comes to the doctrine of God—to describing God's perfect being—the predication of this concept is not typically made in a straightforward fashion, if at all. However, as will be argued over the course of the next three chapters, there is a trajectory of this attribution within the theological tradition that shows sound theological reasons why this concept should be brought into the doctrine of God, and raises important questions about the proper ways to make this act of predication. We will take up and read this tradition beginning with Augustine, whose ambiguity between what we might call theocentrism and Christocentrism militates for a doctrine of divine humility.

3

SCRIPTURE'S SUGGESTIVE TENSIONS
Augustine

B asil Studer's parallel study of Augustine's Christology and Augustine's doctrine of God commences on the premise of a tension in Augustine's thought. On the one hand there is the lofty, unknowable God, the God of philosophical theology—perfect being theology. On the other hand, there is the more ecclesial concept of God revealed in the incarnate Christ.[1] On this basis, Studer's study splits into two independent parts, one on "the grace of God," the other on "the grace of Christ." In his conclusion, he briefly gestures toward a theological rapprochement in a short comment. The reconciliation of these two "opposed tendencies" in Augustine's thought is to be found somehow, Studer says, in Christ's sacrifice. So Studer writes:

> [I]n the final analysis God revealed God's innermost self only in the humiliation of the cross of Christ and that only in God's humility did God give the final and complete proof that God is love. In Augustine's eyes, the death of Jesus was the most convincing proof that behind the impenetrable mystery of the irreversible divine will there was "God is love."[2]

Studer's analyses of Augustine's doctrines of God and Christ stand on their own as helpful contributions to the study of Augustine. Yet it is the recognition of an apparent tension between Augustine's understanding of God proper and his understanding of Christ, and especially the gesture toward "God's humility" as the synthesis to the tension, by which Studer suggests from Augustine's writings a fresh possibility for constructive work in the doctrine of God — a doctrine of divine humility.

This chapter picks up on this suggestive possibility Studer has drawn out of Augustine's work, displaying this fruitful tension in Augustine's doctrines of God and Christ, and exploring the function of the concept of humility in relation to this tension. Augustine does not write a doctrine of God in anything approaching the way of medieval scholastic theologians or contemporary systematic theologians; he does not isolate, categorize, or analyze individual divine perfections. Therefore, in the attempt to find the basis for a doctrine of divine humility in Augustine's writings, this chapter will inevitably begin to push beyond what Augustine has actually said. Yet the question to be asked is not whether this attempt goes beyond Augustine, but whether this going beyond can stake a legitimate claim to "go on in the same way."

Augustine's understanding of God suffuses his entire corpus, and so the question of an ordering principle of the primary source material looms large. As Studer notes, "Anyone wanting to speak of Augustine's picture of God must therefore go into all his writings, which is an impossible undertaking."[3] It is difficult to know how to provide a representative analysis of writings that span the genres of dogma, polemics, prayer, sermons, letters, autobiography, history, and more. Above all, what gives Augustine's corpus its unity and coherence in the face of such diversity is his use of Holy Scripture. Augustine's engagement with key biblical texts presents the aforementioned, theologically generative tension of God *in se* and God *pro nobis*. For this reason, the bulk of this analysis is structured around biblical texts that are especially significant to Augustine, and through which one can see him not only surfacing the tension, but also reasoning toward a unifying concept. In the first section, the foundational giving of the divine name(s) in Exodus 3:14-15 presents Augustine with a tension between God's immutable self-existence and God's merciful response to his distressed creatures. In the second section, some apparently contradictory statements of

Christ in the Fourth Gospel, especially John 5:19-30, present Augustine with a tension between Christ's equality with, and subordination to, the Father. The third biblical text, Philippians 2:6-7, surfaces a tension between Christ's status in the "form of God" and his incarnate "form of a servant." This recurrent tension throughout Augustine's writing provides the structure for a doctrine of divine humility—something that Augustine appears to move toward, but not unambiguously.

Exodus 3:14-15: "The Name of Being" and "The Name of Mercy"

In one of his shortest extant sermons (sermon 6), Augustine provides a theological exposition of God's revelation to Moses in the fiery shrub of Exodus 3:1-15. The biblical text itself pushes the tension between the immutable God of perfect being and God's merciful embrace of the world of mutability. Augustine's first course of action is to rid his congregants of the notion that God's appearance to Moses was such that God was seen "in his substance." This type of direct encounter of God will only be had for those who are pure in heart—and even they cannot have it in this life. Nonetheless, Augustine does believe that God appears to the bodily senses—through specially chosen creaturely objects.[4] The ultimate fact that establishes the possibility of these theophanies is the incarnation.[5] It is the mystery of the Son taking on a human nature that illuminates how God exercises his agency in revelation through angels, prophets, the people of Israel, and of course, the burning bush.[6]

It is out of this burning bush that the divine name is given: "I am who I am" (Exodus 3:14). Augustine teaches his flock in terse fashion that this statement of perpetual is-ness refers, above all else, to the immutability of God: "[T]he unchangeableness of God was prepared to suggest itself by this phrase."[7] Yet in the very next verse, in God's very next breath, "another name" is revealed. The intransitive "I am" is expanded into the transitive. God not only is who God is, he is "the God of Abraham, the God of Isaac, and the God of Jacob" (Exodus 3:15). In the juxtaposition of this second name against the first, Augustine sees within God's very nature the basis for the incarnation. He explains how the second name "means that while God is indeed unchangeable, he has done everything out of mercy, and so the Son of God himself was prepared to take on changeable flesh and thereby to come to man's rescue while remaining what he is as the Word of God. Thus he who is, clothed himself with mortal flesh, so that it could truly be said, 'I am the God of Abraham, the God of Isaac, and the God of Jacob.'"[8] This is no mere homiletical flourish. The two divine names—or two versions of the one name—in their close proximity militate against the notion that one could separate any God of the philosophers from the God who will mercifully take up residence as an individual Israelite. Put another way, there can be no bifurcation between the God of perfect, unchangeable being and the God who lives this perfect being in mercy.

Augustine juxtaposes these two names from Exodus 3 on occasion at key points in his other works. Psalm 102 ends with a statement about the transience of the heavens and earth over against the enduring reality of God's people in God's eternal present: "They shall pass away, but thou endure; like clothes they shall all grow old; thou shalt cast them off like a cloak, and they shall vanish; but thou art the same and thy years shall have no end; thy servants' children shall continue, and their posterity shall be established in thy presence" (102:26-28). Augustine interprets this passage as referring to a cosmic participation in the death and resurrection of Christ. For though it is true that God is the "selfsame," the "I am who I am," "for our consolation he added, 'I am the God of Abraham, the God of Isaac, and the God of Jacob.'"[9] Augustine's interpretation of this perceptively ties together the slavery of the Israelite people in Exodus 3 with the state of humanity and the cosmos under sin and death that is under discussion in Psalm 102, writing: "We are slaves, but for our sake our Lord assumed the nature of a slave; for us mortals he who is immortal willed to die; and for our sake he exemplified our resurrection in himself."[10]

Augustine's treatments of Psalms 122 and 135 are especially instructive in the way he teases out the juxtaposition of these two divine names from Exodus 3. Psalm 122 is a psalm of ascents; a song to be sung while going up to the temple in Jerusalem. Augustine is aware of this *Sitz im Leben,* but the historical fact of Jerusalem's destruction, and especially the Pauline typological reading of Jerusalem (see Gal 4:26), lead him to interpret Jerusalem here as the eschatological unity of God and his people—the "city of God."[11] Using what can only be a

Vetus Latina manuscript, Augustine sees further confirmation of this in Psalm 122:3. His version evidently runs thus: *Hierusalem quae aedificaris ut civitas cuius participatio eius in idipsum.* Augustine places a full stop after *civitas*, allowing the adverb *quae* to be emphasized so as to indicate analogical language: "Jerusalem is built *like* a city." Furthermore, this punctuation and the use of *in idipsum* in place of Jerome's *simul* allow the rest of the verse to be read as "[i]t shares in the selfsame." The "selfsame" (*idipsum*) is for Augustine virtually synonymous with the Tetragrammaton. The Jerusalem under discussion participates in the divine nature—but how? To know God *in se* is too much for feeble creatures to grasp, but Augustine reassures his audience with a christological reading of the divine names in Exodus 3:14-15: "Do not be put off, do not despair. He-Who-Is willed to become a human being like you, so he had more to say when Moses was terrified of his name . . . he said more: 'I am the God of Abraham, the God of Isaac, and the God of Jacob: this is my name forever.'"[12] This condescension of God allows the possibility for the ascent of Israel to Being-Itself. True Israel comprises those who do not aspire to have absolute being themselves, but rather participate in the divine nature through the humility of confessing, or praising, the dually named God (as in Ps 122:4).[13] Furthermore, the ontological stability of the divine nature in which this city participates through praise can be described only in moral terms; Being-Itself is identical with self-giving charity.[14]

The opening of Psalm 135 likewise invites Augustine's reflection on the divine names in Exodus 3:14-15: "Praise the LORD. Praise the name of the LORD" (Psalm 135:1). The motivation for praise is that God is good (Psalm 135:3). God is goodness itself, the ground of all created things which are themselves declared "good" in a derivative sense.[15] God's status as goodness itself is embedded in the Tetragrammaton given at the burning bush, since to exist in sheer actuality is itself an unparalleled good.[16] While the sheer actuality of God as goodness itself is sufficient grounds for endless praise, recalling his experience in *Confessions* 7.17.23, Augustine knows himself to be insufficient to praise on this basis and supposes his hearers are as well.[17] So Augustine announces the good news that God gave the second name of Exodus 3:15 because "he did not will to remain isolated in a majesty which demanded to be praised but was out of reach of anyone who praised him."[18] Answering his rhetorical question as to why God would now change his name, Augustine tells his listeners that the first name is suitable to God *in se*, while the second name speaks of who God is *pro nobis*.[19] Augustine goes out of his way to stress that the second name is not merely a "temporal name" in opposition to the first "eternal name." After all, God says in the passage, "[T]his is my name forever" (Exodus 3:15). Augustine interprets this not in the sense that Abraham, Isaac, and Jacob possess their own eternality with God, but rather that God grants them—and all spiritual Israel with them—to share in his eternality.[20] Thus, this twinning of the names in Exodus 3:14-15 throws light on the structure of Psalm 135. It shows why the praise of the eternal and essential goodness of God—identical as it is with being itself—is enjoined on the basis of God's election of Israel.[21]

Augustine's major works often invoke the first of the two names—"I am who I am" (Exodus 3:14). Augustine takes this name to be one of the rare instances in Scripture in which the divine nature is manifest in a direct fashion, as opposed to the bulk of the biblical witness in which God is revealed through the medium of created things.[22] For this reason, the Tetragrammaton functions as a rule that stands over the rest of biblical interpretation and theological reflection. Take, for instance, *De Trinitate*. In books 2–4 Augustine lays out the unified work of the Father, Son, and Spirit manifest in Scripture and declared by the creeds. He then begins his attempt to understand the ontological presupposition of this scriptural and creedal confession that the one God is Father, Son, and Holy Spirit. To ward off objections, but also to purify his own (and his hearers') logic and language on this front, Augustine devotes three books (5–7) to exploring the way that the church's confession *cannot* be understood. He begins with Exodus 3:14.

The single principle that undergirds this section of *De Trinitate*, and that will keep reason within the bounds of revelation, is the metaphysical simplicity implied by the Tetragrammaton.[23] God's being, which is the origin of all being whatsoever, is entirely actual. God cannot be placed on a plane of being generally and defined in relation to other beings. One corollary of this is that there are no accidental properties that make God God. God is metaphysically simple. Everything that can be predicated of God is an essential property: "With

God . . . nothing is said modification-wise, because there is nothing changeable with him." There are things that can be said of God that are not statements about the divine essence—for instance, the terms "Father" and "Son"—but these are statements of the *relation* of the divine being to the divine being.[24] These statements are not, however, predications of the divine being. "Fatherness" ("unbegottenness") or "Sonness" ("begottenness") are not attributes of God, properly speaking. To say otherwise would lead to the complete unraveling of the doctrine of the Trinity. It would be to say either (1) that there are three divine beings; (2) that there is only one truly divine person, rendering the Son and Spirit less than the Father (Arianism); (3) that there is one truly divine "person" that stands behind three ultimately dissolvable personas presented in Scripture (Sabellianism); or (4) that the three persons effectively add up to the divine being, in which case none of the three could be called God without qualification.

As the divinely revealed name of Exodus 3:14 serves to provide instruments to discipline thought about the "persons" presented in Scripture, so it also, mutatis mutandis, provides instruments by which predications of the divine being are disciplined. The Tetragrammaton is a necessary but not sufficient account of the divine nature. The notion of God's metaphysical simplicity (or the associated concepts of God's aseity, eternality, and immutability) is always one pole within a tension of the doctrine of God. The other pole of this tension consists of the moral or personal attributes of God—God's actions within and toward the creaturely world. But one notices that these two poles function in different ways. Predications of the divine essence derived from Exodus 3:14 function in the manner of *grammar*, providing the rules by which predications of God's moral or personal attributes must be interpreted. This means that even as Augustine often uses Exodus 3:14 alone, he does so only in order to make sense of the name of Exodus 3:15.[25] So in sermon 7 he says that the first name is "eternity's name" ("I am that I am")—a statement of immutability and its attendant doctrines. But "what is much more interesting is that [God] was prepared to have a *name of mercy*: 'I am the God of Abraham, the God of Isaac, and the God of Jacob.' That name in himself, this one for us."[26] And this is no mere conceptual tension, but one that is spiritually generative, enveloping those who understand in a dynamic of proper fear and filial love: "[L]et us then praise, though we cannot find words for it, his being, and love his mercy."[27]

To anticipate the importance of this reading of Augustine's two-fold naming of God: for Augustine, the name of simple being (the Tetragrammaton) is necessary but never sufficient for a doctrine of God. The same is true of the "name of mercy." Augustine's account of the divine life always requires both; there is an indissoluble tension. This means that the notion of condescending mercy—which Augustine calls "humility"—is not merely something God does, it is somehow intrinsic to God. In what way is the disposition toward mercy intrinsic to God's life? The next section moves toward an answer to this question by treating a species of this same tension, this time in Augustine's treatment of John 5:19-30.

John 5:19-30: Trinitarian Processions and Inseparable Operations

The text of John 5:19 "seems to have been a fundamental stimulus in the evolution of Augustine's vision."[28] It is this text, explored in a subset of the tractates on John (18–23),[29] that confronts Augustine with an additional tension that will shape his doctrine of God. The statement of Christ in 5:19 reads: "Very truly, I tell you, the Son can do nothing on his own, but only what he sees the Father doing; for whatever the Father does, the Son does likewise." Within the framework of divine simplicity drawn from the divine name (Exod 3:14) and from the church's trinitarian confession, John 5:19 presents a problem. Arian exegesis of this text seemed to be a piercing riposte to faith in the ontological equality of the Father and the Son. The context of the passage is Jewish anger at what is perceived to be Christ's claim to equality with God (see John 5:18). The declaration of Jesus in John 5:19 that he has no power to act, save for his seeing and imitating the work of the Father, is interpreted by the Arians as a clear statement of Christ's ontological inferiority to the Father.[30] And yet the Fourth Gospel also states that the Son ("Word") shares an association and identity with God from "the beginning" (John 1:2). The Arian interpreter attempts to resolve the tension by creating a hierarchy of being: the Son is less than God proper (the Father) but greater than creation. Augustine takes this effort at constructing a hierarchical ontology—one that envelops a greater God, a lesser God, and creation—to be rank "paganism." It is paganism presumably because, by denying the indivisibility of a simple God, it necessarily places God within the same framework of being as created things, allowing the divine being to be defined by comparison and contrast to other beings.[31] By contrast, Augustine will not resolve the conceptual tension introduced by the Father's doing and the Son's seeing and doing likewise by constructing an ontology of this sort. Instead, disciplined by the grammar of divine simplicity, the tension pushes Augustine toward further definition of the divine being along relational or even moral lines: "I understand this equality in such a way that I also perceive undivided *charity* there; and if undivided charity, then perfect unity."[32]

Divine simplicity rules out for Augustine any interpretation of John 5:19 that states that the Father independently shows the Son what to do, and that the Son in turn acts independently in emulation of the Father. Instead, he glosses the verse as follows: "[T]he Father [does] every kind of work through the Son, so that there are no works whatever done either by the Father without the Son or by the Son without the Father."[33] Thus the trinitarian rule about God's works in time: *opera Trinitatis ad extra indivisa sunt*. John 5:19 reveals that the indivisible nature of God's trinitarian works in time—his "doings"—are rooted in the eternal "showing" and "seeing" of the Father and Son.[34] This text is therefore turned around and used as a rebuke against the Arians, whose theological ontology comes about by projecting materialistic understandings of the works of God in time into the divine being, without allowing a proper understanding of the divine being to discipline, qualify, and correct this effort. The Arians do not give priority to Christ's "seeing" over Christ's "doing." They do not allow the divine being to rule the external divine actions.[35] The question Augustine must seek to answer satisfactorily is what it means for the Father to show and the Son to see.

Augustine's starting point is this: if the Word who created all things (John 1:3) created the senses of sight and hearing, then it is absurd to say that the Word does not see or hear. Yet, per divine simplicity, the fact that the Word sees or hears is not meant in a bodily sense; there is no part of the Word that is an organ of hearing and part that is an organ of seeing. Augustine draws the following conclusion from this: "[I]s he all sight and all hearing? Is that perhaps so? Not at all. There is no 'perhaps' about; that is really and truly so. . . . Both seeing and hearing are one and the same in the Word; hearing is not one thing there and seeing another; but hearing is sight and sight is hearing."[36] The rule of divine simplicity requires that whatever it means for the Son to see, this seeing is identical with his being the Son. The identicality of the Son with his seeing is the first doctrinal principle to emerge from the tension of John 5:19-30. If there is to be any understanding this, Augustine says, one can only hope to reach it by considering the image of God in the human person. Once sights and sounds enter into the inner being (he uses the word "heart" here), it is not one part of the person that sees and another part that hears, but all happens in one and the same heart. Yet this is only an analogy, of course, since, unlike the Word, one is not identical with one's hearing or seeing. In fact, it is the faintest of analogies, since seeing and hearing are not even *essential* properties of a human person.[37] Augustine closes tractate 18 by saying that the aim of reflecting on the divine life is to allow his listeners' darkened spiritual eyes a momentary glimpse of pure divine light, kindling a desire to have their eyes healed so that they can see more fully.[38] This is why, as he opens tractate 19 (given the next day), he says that he has offered not an explanation, but only a way for understanding to make progress toward its infinitely transcendent goal.[39]

In interpreting John 5:19-30 in tractate 19, Augustine moves to what he says is a more difficult tension. The first iteration of the tension is from John 5:20: "The Father loves the Son and shows him all that he himself is doing; and he will show him greater works than these, so that you will be astonished." Augustine notes that the "greater works" to be shown consist in raising the dead at the eschatological judgment. The tension Augustine finds in the statement is based on the verb tenses of the passage: (1) the Father shows (present tense, taken to imply eternally) the Son everything, and yet (2) will show (future, to happen in time) the Son greater things than what the Son has currently been shown. Augustine asks: "[H]ow [can] the eternal Father show things to the co-eternal Son in a time sequence"?[40] He begins to explore this tension by way of John 5:21. The "greater things" of raising the dead is said to be a work not only of the Father, but also of the Son. Based on the principle that the

Father does all that he does through the Son, this cannot mean that the Father raises some and the Son raises others in imitation. Rather, the Father and the Son raise the dead by the same divine power and the same divine will. Yet this is not a resolution: the very next verses (John 5:22-23a) immediately raise the tension anew. They claim that the work of eternal judgment is not carried out by the Father ("for the Father judges no one"), but instead by the Son ("he has given all judgment to the Son"). Augustine propels his listeners further into the text with an implicit promise that Christ himself will somehow resolve this moving tension. After statements that underline the Son's equality with the Father and his status as the Word that raises the dead now (morally) and eternally (bodily) (5:23b-25),[41] Augustine begins to arrive at an insight created by the problems of the text. John 5:26 reads: "For just as the Father has life in himself, so he has granted the Son to have life in himself." The interpretation of this verse issues in a second doctrinal principle from John 5:19-30: "[T]he only difference between Father and Son is this: that the Father has life in himself which no one has given him, while the Son has life in himself which the Father has given him."[42] The Son is given life in a qualitatively different manner. Creatures participate in God's life; the Son has life *in himself*. The life that is given to the Son, as the divine life, is utterly simple—fully identical to the life he is given by the Father. This giving of life is therefore not an act of creation, but an act of eternal begetting. So the second principle means that no distinction whatsoever other than that of "unbegotten" and "begotten" can be made between the Father and the Son. The names "Father" and "Son" simply denote this one eternal distinction.[43]

We can now draw the points of tractates 18 and 19 together. From John 5:19-30, Augustine raises the same basic tension between the Father and the Son in three ways, allowing each to push him to formulate a theological principle in response.

(1) The Son says that he can do only what he sees the Father doing, and yet we know that everything the Father does is already done with, through, and, indeed, by the Son.

This tension, under the discipline of divine simplicity, leads Augustine to formulate the first theological principle to emerge from John

5:19-30: the Son is identical with his seeing. Augustine promises to explore this further.

(2) The Son is shown everything of the Father's eternally, but will be shown by him "greater things" pertaining to the eschatological resurrection.

Augustine's exegetical response to this consists in reasserting the axiom that whatever the Father does is done through the Son. With this the resolution is deferred pending further insight from the text.

(3) All things the Father does are done through the Son, but eschatological, resurrection judgment is said to be done not by the Father but rather is given to the Son.

Here the theological principle that emerges from the exegesis of the passage, and that is said to resolve the tension, is that the only distinction to be made between the Father and the Son is that between unbegottenness and begottenness.

To what extent has Augustine's exegesis actually dealt with the tensions raised? And more importantly, how does this give shape to Augustine's doctrine of God? The principles that were pressed from the text's encounter with the doctrine of divine simplicity are trinitarian in nature. For the sake of clarity here they are one more time:

(A) The Son is identical with his "seeing." In fact, this is really the more expansive principle that "each of the divine three may be understood as identical with the intra-divine acts that Scripture attributes to them."[44]

(B) There is one, and only one, distinction that can be made between the Father and the Son—the distinction between unbegottenness and begottenness.

The theological outcome of Augustine's exegesis of John 5:19-30 is to find an inter-trinitarian basis for the Son becoming incarnate. He has done so in the following manner. To the first tension noted above (1), doctrinal principle A responds by stating that for the Father to show the Son his works, and for the Son to see the Father's works and emulate them "in like manner" is simply for the Father to beget the Son. Nothing less, nothing more. As for tensions 2 and 3, they are closely interrelated. In both of them there is an apparent contradiction between the absolute equality and cooperation of the Father and the Son, and the fact that the Father will show the Son "greater things" in time (2), and that the Son has been given by the Father the role of eschatological resurrection judgment (3). Augustine's response to this apparent contradiction is anticipated in theological principle B. Because the only theologically admissible distinction between the Father and the Son is that of relation (and explicitly not a distinction of being or a division of labor), inasmuch as the texts distinguish between the Father and the Son, they do so only in the sense of the trinitarian relations. Therefore, the Father showing the Son "greater things" (resurrection) is the temporal expression of an eternal reality. The Father raises the dead through the Son in the same way that the Father does all things, even creation—"through the Son." This argument is made by Augustine in tractate 23, given on the third consecutive day after tractates 18 and 19. To make this argument from Scripture, Augustine relies heavily on the text to be treated in the next section: Philippians 2:6-7.

Augustine's exegesis of John 5:19-30 in tractates 18, 19, and 23 is about more than technical distinctions and rules for trinitarian theology. What Augustine has accomplished is to find a basis for the incarnation of the Son in time in the eternal life of God the Holy Trinity, and to do so by employing rather than eschewing the doctrine of divine simplicity. While this may not be surprising to some, it does help to overthrow a certain misreading of Augustine that has been made by contemporary trinitarians. Citing Barth as a key influence, and Gunton, Moltmann, Pannenberg, and Rahner as his compatriots, Robert W. Jenson argues that the entire tradition of Western trinitarianism is deficient, and that blame for this deficiency can be laid at the feet of Augustine's doctrine of God. Jenson contends that the indivisibility of the acts of God in time cannot mean for Augustine that these acts are *mutual* works of the Father, Son, and Spirit, rooted in the trinitarian life of God. His reason for this claim is that it would "posit differentiation in God's intrinsic agency" and that, for Augustine,

> there is no difference at all between the agencies of Father, Son, and Holy Spirit. Either, he thinks, Father, Son, and Spirit must simply do the same thing, or simply different things. . . . Thus he supposes, for example, that the Son's appearances in Israel could as well be

called appearances of the Father or Spirit, or that when the voice speaks to Jesus at his baptism . . . the speaker is indifferently specifiable as the Father or the Son or the Spirit or the whole Trinity.[45]

This is, first of all, largely a misreading of Augustine. As shown above, Augustine does not say that there is "no difference at all" between the Father, Son, and Holy Spirit. In fact, in that very passage, Augustine says plainly that only the Father's voice was heard at the baptism, that only the Spirit came in the form of a dove, and that only the Son took on flesh (*Trin.* 1.8). Augustine explicitly disagrees with Peter Lombard, whom Jenson cites as a direct heir of Augustine, that any of the three could have been incarnate.[46] However, Augustine of Hippo would agree with Jenson's Augustine in this: that there are not multiple "agencies" within the Trinity. Whatever "persons" are for Augustine (and he resists attempts to bring clarity to this term), they are not separate agents or actors, on the pain of either splitting God into three parts or creating three separate gods. Whatever the merits of this "trinitarian renaissance" of which Jenson is part, it is wrong to claim that Augustine's understanding of the Trinity within the strictures of divine simplicity supposes that there can be no intrinsic connection between the "structure" of the immanent Trinity and the work of the economic Trinity.[47] For Augustine, God's merciful condescension manifests God's simple, immanent life. In fact, it is only on the basis of the outworking of this mercy that one knows God to be Father, Son, and Spirit.

For Augustine, the doctrine of God has two necessary and mutually complementary components: God *in se* and God *pro nobis*. Taking his cue from the keystone text of Exodus 3:14-15, he refers to God's life under the rubrics "the name of being" and "the name of mercy." The former, it was argued, was a sort of "grammar" of the latter. Augustine's doctrine of trinitarian processions, seen in his exegesis of John 5:19-30, further demonstrates this claim by making the case that God's condescending mercy toward creatures in the incarnation of Christ cannot be something accidental to God, but rather is somehow rooted in the life of the Holy Trinity. The outstanding question Augustine now faces is how God shares his life with contingent creation. To answer this question, we turn now to the *forma dei / forma servi* christological schema that Augustine develops from Philippians 2:6-7.

PHILIPPIANS 2:6-7: THE *FORMA DEI* AND THE *FORMA SERVI*

Lewis Ayres says that it is in Philippians 2:6-7 that Augustine finds his hermeneutical key to overcoming Arian readings of passages that imply a lesser status for the Son in comparison to the Father.[48] It is Philippians 2:6-7 that provides Augustine with a twofold schema of Christ's life—*forma dei, forma servi*—that makes sense of both the statements of equality with the Father as well as statements of the Son's inferiority to the Father. Indeed, Augustine writes in *De diversis quaestionibus octoginta tribus*: "[T]he rule of Catholic faith [*regula . . . catholic fidei*] is this: when the Scriptures say of the Son that he is less than the Father; the Scriptures mean in respect to the assumption of humanity; but when the Scriptures point out that he is equal, they are understood in respect to his deity."[49] For Augustine, Philippians 2:6-7 both establishes this rule and is made sense of by this rule.[50] As noted above, it is the discipline of this rule that undergirds the exegesis of John 5:19-30 (tractate 23). The tension between the Son as God (*forma Dei*) and the Son as divine-human (*forma servi*) is, for Augustine, theologically generative.

Before analyzing Augustine's treatment and use of Philippians 2:6-7, it will be helpful to comment on the biblical text and a notable debate in contemporary New Testament scholarship. Philippians 2:6 reads in Greek: ὃς ἐν μορφῇ θεοῦ ὑπάρχων οὐχ ἁρπαγμὸν ἡγήσατο τὸ εἶναι ἴσα θεῷ. Michael J. Gorman argues that the participle ὑπάρχων should be taken causally rather than concessively. On this basis he asserts that the Son does not hoard his divinity (2:6) but rather takes on a human nature *because* he is God (2:7-8). This is in contrast, Gorman says, to the "vast majority" of translators (see NIV, ESV, NRSV, NASB) who take the participle to mean that the Son takes on a human nature *although*, or despite the fact, that he is God.[51] Theologically, this allows Gorman to develop the statement that the divine life itself is "cruciform." A third option that Gorman mentions, only to ignore, is that the participle could have a temporal or neutral translation of "while" or "being"—"being in the form of God."[52] This third option is the tack taken by the older English translations, like the KJV ("being") and Wycliffe ("when"). This third, more neutral, option is also what is taken by the Latin Vulgate, which Augustine relies on when it translates ὑπάρχων as *esset* (*"qui cum in forma Dei esset non rapinam arbitratus est esse se aequalem Deo"*). Greek participles are by nature ambiguous, requiring their meaning to be supplied by context and content. The more neutral translation of ὑπάρχων as simply "being" or *esset* as well as the concessive translation ("although") both maintain the theological tension in the text between the Son in the *forma dei* (divine) and the Son in the *forma servi* (divine-human). Gorman believes that adopting a causal ("because") translation of ὑπάρχων will alleviate the theological tension of the passage. Yet things are more complicated than this.

To make his argument for a causal translation of ὑπάρχων in Philippians 2:6-7, Gorman appeals to a general narrative pattern wherein Pauline texts that appear to follow the formula "although [x] not [y] but [z]" are to be interpreted "because [x] not [y] but [z]." His examples are 1 Thessalonians 2:6-8 and 1 Corinthians 9:17. These texts do not employ the specific participle ὑπάρχων, but Gorman's interpretation is based on the fact that these passages are about the *imitatio Christi*. Paul adopts voluntary limitations, not in spite of ("although") his identity as an apostle of Christ, but precisely *because* he is an apostle of Christ.[53] Gorman retains the "although" translation at a superficial level ("surface structure"), since, he says, what Paul and Christ do contradicts normal human expectations about what it means to wield power. Ultimately, however, the "deep structure" of the passages have the meaning of "because," so that kenotic "power-in-weakness" is the truest expression of Paul's and Christ's persons. But this interpretation is not established, even if one grants Gorman's translation of ὑπάρχων. The statements that God is *essentially* "vulnerable," "cruciform," and "kenotic" all assume that a causal conjunction exists between 2:6 and 2:7. However, there appears to be no causal conjunction joining them. The participial clause of 2:6, ἐν μορφῇ θεοῦ ὑπάρχων, subordinately modifies only the immediate clause ὃς . . . ἁρπαγμὸν ἡγήσατο τὸ εἶναι ἴσα θεῷ. The next main clause, in 2:7, begins with an adversative conjunction, providing a separate, contrasting statement about the subject of the sentence (Christ Jesus): ἀλλὰ ἑαυτὸν ἐκένωσεν μορφὴν δούλου λαβών, ἐν ὁμοιώματι ἀνθρώπων γενόμενος· καὶ σχήματι εὑρεθεὶς ὡς ἄνθρωπος. This second main clause has its own subordinate participial clause (which in turn has its own subordinate participial clause introduced by an ascensive conjunction, which continues on through 2:8). There are therefore two statements about Christ Jesus here: (1) "though he was in the form of God, [he] did not regard equality with God as something to be exploited" (2:6), and (2) "but (ἀλλὰ), [he] emptied himself, taking the form of a slave, being born in human likeness. And being found in human form, he humbled himself, and became obedient to the point of death—even death on a cross" (2:7-8).

Gorman takes his interpretation of Philippians 2:6-7 to be proto-Chalcedonian. What he finds proto-Chalcedonian is that "kenosis is thus the *sine qua non* of both divinity and humanity, as revealed in the incarnation and cross of Christ, the one who was truly God and became truly human."[54] Thus, for Paul, "true humanity and true divinity are analogous at the most fundamental level."[55] Gorman makes what the Son does in becoming human and suffering an eternal attribute of God. However, while the Chalcedonian definition confesses the unity of Christ's two natures in one person, it also establishes that each nature retains its distinctive attributes: "[T]he distinctiveness of each nature is not nullified by the union. Instead, the 'properties' (*idiotētos*) are conserved and both natures concur (*suntrechousēs*) in one 'person' (*prosōpon*) and in one *hypostasis*."[56] Gorman's interpretation of Philippians 2:6-7 goes beyond the Chalcedonian definition in that it is not merely a statement of the concurrence of the properties, but rather a statement about the *communication* of the properties. Further, Gorman does not merely indicate a communication of the properties that occurs in the divine and human natures of the incarnate Christ, but instead reads the properties of this divine-human Son (the *forma servi*) into the preincarnate Son, and therefore the doctrine of God (the *forma Dei*). (Gorman is aware of the objection that this would make "kenosis a divine necessity rather than a free act of love and grace," but all he can do is acknowledge a paradox in his own theological conclusion.[57]) This is one direction for a Christology that claims Chalcedonian legitimacy, and it is a direction that will have to be reckoned with in the next chapter, on Karl Barth. Yet, again, this is not a direction that is established on the grammatical and lexical grounds, specifically by the translation of a single participle. Both Chalcedon and Philippians 2:6-7 admit other possibilities.

For Augustine, Philippians 2:6-7 does not enable one to say that God is essentially "cruciform" or "vulnerable" or "kenotic." In Augustine's reading, the text does not allow one to speak of a communication of properties in the way that certain kenotic theologians have. Augustine is careful not to make a causal connection between the *forma Dei* and the *forma servi* and careful not to allow the latter to determine the former without qualification. Yet clearly there is some sort of communication, or rather, "participation" that takes place. Consider this important excerpt from *De civitate Dei* that depends, characteristically, on a terminology developed out of Philippians 2:6-7:

> It is not because he is the Word, however, that he is the mediator. For the Word, of course, is supremely immortal and supremely blessed in so far as he is removed from miserable mortals. He is the mediator, rather, due to the fact that he is man. . . . It is God who is blessed in himself and also makes us blessed, and, because he became a participant in our humanity, he provided a shortcut to participation in his divinity. . . . That is why, when he willed to be lower than the angels, in the form of a servant [*forma servi*], he still remained higher than the angels in the form of God [*forma Dei*]. At one and the same time he was both the way of life here below and life itself in heaven above.[58]

The context is a refutation of the Neoplatonist notion that mediation occurs through angels. In place of this, Augustine shows how a two-natures Christology provides mediation. He says that there are two categorical attributes possessed by the divine life: "immortality" (*inmortales*) and "blessedness" (*beati*). By contrast, there are two categorical attributes possessed by human beings: "mortality" (*mortales*) and "misery" (*miseros*). To be God is to be immutably blessed. To be human is to be mutably miserable—miserable but, hypothetically, with time to change. Since mediation is situated between the two spheres, Augustine reasons, then mediation entails sharing one category of attribute each with both God and humanity.[59] Good angels (*eudaimones*) themselves share in a derivative sense of immutability and blessedness and therefore can be of no help. Demons (*daimones*) are immutably miserable, since they have no opportunity to repent of their rebellion.[60] Augustine's argument here works on the following assumptions: (1) that sharing in blessedness is the path whereby mutable creatures gain a share in immutability, and (2) that a share of immutability, once gained, cannot be lost; with the mutual entailment (3) that a creature that through blessedness gains a share of immutability and subsequently ceases to share in blessedness will henceforth be immutably miserable.[61] Thus, a mortal person could, by sharing in blessedness, attain a share in immutability as well. This is precisely what Augustine sees the union of the two natures of Christ accomplishing: "We must seek a mediator who is not only man but is also God, so that the blessed mortality of this intermediary may, by his intervention, lead men from their mortal misery to blessed immortality."[62] The blessedness of the divine nature is communicated to Christ's human nature, such that his human nature subsequently shares in the immortality of God through participation in blessedness. At the level of blessedness there is direct communication, while at the level of immutability there is only indirect communication.

When Augustine describes Christ's mediatory role in terms of "blessedness" and "immortality," he is, in effect, speaking of the divine life at two different, though complementary levels. The former speaks in terms of the personal, moral character of God's being—his love. The latter speaks in terms of what we have previously called God's being—his immutability, which is shorthand for his metaphysical simplicity. The moral character of God's life is directly communicable, while the immortal character of God's life is something ineffable that remains proper to God alone and can only be shared indirectly, with moral blessedness leading to the beatific vision. This is virtually identical with the dual divine naming that Augustine drew out of Exodus 3:14-15—"the name of mercy" (3:15) and "the name of being" (3:14). The former corresponds to the *forma servi* and the latter to the *forma Dei* (where it is understood that the *forma servi* does not denote merely the human nature of Christ, but the person of Christ as divine-human). The fact that the divine nature communicates to the human nature of Christ at the level of moral character but not at the level of immutable being explains why Augustine can say, without paradox or contradiction, that even in the *forma servi* Christ remained in the *forma Dei*. Within this schema it is unintelligible to describe the divine life *simpliciter* as "kenotic" or "vulnerable" or "cruciform." For what God does in the incarnation of Christ is to allow a human life to participate in his own immeasurable life. The incarnation, and even the suffering and death, of Christ is an expression of the divine identity that makes the most profound impact on the human nature but does not determine the divine nature. The divine life determines the life of Christ, but the relation cannot be reversed. To put it in the terms of later medieval scholasticism: the creature exists in a real relation to God, but God does not exist in a real relation to the creature. Before there was an *extra Calvinisticum*, there was an *"extra Augustinum"*—developed by way of the generative tension inherent in Philippians 2:6-7.[63]

This *forma Dei / forma servi* schema taken from Philippians 2:6-7 is recurrently used by Augustine in order to make sense of those passages in Scripture that speak of the Son being less than the Father—for example, John 14:28: ". . . the Father is greater than I." A key instance of this use of *forma Dei / forma servi* occurs in the first book of *De Trinitate*. Heretical readings of Scripture, and here Augustine has in mind chiefly Arian interpretations, are based on a failure to consider such statements in light of "the whole range of the Scriptures," leading to the erroneous attempt "to transfer what is said of Christ Jesus as man to that substance of his which was everlasting before the incarnation and is everlasting still."[64] The fundamental Arian error is thus to see any statement about Christ as referring to the Son *simpliciter*. Augustine argues, by contrast, that a proper understanding the two *formae* of Christ will allow one to make sense of texts that speak of the inferiority of Jesus Christ to the Father without detriment to those texts that speak of the equality between Father and Son. In one sense, therefore, Augustine affirms that Christ *is* less than the Father. Yet, on the other hand, Christ retains full and absolute equality with the Father. Christ is both less than God and equal with God. "So if the form of a servant was taken on in such a way that the form of God was not lost . . . who can fail to see that in the form of God he [Christ] too is greater than himself and in the form of a servant he is less than himself." Therefore the two natures of Christ are to be carefully maintained, "without any confusion. . . . Neither of them was turned or changed into the other by that 'take-over'; neither godhead into creature and ceasing to be god-head, nor creature changed into godhead and ceasing to be creature."[65]

Augustine's careful distinction between the *forma Dei* and *forma servi*, and the insistence that the two not be confused, does not undermine the personal union of the two natures. Recall again the distinction between the grammar of God's life—his simplicity—and the moral character of God's life—his love. Since the latter is *directly* communicated to Christ, there is an identicality between the two natures, but not an absolute identicality. That is to say, the human nature of Christ does not share all the properties of the divine nature of Christ, for were the two natures to share all properties in common, there would not be two natures but one. However, since it is the personal, moral character of God's life that is directly communicated to the human nature of Christ, there is an identicality of true self-expression of one's person but such that the expression is not an exhaustive expression. Paul Ricoeur calls this self-expressing form of identicality "*ipse*" identicality. (By contrast, that identicality that states complete sameness he calls "*idem*."[66]) Augustine's *forma Dei / forma servi* schema relies on something like this *ipse* identicality at the level of personal expression, and it is this that allows Augustine to maintain a distinction between the two natures while affirming that Christ is always and ever a single, personal subject. This is why Augustine can state, without contradiction, "each (*forma*) is God because of God taking on, and each (*forma*) is man because of man taken on." Were the is-es in this statement that of *idem* rather than *ipse* identicality, Augustine could not add in the next breath: "Neither of them was turned or changed into the other."[67] For this one person, God the Son, exists eternally in the *forma Dei* but gives a true self-expression in a human nature in the *forma servi*. These *formae* are distinct and yet continuous, since it is one and the same personal, moral agency that is expressed.

Augustine's understanding of Christ's personal unity in the two *formae* calls for a brief anticipation of a later christological controversy. On the face of it, it may be thought that the one personal, moral character that unifies the two natures implies a monothelite Christology—the teaching that Christ, while having two natures, had only one will. This would be one way of understanding what it means for Christ's two natures to remain distinct and yet have a personal unity. Yet this version of Christology would thus require that the human nature Christ assumed did not have a will. Dominic Keech seems to read Augustine in this manner when he writes: "In spite of Augustine's assurance that Christ is one person in two natures, that personality appears to be predominantly characterized by the nature of the Word who assumes it." However, within Augustine's schema there is no reason why the personal expression of God cannot be both (1) God's personal expression, and (2) a genuinely human expression of God's personal character. The idea that this creates a "difficulty of assigning the source of the acts or experiences of Christ to either one of his natures" misses the point.[68] Within Augustine's schema the personal union of the two *formae* means that the source of "the acts or experiences of Christ" is the *forma dei*, while their outworking in the *forma servi* is fully and genuinely human. The claim that Augustine's "Christ possesses an ambiguous will, imprecisely apportioned between his divine and human natures" misses the mark in that it presupposes a competitive relation, alien to Augustine's Christology, between the divine and human natures of Christ.[69] The presupposition of such a zero-sum relation between the divine and human willing in Christ is what led to the Third Council of Constantinople in 681. The conciliar definition rejected this account as a false dilemma. Far from running afoul of the later conciliar definition, Augustine's Christology easily accommodates, if not implies, a dyothelite Christology.

As noted above, this highly nuanced *forma dei / forma servi* christological schema, derived from Philippians 2:6-7, is exhibited most evidently in Augustine's interaction with subordinationist texts. Nowhere is the comprehensiveness of this schema seen as clearly as when it is put to use to interpret 1 Corinthians 15:24-28. This biblical passage confronts Augustine with the statement that, even in the eternal kingdom, when all things are said to be subjected to Christ, that Christ himself will be subject to the Father: "When all things are subjected to him, then the Son himself will also be subjected to the one who put all things in subjection under him, so that God may be all in all." Augustine offers extended reflections on this text in *De Trinitate* 1 (as well as in the closely paralleled earlier *De diversis quaestionibus octoginta tribus* 69).

Augustine makes it clear from the outset, regarding his treatment of 1 Corinthians 15:24-28, that he does not take the text to imply that the human nature of Christ will be "changed into divinity itself."[70] In interpreting the statement that all things are subject to God—with the exception of God himself (1 Cor 15:27)—Augustine is careful to follow the rule of inseparable operations. Thus, when the Son subjects all things in handing over the kingdom to God the Father, he also thereby subjects all things to himself by the very act of handing over the kingdom and destroying all rule and authority (1 Cor 15:24).[71] Moreover, the temporal language of the passage—"when [Christ] hands over the kingdom to God the Father" (1 Cor 15:24)—does not imply either that there are things that are not now subject to the Son, or that the Son is not now subject to the Father.[72] Likewise, "[f]or he must reign until he has put all his enemies under his feet" (1 Cor 15:25) does not mean that the Son will one day relinquish the kingdom when he hands it over to the Father.[73] Instead, the text should be read so as to indicate that the eternal rule of God will become manifest once and for all, both to those who do not currently acknowledge God's rule and to those who believe in God's rule through faith.[74] For the former this will mean judgment, while for the latter this will provide direct, face-to-face contemplation of God, rather than the "regime of symbols" through which they currently "see in a mirror [riddle], dimly" (as in 1 Cor 13:12).[75] Thus the temporal change implied by the passage is the translation of the church to full and unchanging blessedness in the presence of God: "for the fullness of our happiness, beyond which there is none else, is this: to enjoy God the three in whose image we were made."[76] For the time being, the church is in a state of longing, rejoicing with faith in, and hope for, this vision. This longing is created by the twin action of the advent and subsequent departure of the Son in the *forma servi*. Paraphrasing John 16:26 by way of Philippians 2:7, Augustine writes:

> "I came forth from the Father," that is, surely, "It was not in the form in which I am equal to the Father that I was manifested, but in another guise, namely as less than he in the creature I took on"; and "I have come into this world," that is, "I have shown the form

of a servant, which I emptied myself to take, even to the eyes of sinners who love this world"; and "Again I am leaving this world," "from the sight of those who love the world I am removing what they have seen"; and "I am going to the Father," "I am teaching my faithful ones that I can only be fully understood in my equality with the Father."[77]

Christ as the *forma servi*, the divine-human, thus manifests the glory of the triune God to humanity, creating a condition of faith seeking contemplation. By his departure, and the sending of the Spirit, he signifies that this manifestation is indirect—that they must look through the temporal manifestation of Christ to the eternal God mirrored therein. Thus as the *forma servi*, Christ is the mediator—the way. And as the one who remains the *forma Dei*, he is the goal. As Augustine will say in *De Trinitate* 13: "It is [Christ] who plants faith in us about temporal things, he who presents us with the truth about eternal things. Through him [the God-man, the *forma servi*] we go straight toward him [the eternal Son, the *forma Dei*] . . . without ever turning aside from one and the same Christ."[78] First Corinthians 15:24-28, interpreted by way of the *forma servi / forma Dei* schema from Philippians 2:6-7, describes what it means to arrive, by way of Christ, at the goal of Christ (and therefore the Father and the Spirit too)—with the outcome that God is "all in all."[79]

So for Augustine there is again a theologically generative tension embedded in the *forma Dei / forma servi* christological schema. The Son in the *forma Dei* cannot be dissolved into the *forma servi*. It is this tension that allows Christ to be the mediator: bringing God and humanity together in genuine fellowship, all the while God remaining God and humanity remaining humanity. This possibility is rooted in God's life, which is manifest in the Old Testament twinning of the divine names of "being" and "mercy," and in the New Testament revelation in time of God as Trinity: Father, Son, and Spirit in inseparable operations. With this recurrent tension in Augustine's theology established, all that is left to do is to draw this together by showing explicitly how this results in a potential account of humility as an attribute of God.

CONCLUSION: AUGUSTINE'S AMBIGUOUS
DOCTRINE OF DIVINE HUMILITY

This chapter has treated three scriptural passages that are theologically generative for Augustine (and, of course, for much of the Christian tradition as well). These passages bring Augustine face-to-face with different versions of the same conceptual tension between God *in se* and God *pro nobis*. On the one hand, God is the self-existent, immutable, metaphysically simple being that cannot be defined by anything other than God himself. On the other hand, God can be known as such only because he manifests his divine life to creation. God mercifully grants creatures participation through the incarnation. Whether this tension is present in the passages on divine name, the doctrine of the Trinity, or Christology, Augustine resists conceptual resolution. For example, at a key point in *De Trinitate*, Augustine discusses the relation of the temporal content of faith to the divine life of God. He explicitly states that the incarnation was not a necessity for God since no power can compel God.[80] Yet not long after this he speaks of God delaying what is within his power, in order to fulfil his justice—"that is why he needed to be both God and man."[81] Augustine makes a distinction between God's power and God's justice, knowing full well that the two things are both somehow one in the divine life. God cannot be exhaustively defined by either his power or his justice—either his sheer freedom or his being merciful. This tension is theological bedrock. Rather than attempt to resolve the tension in the doctrine of God, then, Augustine tends to give this tension a name—humility.

Augustine is the theologian of humility par excellence. The concept is central to his entire theological project. Humility is the greatest power conceivable—a power of divine grace that transcends the faux power of pride.[82] It is the beginning of all virtue.[83] Humility overthrows the superstitions of false religions.[84] It is the complete reversal of the first and summary sin of pride; by lifting themselves up, human beings "fell," and by Christ bringing himself down, human beings are lifted up.[85] Humility is the perfection of charity, as God shares his power with his powerless creatures.[86] This humility is a cure for human sin.[87] Christ's humility is defined as God stretching out his hand to fallen humanity.[88] Humility is the only path by which one can travel to

God, a path that was blazed by the Word becoming human.[89] "But the humility of our Lord in undergoing human birth was too little for him to do for us" so he even went as far as to die on a cross.[90]

While humility is a pervasive theme in other patristic authors, the emphasis in Augustine's writing falls startlingly on God. There are a number of places in Augustine's writing where he refers explicitly to "divine humility" or "the humility of God," or where the subject of the verb "humble" is God. He thus speaks of "the power of the humility of God which appeared in Christ."[91] Similarly he refers to "the humility of our Lord God."[92] He writes of "the abject humility of God who humbled himself."[93] And it is "the humility of God" that shows up pride and beckons humanity back to God.[94] The "pride of earth" is said to pale in comparison to the transcendent power of "divine humility."[95] In sum, the association of humility with God "is one of the most characteristic themes in Augustinian theology. The incarnation of the Word of God is God's humility, God's humiliation, the divinity at our feet."[96]

Despite the litany of references, one might wonder whether Augustine really means that humility to be taken as a divine attribute with the same force that one might say "God is omnipotent" or "God is wise" or "God is good." Perhaps statements about God's humility are simply rhetorical flourishes—stylistic variations that require theological nuance if they are to avoid misunderstanding. The majority of the time Augustine refers to humility, he is speaking simply of the humility of "Christ" or "the Son" or "the Lord." These instances might conceivably be interpreted as referring to a quality that pertains to the Son only in the *forma servi*. Indeed, there are instances in which Augustine seems to contrast humility with divinity: "[B]y his humility he has been made a road for us in time, in order that by his divinity he might be for us a mansion in eternity."[97] Or, similarly, Augustine says that Christ "does not lose his divinity when he teaches us humility; in the former [divinity] he is equal to the Father, in the latter [humility] he is like us."[98] Augustine can write of humility in instrumental terms, as a means to an end: "for so great is the utility of human humility that even the divine sublimity commended it by his example."[99] Or, again in a similar way, he says that "our milk is Christ in his humility; our solid food is the very same Christ, equal to the Father."[100]

One way of understanding the instrumental references to humility in Augustine's works is to take humility as something God does—synonymous with the incarnation itself—rather than as a description of the divine being. If this is the case, just as one cannot make the incarnation an attribute of God, so neither can one make humility an attribute of God. While humility does at points appear to function for Augustine as a synecdoche for the incarnation, even more often it appears as the basis for the incarnation. Another, more plausible, way of understanding the ambiguity in Augustine's references to humility in relation to God would be to see humility as a divine attribute that falls squarely on one side of the tension discussed throughout the chapter. To employ the terms of Exodus 3:14-15, humility as an attribute is akin to "the name of mercy." In other words, humility is a descriptor of God *pro nobis*, but not of God *in se*. This interpretation of Augustine's use of humility is problematic, however. It has the same problem noted above—namely, that it undercuts the way Augustine takes humility to be the motivating factor for God's movement toward creatures in mercy. As such, it would seem to require something other than humility to bridge the gap between God *in se* and God *pro nobis*, the likeliest candidate being a bare conception of the divine will.

For Augustine, humility is applied straightforwardly to God, but Augustine offers no explicit exposition of how, precisely, one should take these statements. The humility of Christ clearly has a soteriological function for Augustine—it counters the pride that has corrupted the world. Yet an instrumental understanding will not suffice, since it is evident that he also sees humility as the basis for the incarnation. Furthermore, humility cannot be regarded as something merely God the Son does, since Augustine abides strictly by the rule that there can be no real division of the works of the Father, Son, and Spirit—not even with regard to the incarnation itself. With this, Augustine never advances beyond the basic feature of his understanding of God that holds together "the name of being" and "the name of mercy" in a generative tension. In the end, Augustine's understanding of divine humility is highly suggestive, but necessarily remains ambiguous. It is ambiguous in the sense that it says two things at once—that the self-sufficient God *in se* is freely but eternally God *pro nobis*.

4

DIVINE HUMILITY AS
AN "OFFENSIVE FACT"
Karl Barth

K arl Barth offers a full-throated statement of divine humility in the fourth volume of his *Church Dogmatics*: "[T]here is a humility grounded in the being of God."[1] Yet for all its boldness, Barth's statement manifests ambiguity of its own peculiar sort. In concluding his careful exposition of Barth's doctrine of the divine attributes in volume 2.1 of *Church Dogmatics,* Robert B. Price raises a series of questions about the new direction Barth takes as he refers to the humility of God:

> Barth speaks of humility and obedience as divine perfections. . . . At the same time, however, humility and obedience are not merely appropriated to the Son, as they would have to be if they were truly divine perfections. They are exclusively those of God the Son. Why does Barth speak of humility and obedience as divine perfections when dogmatically it seems they must be personal properties of the Son? Does this represent development in his doctrine of the divine perfections, even though Barth continues to insist on the same, traditional definition of a divine perfection as describing the whole essence of God? Or has Barth reconciled the categories

of "essence" and "person," so that this actually represents development in his doctrine of the Trinity?[2]

With this line of inquiry, Price provides an entry point into the difficulties surrounding one of the most beloved and influential sections of Barth's *magnum opus*, "The Way of the Son of God into the Far Country."[3] Clarity is needed as to what sort of theological pressures move Barth toward his bold statement.

G. C. Berkouwer's *The Triumph of Grace in the Theology of Karl Barth* contains perhaps the deepest interaction with Barth's position among older texts. Berkouwer sees Barth uniting the theological tradition's successive states of humiliation and exaltation into one moment, making it "possible to speak of a new form of 'theologia crucis,' a theology of the cross. The power of God, the omnipotence of God is revealed in the cross."[4] When Berkouwer turns from summary analysis to criticism, he decries Barth's inclusion of an intra-trinitarian "obedience of God" as something that exceeds the boundaries of revelation and leads inevitably to a Theopaschitism that will have to posit the death of God, God's own division against himself.[5] Berkouwer's contention with Barth is that he goes beyond the proper location of mystery and attempts to "comprehend the incarnation."[6] Barth attempts to qualify the notion of conflict by describing God's self-humiliation as omnipotence, against which Berkouwer argues that this only works if by omnipotence Barth makes recourse to a notion of omnipotence that, while biblical, cannot be developed narrowly out of Barth's christological conception.[7] In this reading, Barth's problem ultimately lies in the way he takes the human Jesus Christ to be in the strictest identity with God. Countering Barth's section title, "The Lord as Servant," Berkouwer states that in the mystery of the incarnation "God confronts us . . . as the *Servant* of the Lord."[8] Darren Sumner's recent monograph aims to counter Berkouwer's criticism by showing that the actualistic nature of Barth's theological ontology entails Barth's christological conclusions.[9] But the question Berkouwer raises is precisely the theological legitimacy of the strict identity statement implied by this type of actualism. Since, as Sumner admits, his "starting point" is simply Barth's actualistic understanding of theological ontology, his counter of Berkouwer can amount to little more than a reassertion, rather than a full defense, of Barth's position.

One of the more detailed recent treatments of "The Way of the Son of God into the Far Country" is that found in Paul Dafydd Jones' *The Humanity of Christ*. Jones argues that Barth takes the divine *kenosis* to be consequent, logically posterior, to the divine election, such that the incarnation is said to be "ontologically transformative for the divine Son."[10] He also states that the most novel and provocative aspect of Barth's statement of divine humility, that there is an intra-trinitarian obedience, is "ethically and doctrinally injurious," "crudely hierarchical," and an example of Barth's "incorrigible sexism."[11] Kevin Giles argues against Jones' type of reading, insisting that Barth's focus on divine unity negates and reinterprets the language of subordination so as to make the one God, rather than merely the Father or the Son, the subject of the divine commanding and obeying.[12] Giles sees Barth's position that Christ is eternally God and man, and eternally the electing God, as leading Barth to a breaking point at which he "resorts to convoluted, poetic language in which he speaks of a 'subordination of God in himself.'"[13] Paul Molnar, for his part, agrees with Jones that Barth improperly introduces hierarchy into the life of the Trinity, and proposes that Barth does so out of a motivation "to say that the obedience of the incarnate Son acting for us is an act of God himself."[14] One presumes that Molnar means to oppose this to an account in which the obedience of the Son is merely a human obedience, but he does not elaborate.

The divergent results of these studies of Barth's theology of divine humility show the confusing and potentially problematic nature of Barth's insistence on obedience within the divine life, and ambiguity as to what might motivate Barth to make this move. One begins to wonder if Rowan Williams was correct when he wrote in 1979 of Barth's particular conception of divine humility: "What, if anything, this can possibly mean, neither Barth nor his interpreters have succeeded in telling us . . . [the material on divine humility] produces one of the most unhelpful bits of hermetic mystification in the whole of the *Dogmatics*."[15]

This chapter's purpose is to test the viability of Barth's doctrine of divine humility, specifically with reference to the extension of the concepts of command and obedience, superiority and subordination, into the divine being. Does Barth's particular way of attributing humility to the divine being represent an advance that one can say "goes on in the same way," or is there here an intrusion of a flawed conceptuality? The first step in accomplishing this purpose is to analyze Barth's christological subsection "The Way of the Son of God into the Far Country" with as much clarity as possible. Laying out Barth's argument will allow the questions to emerge that will facilitate a theological stress-test on this most important and representative section of Barth's theology—his account of divine humility.

"THE WAY OF THE SON OF GOD INTO THE FAR COUNTRY"

Barth's Dogmatic Argument for Divine Humility

Berkouwer sees Barth as combining the tradition's successive states of humiliation and exaltation into one moment. There is something deeply right about this, but it is bluntly put. Barth brings humiliation and exaltation together by appropriating them to the divine and human natures of the one person, Christ. The manner in which God the Son humbles himself results in the exaltation of the man Jesus. There is a twofold movement to this unified act of atonement, and Barth refers to this as a "history" (*Geschichte*).[16] The history that is atonement is the temporal execution of God's eternal decree.[17] In "The Way of the Son of God into the Far Country," Barth treats the first movement—the condescension of God.[18] Barth then moves from dogmatic argumentation to exposition of his dogmatic conclusion.

Barth's dogmatic argumentation in this section of the *Church Dogmatics* can be summarized by the following four propositions: (1) The activity of the man Jesus Christ is identical with God, and therefore God is identical with the activity of the man Jesus Christ. (2) The defining activity of Jesus Christ, and therefore of God, is obedience defined as humility, or a willingness to suffer on behalf of others. (3) This obedience-as-humility is the mystery of the divine being—it is a foundational reality. Together, (1)–(3) issue the stunning conclusion: (4) Since obedience-as-humility is the mystery of the divine being, it must be said not only of God's life *ad extra* but also God's life *ad intra*.

(1) *The activity of the man Jesus Christ is identical with God, and therefore God is identical with the activity of the man Jesus Christ.* Barth

begins with the basic axiom that the man Jesus Christ is identical with the Lord of all. This is the contention of the New Testament documents, the earliest Christian confessions, and the dogmas of the fourth and fifth centuries.[19] This is an axiom established only by God's self-revelation, something that is either known and recognized or not at all. This self-revelation is the premise that must be granted if one is to understand the New Testament texts.[20] Barth reasons that, if we accept the basic premise that "Jesus is the Lord" in the sense of strictest identity, we must also accept the controvertible statement: "The Lord is Jesus." The result is that Lordship (i.e., the divine being) comes to be defined by reference to Jesus Christ.[21] When Barth says that the divine being is known and defined only in reference to Jesus Christ, he understands this to mean what Jesus Christ does—his action or history—and not some static conception of a "nature." This is what is commonly referred to as Barth's "actualism."

(2) *The defining activity of Jesus Christ, and therefore of God, is obedience defined as suffering on behalf of others—humility.* The defining characteristic of the life of Jesus Christ, Barth argues, is his unflinching obedience to God, his Father.[22] Therefore the statement "the Lord is Jesus" results in the difficult, but nonetheless properly deduced, conclusion that "the true God—if the man Jesus is the true God—is obedient."[23] This obedience that defines God is offered in the particular manner of a willingness to suffer on behalf of others—to take upon himself all the negating consequences of the disobedience of others.[24] God's willingness to take upon himself weakness, impotence, temporality, and perishing, this type of obedience is what Barth calls "the deepest humility."[25]

(3) *This obedience-as-humility is the mystery of the divine being—it is a foundational reality.* "Mystery" for Barth means not something that is unknown, but something that cannot be known in any way other than through divine revelation.[26] A mystery in this sense is a datum, a given fact for faith. While one cannot reason *to* mystery, one can reason *from* mystery. This means, Barth says, that the basic starting point for knowing the divine nature is the fact of the Son of God's condescension in the incarnation and his suffering in the flesh. This means, by contrast, that the divine nature is not known either by abstraction, negation, or maximization of general concepts of being.[27] Humility is the mystery of the divine being; it is mystery in the same sense that God is mystery.

(4) *Since obedience-as-humility is the mystery of the divine being, it must be affirmed not only of God's life ad extra but also of God's life ad intra.*[28] If obedience-as-humility were affirmed of God's life only *ad extra*, then God's life *ad intra*—God's proper being—would neither be revealed nor reconciled to humanity in time. The divine life *ad extra* would not be the divine life at all. The obedience-as-humility that actualizes reconciliation in time must be a reality in the very depths of God's eternal being. It might be wondered at this point why Barth is compelled to maintain the distinction between God's life *ad intra*, the immanent Trinity, and God's life *ad extra*, the economic Trinity, at all. After all, would not the strict identity between the activity that is Jesus Christ and the being of God allow for this distinction to be done away with? The distinction is necessary to maintain the freedom of God—the counterfactual possibility that God would be God without the work he does in time.

After establishing this basic dogmatic argumentation, Barth turns to an exposition of the reality denoted by the stunning conclusion in proposition (4). He moves from faith to an attempt to understand what it means for humility to be part of God's immanent life from all eternity.

Barth's Exposition: Obedience as an Inter-Trinitarian Reality

Barth begins with the manifestation of divine humility *ad extra* because the first, inner moment of the divine being is known by creatures strictly by way of its second, outer moment of manifestation. This outer manifestation of the divine being is the activity of Jesus Christ—his humble obedience to the Father on behalf of his fellows. Barth reiterates that this must be a free act—something that is contingent upon nothing other than God's own will. Negatively, this means that God does not change himself nor limit himself in any fashion when he humbles himself (contra Lutheran kenosis accounts), but rather maintains and expresses his own unalterable will and being[29]—otherwise, reconciliation has not taken place and revelation is an impossibility.[30] Positively, the fact that humility is God's eternal will leads to the bold statement "that God for his part is God in his unity with this creature, this man."[31] In other words, it is impossible in any way to define God's immutable being without referring to his movement of humility toward incarnation and crucifixion.

According to Barth, Christian theology has traditionally been ambiguous with respect to defining the being of God by the humility of Jesus Christ, wavering between deep christocentric impulses and general conceptions of the divine being.[32] One path toward alleviating this ambiguity that has occasionally been attempted is to posit an absolute paradox between God's being *in se* and *pro nobis*—a cleft wherein what God assumes in the incarnation and the cross (limitation, temporality, weakness, powerlessness, lowliness) is arrayed in opposition against the attributes of God's proper being (omnipresence, eternity, omnipotence, glory). On this account, God's identity with himself would consist only in a sheer act of will to be the reconciler by positing himself in antithesis to himself. God would give himself away.[33] Barth affirms that in the atonement God gives himself to the world in the most radical way, but if this means that he gives up his being of God, then, again, no reconciliation of the world with God is achieved.[34]

But faith says that reconciliation has been achieved. God is not a God divided against himself, but a God who lives in perfect unity with himself even as he enters the contradiction of his creature against him: "If we think that this is impossible it is because our concept of God is too narrow, too arbitrary, too human—far too human." Barth says all concepts of God, or concepts of divine attributes, that rely principally on a contrast between God and creation are to be ruled out (taking a not-so-subtle jab at his earlier self's fixation on the "Wholly Other").[35] Instead, the mystery of God's humility—the Son's humble obedience in the atonement—must be the starting point for reflection on the divine being. In humbling himself God conceals his glory, but this act of concealment is itself "the image and reflection in which we see him as he is."[36] Barth goes so far as to say that the *forma Dei* is not in opposition to the *forma servi*, and that the two do not stand alongside one another in an ambiguous relationship. Instead, "the *forma Dei* consists in the grace in which God himself assumes and makes his own the *forma servi*." This is the true mystery of the divine being, Barth says, before which theology must bow its knee in worship; it is because

Jesus Christ is humble, and not in spite of this fact, that he bears the divine name and receives all glory (Phil 2:9).[37]

The conclusion drawn from the divine life *ad extra* is that humility (in the sense of obedience in the way of incarnation and suffering) is proper to the divine being: "[F]or God it is just as natural to be lowly as it is to be high, to be near as it is to be far, to be little as it is to be great, to be abroad as to be at home."[38] Barth is adamant that this can be understood in such a way that it does not entail that God's relation to creation is necessary for God to be God: "He does not have to choose and do this. He is free in relation to it."[39] Yet while he affirms that God does not have to be humbly obedient, Barth also says: "There is no possibility of something quite different happening."[40] So Barth's claim is that God's movement toward incarnation and crucifixion is both unnecessary and necessary. This is so because we are here encountering "a divine decree."[41] A divine decree is unconditioned by anything other than God himself; it is entirely free. And yet, once given, a divine decree has the characteristic of absolute necessity. Based on the suppositions

(1) that the activity of Jesus Christ (humility) is something freely willed by God, and

(2) that this freely willed activity of Jesus Christ (humility) is identical to God,

Barth draws the conclusion

(3) that God freely wills his own being in willing the humility of Jesus Christ.

The danger in this formula is that it could be taken in such a way that God is said to become God only in his life *ad extra*, so that the God who determines to be Jesus Christ in time is, in eternity, a "sovereign *liberum arbitrium*."[42] This would either mean that God's own proper, eternal being remains an entirely unknown quantity, or it would mean that creation itself is necessary to God's eternal being (and thus not creation at all).[43] For Barth, the former would deny that reconciliation has occurred, while the latter would deny that reconciliation needed to occur at all. Both of these alternatives are inadmissible for Christian theology. Thus when Barth draws the conclusion (3) that God freely wills his own being in the (*ad extra*) humility of Jesus Christ, this must—on pain of total theological shipwreck—be taken to mean that when God wills his humility *ad extra*, he is reproducing his own, already complete, being *ad intra*. Thus Barth:

> Is it a fact that in relation to Jesus Christ we can speak of an obe-
> dience of the one true God himself in his proper being? . . . We
> not only can do so but have to do so. . . . We have not only to deny
> but actually to affirm and understand as essential to the being of
> God the offensive fact that there is in God himself an above and
> a below, a prius and a posterius, a superiority and a subordination.
> And our present concern is with what is apparently the most offen-
> sive fact of all . . . that it belongs to the inner life of God that that
> there should take place within it obedience. . . . For everything the
> creature seems to offer him—its otherness, its being in antithesis
> to himself and therefore his own existence in co-existence—he has
> also in himself as God, as the original and essential determination
> of his being and life as God.[44]

Barth is thus driven, by his own theological axioms, to the conclusion that there is obedience within God's life—a commanding and an
obeying. He will attempt to make sense of this "offensive" conclusion
by way of a doctrine of trinitarian relations.

Negatively speaking, Barth rules out both the subordinationist
understanding whereby intra-trinitarian obedience would make the
Son inferior in being to the Father, as well as a modalist understanding in which the humble obedience of the Son to the Father is only
an epistemic reality that is somehow dissolved in some higher, divine
essence. By contrast, Barth states positively the "perfect unity and
equality" of the one who commands (the Father) and the one who
obeys (the Son), united as they are in affirming one another in fellowship through a third (the Spirit).[45] What Barth has done is to sketch
a trinitarian account of the divine will, so that just as the one divine
being is said to exist eternally in three "persons" or "modes of being," so
this same reality must be explicated in voluntaristic terms, so that the
one divine will (that is itself identical to God's being) exists in three
modes of willing. There is no possibility of getting above or behind
this threefold will of God to some naked will of God in itself, because
there is no getting behind the modes of being of the Father, Son, and

Holy Spirit.[46] It is in and only in the Son being begotten that he is *homoousian* with the Father, and it is in and only "in his humility and compliance as the Son that he has a supreme part in the majesty and disposing of the Father."[47] And just as, in the *filioque* tradition at least, the Father and Son are said to be united in their mutual generation of the Spirit, so Barth's voluntaristic account casts the Spirit as an eternal act of "mutual affirmation and love."[48]

In place of the Father's eternal begetting and the Son's eternal begottenness, and a mutual procession of the Spirit from both Father and Son, Barth speaks of the Father's eternal commanding, the Son's eternal obeying, and the Spirit as a mutually voluntaristic act of affirmation. Barth does not intend by this to posit multiple wills in the divine being, but rather to recast the three modes of the one God's being in voluntaristic terms. Barth takes it that willing is something that can be predicated of the trinitarian modes of being in their relations, rather than the essence shared by each of the three. But if the only thing that makes the modes of being (or "persons") *three* is the relations or processions between them, then it is difficult to see how moving the will into the category of processions does not ultimately introduce three irreducibly distinct wills into the divine being. And if, by implication, the divine will (being identical with the divine essence) can be recast in terms of the three irreducible processions, then has not the notion of essence itself been done away with entirely, collapsed into pure relatedness? And yet it appears to make no sense to speak of *relationes* without *relata*, or rather, in this case, to modes of a *relatum*.

QUERYING BARTH'S ACCOUNT OF
INTER-TRINITARIAN OBEDIENCE

At the very least, there is something deeply questionable about what is entailed by Barth's account of divine humility.[49] The rest of this chapter attempts to make sense of that account. This is not to say that we are engaged here in an effort to show his account to be ultimately coherent, or to fit within the bounds of creedal orthodoxy. Rather, the effort here is aimed at understanding more clearly what deep theological convictions led Barth to this point. Only then can approbation be distributed, disavowal issued.

The operative assumption here is that at this important point in his theological project, and at this late point in his career, Barth is not merely losing the dogmatic plot. Accordingly, one must penetrate more deeply into some of the underlying ambiguities present in Barth's account of divine humility. Based on the interpretation above, two fundamental theological moves undergird Barth's account of intra-trinitarian obedience, each opening up its own difficult questions:

(1) Barth posits a strong relation of identity between the man Jesus Christ and the eternal being of God—but just what is the nature of the relation he means to posit? Barth says that Christ's life in time is "the mirror . . . of the divine nature."[50] But what precise qualifications, according to Barth, stand between this creaturely mirror and the eternal life of the Creator?

(2) Barth sees the life of Jesus Christ defined principally by a voluntaristic relationship of obedience to the will, or command, of the Father. He appears to refer to Christ's will *simpliciter*, making no reference to either the human will or the divine will. So how does Barth see the divine and human natures of Christ to be related, specifically with reference to the divine and human willing?

The confluence of (1) and (2) leads Barth to mirror his strongly voluntaristic account of Christ into the trinitarian processions, with the novel outcome of a differentiation within the divine will that undergirds intra-trinitarian obedience. The analysis in this section will show that there are legitimate concerns about both the way that Barth has reached this conclusion and the dogmatic value of the conclusion. Uncovering the difficulties inherent in both (1) and (2) in this manner allows the revision of Barth's problematic, straightforward equation of humility and obedience.

Christ and God's Being: The Mirror of Mystery

Barth says that it is Christ's "becoming flesh" that is the "mirror" in which the divine nature can be known. This mirror—Christ—is the "mystery" of the divine nature in the sense that he is the one creature wherein the knowledge of God being is made known. There are "two moments" in this mystery—the reflection (the outer moment of the incarnation of the Son of God) and the thing reflected (the inner moment of the eternal trinitarian life of God).[51] This parallels, in important ways, Barth's treatment of the event of revelation in volume 1.1 of *Church Dogmatics*. In order to shed light on the way this theological mirroring works in *Church Dogmatics* 4.1, it will be helpful to see this type of analysis in action at length in the doctrine of revelation in *Church Dogmatics* 1.1.

The event of revelation is a mediated, creaturely encounter with the uncreated reality of God's own life. In his doctrine of revelation, therefore, it is not enough to stop at a surface-level description of God's Word as it is encountered in the life of the Christian Church, but rather he must go on to describe the nature of the Word of God. The event of revelation (the Word of God) gives the identity of God as Father, Son, and Holy Spirit. In order to move from this declaration of divine identity (the outer moment, the "who"), to some knowledge of the nature of the word of God (the inner moment, the "what"), Barth insists that one can do so only indirectly—by attention to the "how" of God's word. Just as in volume 4.1 of *Church Dogmatics*, the eternal life of God must be known indirectly through a structural analysis of the incarnation, here in volume 1.1 Barth proposes to know the eternal nature of God through a structural analysis of the event of revelation in the life of the Christian. In both cases, there is a content that is given in an event, and then there is analysis of the structure of this event that yields a "mirror" or "reflection" of the eternal divine nature. "Thus we can certainly say what God's Word is, but we must say it indirectly. We must remember the forms in which it is real for us and learn from these forms *how* it is. This 'how' is the attainable human reflection of the unattainable divine 'what.'"[52] Barth thus describes his particular mode of mirroring, at least with respect to the event of revelation, like this: "[T]here is on the basis of the doctrine of the Trinity a doctrine of divine attributes in which is manifested the nature of God that is hidden from us."[53] Similarly the movement in his section on Christology proper is one from a (divinely) given temporal reality to a depiction of the divine nature.

In analyzing the structure of the Word, Barth begins with the verbal concept—speech. The structural analysis of divine speech yields particular attributes of the divine nature. In the first place, the divine nature, the Word of God, is what Barth calls "spiritual." This is in contrast to every type of speech that occurs on the created plane of nature or *physis*. The Word of God is always embodied in some creaturely act (preaching, sacraments, Scripture, and ultimately the human nature of Christ), but it is embodied or expressed in these in such a way that they are taken up and used as instruments—they are not essential to the Word's nature.[54] The Word acts in and upon nature, but nature does not act upon the Word. This functions, Barth says, as "an admonition to concentrate on the spiritual sphere and to beware of straying into the natural sphere."[55] The second attribute Barth finds in divine speech is its "personal" quality. By this, Barth means (1) that God's word is identical to God and therefore (2) is always a free subject and never an inert object in the realm of creation.[56] The third attribute that makes the Word of God specifically divine speech is its "purposive" quality— the way it exists for a purpose beyond itself.[57] Put another way, the divine Word is communicative. Barth is aware of the danger that this makes the human recipients of divine address to be necessary to the being of God, something he admits he "most astonishingly stated" in the precursor to the *Church Dogmatics* but now rejects. Instead, he gestures toward two types of necessity. In contrast to God's being which has logical (or absolute) necessity, the existence of creaturely recipients is included in God's being as a factual necessity.[58] Simply put, logical necessity means that it is impossible that God not exist, since by God one means not merely an existing thing, but the ground and possibility of all existence whatsoever. Factual necessity means that it is impossible that there ever was, or ever will be, a time in which God's word does not have a creaturely recipient. Dogmatically, this enables Barth to maintain a distinction between the absolutely necessary character of the Word of God within the life of God, as opposed to the gratuitous nature of the Word of God's outward movement in his unified acts of creation and reconciliation. Unless one maintains at this point that God could not have done what he has actually done, one has not understood the implications of God's being.[59]

After analyzing the Word of God in terms of its structure as speech, Barth moves to a consideration of what it means that divine speech is at the same time divine act. Here he recognizes first that this requires the attribute of "contingent contemporaneity." By this Barth means that the contemporaneity of the event of revelation is not to be vouchsafed by any historical continuity between the authors of Scripture and contemporary persons, but neither is the contemporaneity threatened by any historical discontinuity. Instead, the contemporaneity is contingent only on a divine act working through the medium of the divinely ordained historical witness.[60] The second aspect of the word of God understood as act is its "power to rule."[61] The speaking of the divine word, because it is God himself, accomplishes the transfer of the one spoken to into the realm of the divine lordship.[62] Third and finally, Barth indicates that the divine speech as divine act means that it is an act of "decision" rather than a mere event. The difference is that the former (decision) is unconditioned by some historical causation, whereas the latter can be interpreted as having a cause. A decision is an act of will that transcends historical causation, and in the case of the divine will it is entirely unconditioned by other creaturely events.[63] This means that the divine word is known only through an act of chosen self-revelation that produces a state of decision in the recipient.[64] The accomplishment of lordship in the act of revelation is therefore "the act of the inscrutable judgment of God."[65]

The third set of attributes Barth develops as a description of the Word of God is organized under the heading of "mystery." These attributes are put forward as a "theological warning against theology," designed to ensure that the previous description of the event of divine revelation cannot be seen as a formula to be mastered by the recipients thereof. Here Barth notes that the divine word is mystery in the sense that it is always veiled in "secularity"—that the event of divine revelation always occurs through a temporal event that can, in fact, be interpreted within the cause-effect nexus of created reality.[66] Yet this secularity of God's word—its temporal content—"is not itself and as such transparent or capable of being the translucent garment or mirror of God's Word."[67] Stating the matter in terms of another attribute, Barth says that, though it is always a real historical happening, the event of revelation is mystery in the sense of being characterized by "one-sidedness." No account can be given of the relation between the two sides, since "if we could know and state this, the Word of God would obviously cease to be a mystery, and would just be a paradox like others, a paradox behind whose supposed mystery one can more or less easily penetrate."[68] Instead, the one-sidedness of revelation is the fact that the divine content is mediated through (and only through) the secular form without becoming strictly identical with it—the coalescence of the two always remains a free decision of God.[69] This free decision is what Barth means when he gives his final attribute related to mystery: "spirituality." The spirituality of revelation is nothing less than the Holy Spirit, for God himself is the event of revelation on both the divine and human sides, uniting secular form and divine content in accomplishing the human act of recognition that is faith.[70]

Barth's catalogue of descriptors of the nature of the Word of God is really nothing less than a first draft of the doctrine of the Trinity from three different perspectives: that of God *in se*, that of God's active relation to creation, and that of creation's receptive relation to God. The following table (in which *Church Dogmatics* is abbreviated CD) attempts to display the architectonics of Barth's account.

CD §5, "The Nature of the Word of God"	CD §5.2, SPEECH God *in se* CD §8–12, "The Triune God"	CD §5.3, ACT God → Creation CD §13–15, "The Incarnation of the Word"	CD §5.4, MYSTERY Creation ← God CD §16–18, "The Outpouring of the Holy Spirit"
REVEALER Father CD §10.1, "God as Creator"	Spiritual	Contingent Contemporaneity	Secularity
REVELATION Son CD §11.1, "God as Reconciler"	Personal	Power to Rule	One-Sidedness
REVEALED-NESS Holy Spirit CD §12.1, "God as Redeemer"	Purposive	Decision	Spirituality

The horizontal axis (from left to right) shows the movement from God's being outward (so to speak) to creation; the vertical axis (from top to bottom) shows the appropriation of the attributes within the doctrine of the Trinity.

This table enables one to see more clearly how it is that Barth conceives of the relation between the accomplished state of revelation in the knower (mystery) to the being of the Triune God (speech). Epistemologically, the order goes from right to left, and this mirrors (in the sense of reflecting-in-reverse) the ontological order, which moves from left to right. As Barth puts it: revelation is "the root of the doctrine of the Trinity" and the doctrine of the Trinity is "the interpretation of revelation."[71] In the center (act) is the event in which divine subjectivity becomes objective without surrendering its subjectivity thereby—the incarnation of the Word. Barth's claim is thus that there is a relationship of indirect identity between the doctrine of revelation and the doctrine of the Trinity—and indeed an indirect identity with the being of the Triune God. One may move through a formal or structural analysis of the event of revelation to an account of God's triune being and then subsequently interpret revelation in light of God's triune being.

In order better to understand Barth's concept of mirroring here, it is instructive to read a critique of his theology that was written before the first volume of the *Church Dogmatics*. Barth apparently did not discover Dietrich Bonhoeffer's *Act and Being* until after the latter's death. Bonhoeffer, however, was keenly aware of Barth's theology and, while deeply appreciative, was also concerned about what he perceived as its inadequacies. Bonhoeffer contends that Barth's method embodies a transcendentalism that has its roots in medieval nominalism and in which the concept of objectivity is altogether lost and God's being is interpreted only as act:

> This attempt is bound to come to grief against the fact that (according to Barth) no "historical" moment is capax infiniti, so that the empirical action of man—"belief," "obedience"—becomes at most a pointer to God's activity and can never, in its historicality, be faith and obedience themselves. . . . God recedes into the non-objective, the non-available. That is a necessary consequence of the formal conception of his freedom.[72]

Indeed, for Barth, all that can be said from the human side of revelation is that it is a one-sided, punctiliar happening that retains its total secularity. This leads to an account of God's relation to the creaturely means of revelation in terms of pure contingency—dependent on an ever-new decision on the part of God. A structural analysis of this event yields an account in which God is described as beyond all created things ("spiritual"), pure subjectivity ("personal"), and self-sufficiently communicative ("purposive").

Barth's transcendentalist approach inevitably morphs from within. The doctrine of election in *Church Dogmatics* 2.2 explicates the decision of God not merely in relation to an event of revelation in time, but now from the perspective of God's eternal decision that logically precedes creation. God's eternal decision cannot have something other than God as its primary object, and so the decision of election is the decision that determines God's own being as Creator, Reconciler, and Redeemer. As God determines his own being in this manner, creation as a reality other than God is included. This account of the divine decision that is logically prior to creation requires of Barth a greater specificity in terms of the content of that decision, and it is here that his theology becomes radically and uniquely christocentric. This transcendentalist approach moves from an analysis of the act of revelation in the human knower(s) to an analysis of the concrete act of revelation that is Jesus Christ.

In volume 4.1 of *Church Dogmatics*, when Barth turns to the doctrine of reconciliation and Christology proper, he picks up where he left off with the doctrine of election. He proceeds to move transcendentally from a structural or formal analysis of Christ's being-in-act in the economy (his condescension, obedience, and humility), to an account of God *in se*. Thus, as has been shown above, the volitional structure of Christ's obedience in time is read into the doctrine of God such that it becomes necessary to refer essentially to what above was called three "modes of willing"—commanding, obedience, and mutual affirmation.

One helpful way to analyze Barth's method of transcendental mirroring is to situate it vis-à-vis Augustine's search for analogies in books 8 to 11 of *De Trinitate*. Having dealt with the doctrine of the Trinity at the exegetical and linguistic levels in the first half of

De Trinitate—that is, having demonstrated from Scripture the rules of trinitarian faith—Augustine proceeds in the remainder of the work to seek an analogy that will bring understanding.[73] What is ruled out in his quest is any bodily conception, since this would require metaphysical composition. So too, for the same reason, are spiritual conceptions that involve changeability ruled out.[74] Rather than seek God in terms of an object in the world, Augustine enjoins the reader to seek an image of God in the structural analysis of the human acts of knowing the truth or loving the good—the implied assumption here being that there must be a transcendent and absolute goodness and truth—namely, God—that grounds every other instantiation of these qualities.[75] And this transcendent and absolute goodness or truth must be present in or to the human knower, and it is that which allows for the recognition of the various creaturely instantiations.[76]

Augustine's quest for an analogy of the Trinity in the structure of human life takes him to the specific act of human loving. Augustine's argument runs as follows. At the highest level of reality, truth and goodness must have a certain identicality and coequality, since if something were truer than the greatest good, it would be the greatest good, and vice versa. This means in turn that knowing the truth and loving the good are part of a single, unitive act. (Undergirding and confirming this assertion, of course, are the dogmatic tenets of the trinitarian faith that see the one simple, undivided essence of God as being irreducibly Father, Son, and Holy Spirit.[77]) It is this single, unitive act of knowing and loving that Augustine sees as the only possible locus for an analogy of the Trinity.

In his explorations of an analogy within the unitive act of knowing and loving, Augustine is careful to hone in on the act of self-knowledge and self-love. His analogies thus morph from "lover, loved, and love" to "mind, self-knowledge, and self-love," and then to "memory, understanding, and will." In *De Trinitate* 9–10 Augustine thus intentionally abstracts and purifies the act as much as possible from any notion of multiple subjectivities or dependence on outward objects. Only once he has purified the image in this way does he venture in the subsequent books (*De Trinitate* 11–14) to analyze it *in vivo* in relation to temporal objects (11), demonstrating its fallen (12), redeemed (13), and perfected (14) modes of operation. In book 15 he makes it clear that he has not found an image that is identical or even adequate to the Trinity, since no image within the person can adhere to the rules of trinitarian faith, with its three "somethings" in the simple, undivided essence: "In this mirror, in this puzzle, in this likeness of whatever sort, who can adequately explain how great the unlikeness is?"[78] Nonetheless, by seeking to know the self in light of the doctrine of the Trinity, and vice versa, Augustine sees this as a valuable spiritual exercise, one that will allow for a greater integration such that what one loves is the good and what one knows is the truth—all in a unified operation.

Augustine's project of mirroring from created reality to the Trinity appears at first to share the marks of Barth's transcendentalist method. It seeks, through a formal or structural analysis of a given reality, to arrive at some analogical description of the divine being. However, the differences between the two approaches are important. For Augustine, a certain parameter is put in place that must rule over any subsequent analysis—the rule of divine simplicity. In *De Trinitate* 5–7, the statement that God's being (*esse*) is simple has the implication that, while what is said about God (*dictio*) may imply linguistically that God has contingent properties, upon theological reflection (*cogitatio*) what must be thought is that it is creaturely contingency (that is, the possession of accidents) that provides the truth conditions for such statements.[79] The only terms that receive a different outcome as they are interpreted by the rule of divine simplicity are the predicates "Father," "Son," and "Holy Spirit" (and perhaps other scriptural correlates) that are exegetically established as having an eternal take on God's identity.[80] In sum, Augustine's statements about the divine being per se are strictly minimalistic—simple.

By contrast, Barth's method of mirroring is not set in the same way under the discipline of the axiom of divine simplicity. It is not explicitly the result of scriptural reasoning. Consider the first volume of the *Dogmatics*, in which Barth self-consciously places the doctrine of the Trinity near the beginning of his project, contrasting this approach with those who have started with the existence or attributes of God. He wants to, as he admits, delay the treatment of divine unity until later (in *Church Dogmatics* 2.1), but nonetheless feels compelled to establish that triunity is not only not opposed to unity but is rather "the basis of the Christian concept of the unity of God."[81] The trouble is, the concepts of triunity that he employs authoritatively here arose only on the prior basis of a strong commitment to divine unity, indeed, divine simplicity. Thus, prior to treating divine unity, Barth assumes already that whatever triunity means, it can denote only a single "willer and doer."[82] The three-ness of "persons" does not and cannot denote "a plurality of individuals or parts within the one Godhead."[83] Only on the basis of this assumed divine unity or simplicity—which are really assumptions about a whole package of divine attributes—can Barth make his key move of foregrounding triunity. In effect, only because the theologians before did not simply start (conceptually) with triunity can Barth now do so.

Barth assumes the trinitarian deliverances of creedal Christianity and proceeds from them in a new direction, building upon the insights of the past by starting with triunity as a reality given immediately in the event of revelation (Revealer, Revealed, Revealed-ness), pointing to the Trinity that is God (Father, Son, and Holy Spirit). It is his taking triunity as a revealed datum that enables Barth's particular method of transcendental mirroring. By starting with the givenness of triunity, both in revelation and conceptually, Barth has no need for, and in fact, eschews, the Augustinian method of mirroring that plays the triplicity of the economy off of the divine simplicity given in the divine name. Instead, Barth's general approach is to reflect what is in the economy into the doctrine of God's immanent life with a more minimalistic, and indeed volitional, rule to govern this process—the rule of freedom.

One might even put the matter like this: for Augustine the given data of revelation are the divine names: "I am who I am," "Father, Son, and Holy Spirit," "Jesus Christ." The doctrine of the Trinity is not a given datum in revelation, but rather a synthetic conclusion from the divine names. Since this is the case, for him the doctrine of the Trinity does not come to overrule and determine his understanding of the divine attributes. In fact, the doctrine of the Trinity is possible only within the matrix of the divine attributes associated with divine simplicity. In this, Augustine is representative of a broad patristic consensus.[84] By contrast, Barth takes as the primary given datum of reality the Trinity in the event of revelation as mentioned above. This has the strange outcome of causing Barth to assume the divine attributes associated with simplicity in order to get his work off the ground, all the while leaving him without a strong doctrine of divine simplicity as a principle by which to discipline his transcendental mirroring from the economy. Thus, with respect to divine humility in volume 4.1 of *Church Dogmatics*, the divine being that is the divine will (per an assumed doctrine of simplicity) is revealed, according to Barth, in the relation of command–obedience between the Father and the Son, a feature that is then mirrored into the eternal divine being as an eternal commanding and obeying. In effect, Barth's method only works if it is an epistemological loop that proceeds from the knowledge of God's eternal, trinitarian being downward into the economy of redemption and back up again into the immanent life of God. But this, in the end, is precisely what Barth seeks to avoid—namely, starting with any conception of the divine being that cannot arise out of a formal analysis of the event of revelation.

One main factor in Barth's provocative account of divine humility as intra-trinitarian commanding and obedience is his understanding of how revelation mirrors or reflects the eternal being of God. There are serious questions as to whether (1) this method would be possible if not for the previous methodology of mirroring that Barth rejects, or (2) whether Barth's method can even remain true to its own stated aims. This is not, however, the only significant theological factor that underlies Barth's account of divine humility.

CHRIST'S WILL(S): DYOTHELITISM OR MONOTHELITISM?

Barth's Christology is novel in that it attempts to see Christ in terms of "history"—radically dynamic rather than static. He thus deliberately eschews the traditional suite of christological terminology, like "natures" or "persons." In a seminal essay, Bruce McCormack takes up the question of the sense in which, if at all, Barth's Christology may be considered "Chalcedonian." McCormack's contention is that Barth preserves the "theological values" of the definition of 451 but does so "under the impress of ontological commitments which are other than those of the fathers at Chalcedon."[85] Barth maintains the basic intention of affirming the full humanity and full divinity of Christ, but his actualistic doctrine of God, as expressed in his doctrine of election, has led him to affirm this in a striking new way. God's being, in this reading, is eternally determined by the free decision of the Son to become human in Jesus Christ.[86]

The conceptual shift that the doctrine of election effects within the realm of Christology is the replacement of the concept of "nature" with the category of "history" and the integration of "history" into the concept of "person." Because, within Barth's formulation, the divine-human Jesus Christ (and not the *Logos simpliciter*) is the eternal subject of election, it is impossible to speak of two "histories," but rather one must speak of "two aspects of one history."[87] Reversing the traditional order, the unified subject (traditionally, the "person" of the "hypostatic union") of Jesus Christ is basic, and his simple history can be considered from the perspectives both of eternity and of time. According to McCormack, then, Barth turns both the divine and the human natures into conceptual parts ("two aspects") of the eternally simple divine-human person ("one history").

> The first and eternal Word of God, which underlies and precedes the creative will and work as the beginning of all things in God, means in fact Jesus Christ. It is identical with the One who, very God and very man, born and living and acting and suffering and conquering in time, accomplishes the atonement.[88]

Though Barth himself regards the *Logos asarkos* concept (the Son considered apart from his incarnation) as "necessary and important," McCormack declares this a false step.[89] Indeed, since Barth's rare payment of homage to the concept of a preincarnate Son is given in the context of rendering further talk about this subject as "pointless" and even theologically "impermissible," McCormack's reading is cogent.[90]

The purpose of this section is neither to contest nor to acquit McCormack's reading of Barth. Rather, taking it for granted, this section aims to test Barth's historicized Christology against the Christology of Maximus the Confessor—specifically, situating Barth's revised understanding of "natures" and "person" and their interrelation in relation to Maximus' seventh-century battle against monothelitism, and the eventual triumph of Dyothelitism at Constantinople in 681. This comparative endeavor will shed light on Barth's understanding of the volitional agency of Jesus Christ, which is so central to his account of divine humility. The contention here is that Barth, though retaining a nominal commitment to Christ's two wills, is constrained by the internal forces of his doctrine of election from employing the full resources of dyothelitism at the key point for an understanding of divine humility—the obedience of Jesus Christ in relation to God. In order to make this case, we will examine Maximus' and Barth's respective treatments of Christ's prayer in Gethsemane. But first it is important to establish the basic background of the monothelite Christology with which Maximus did battle.

Once ecumenical consensus regarding the divinity of Christ was achieved in the Nicene Creed, the dogmatic debate became focused on how to understand and articulate the fact that while the Son was fully God, he was also fully human. The Apollinarian solution was to say that Christ's human nature lacked a rational soul, since this space was filled by the Logos. Opposed to this was the Nestorian solution which, to maintain the full and complete humanity of Christ, spoke about both natures in hypostatic (or personal) terms. The Apollinarian solution attempted to achieve real, personal union but had to modify Christ's human nature in order to do so. The Nestorian solution upheld the full integrity of both of Christ's natures but in turn had to sacrifice the possibility of real union.[91] For all their differences, both parties in this christological struggle were united in their shared assumption that two complete natures necessarily entailed two persons.[92] It was this underlying assumption that Cyril's Christology subverted. Cyril agreed with the Apollinarian impulse that Christ must be a real, and not merely apparent, union of divinity and humanity. To maintain this without subtracting from or mixing together Christ's two natures, Cyril posits that the one indissoluble link between the two natures is that they share one and the same hypostasis—the same personal, though not natural, identity. For Cyril Christ is one, and only one, personal subject—"God made man." And yet this one subject is himself, after the incarnation, "a mysterious and incomprehensible union" of two natures "without confusion or change."[93]

Cyril thus denies any confusion, change, or mixture of Christ's two natures by positing that the two natures are united not through their inherent compatibility with one another, but because they are both the natures of one and the same hypostasis. Thus, the ecumenical Definition of Chalcedon, with Cyril's Christology as its basis, declares Christ to be:

> perfect in both deity and also in humanity . . . actually God and actually man, with a rational soul and a body . . . like us in all respects, sin only excepted . . . only-begotten in two natures without transmuting one nature into the other, without dividing them into two separate categories, without contrasting them according to area or function. The distinctiveness of each nature is not nullified by the union. Instead, the properties of each nature are conserved and both natures concur in one person and in one hypostasis.[94]

The hypostatic union means that to Jesus Christ can be attributed everything pertaining to the divine nature and everything pertaining to the human nature. As Cyril says: "[B]oth the recent characteristics of humanity, and the eternal characteristics of the deity apply to him."[95] The attributes of both divinity and humanity accrue to one and the same Jesus Christ, since he possesses a divine nature from eternity and has taken on an additional, human nature in time. Note, however, that this does not mean that everything that can be attributed to Jesus Christ can thereby be attributed to the divine nature (or the human nature). The propositions "Jesus Christ is God" and "Jesus Christ is human" are not reversible. If they were, one would also have to affirm the identicality of the divine and human natures with the proposition "God is human." This is clearly not what Cyril has in mind: "Godhead is one thing, manhood quite another. . . . One cannot speak of things 'united' when there is only one thing to start with; there must be two or more."[96]

By the time of the sixth century, Cyril was claimed by certain interpreters, the Monophysites, who argued that after the incarnation Christ united divinity and humanity in one composite nature.[97] Maximus rejects Monophysitism on the grounds that such an account would not at all do justice to Christ's divine nature. That is, if the divine nature that the Logos hypostasizes is simple, free, and sovereign, then the divine nature cannot exist in a dependent relationship with the human nature.[98] For this reason, Maximus was careful to rigorously apply to Christology the distinction between hypostasis and nature. For Maximus, "hypostasis" refers to something subsisting by itself. Whereas the term "nature" identifies *what* Christ is, the term "hypostasis" identifies *who* Christ is. Christ is therefore not a composite nature, but a composite hypostasis; his single identity is composed of two distinct natures.[99] The divine nature of the Son is therefore always hypostasized, but the humanity of Christ is a second nature taken on by the Son's hypostasis and is therefore of itself anhypostatic. This has the curious but important implication that one can, indeed must, speak of the identity of the Son at two different levels. On the level of nature, the Son is identical with the divine nature but is not identical with the human nature. On the level of hypostasis, however, the Son has a dual identity, being identical with both the divine and human natures.[100] (It will be noticed that this is similar to the way Augustine posits a direct participation of Christ's human nature in divine "blessedness" but an indirect participation of Christ's human nature, through blessedness, in divine "immortality"—the divine being or nature.)

On the basis of the dogma that Christ is one hypostasis in two natures, the debate between monothelitism and dyothelitism—the question of whether Christ has one or two wills—turns on whether the faculty of the will is a hypostatic property or a natural property. If the will is a hypostatic property, then Christ can have only one will. If, however, the will is a property that belongs to a nature, then Christ must have two wills. Of course, the question of what is implied by each potential location of the will must also be brought into focus at this point. If the will is a natural property, as Maximus will argue, then it is principally a nonrational faculty that desires what is proper to one's nature. Deliberative reason is ancillary to this type of willing in that it will decide how best to achieve what one wills. If, on the other hand, the will is a faculty of the hypostasis, a rift is introduced between one's nature and one's particular identity, such that willing would involve deliberating about what one wants to do or what one should want to do. (This deliberative type of will Maximus refers to is a "gnomic will," a type of willing that does in fact exist in human beings but only as a mark of their fallen disconnectedness from their nature.) Because gnomic willing is predicated on a (potential or actual) rift between one's nature and what one wills, God cannot be said to

134 // DIVINE HUMILITY

have a gnomic will, since God always wills, non-deliberatively, what is in accordance with the divine nature. Were the divine hypostases of the Trinity said to possess deliberative wills, then there would be three wills that could be said to be one only in the sense that all three will the same object. Furthermore, as Maximus says, this would introduce at least the potential that the three distinct wills would not will the same object and therefore be at odds with one another.[101] Thus, it follows on from trinitarian logic that the will is not a property that belongs to the three divine hypostases, but instead belongs to the single divine nature.

Since the will belongs properly to nature, and since Christ has two natures, then Christ has two wills—one divine and one human. This brings me to a brief consideration of Maximus' treatment of Christ's prayer in Gethsemane: "Father, if it is possible, let this cup pass from me; yet not what I want, but what you want" (Matt 26:39). In *Opusculum* 6 Maximus parses Christ's prayer to show the failure of monothelite interpretations. On the one hand, if the prayer expresses a will of Christ's human nature alone, then Christ's human nature contends with and resists God in one breath ("let this cup pass from me") and yet expresses harmony and concurrence in the next ("not as I will, but as you will").[102] On the other hand, Maximus argues that the prayer also cannot admit an interpretation that takes it as simply the expression of Christ's divine nature. It is impossible, he says, for the Son to will something different from the Father (since the will is a natural property of the divine nature, common to the three hypostases), and thus what is expressed in the prayer would be the will of God *simpliciter*, so that the divine will would be vacillating within itself, expressing both negation ("not what I will") and affirmation ("but as you will").[103] In both of these interpretations, the type of willing implied is of a gnomic, deliberative sort—that which is characteristic of human fallenness. And in both cases, it introduces a volitional cleft into either the person of Christ or the divine nature itself.

In light of these failed one-will interpretations of the prayer in Gethsemane, Maximus argues that Christ's petition "demonstrates harmony between the human will of the Savior and the divine will shared by him and his Father, given that the Logos assumed our nature in its entirety and deified his human will in the assumption."[104] Christ's flinching from the cup he is to drink is an expression of a natural human aversion to death, but the prayer demonstrates that, despite this reflex, Christ's human will harmoniously affirms and follows after the divine will.[105] So Maximus writes: "As God, he approved that salvation along with the Father and the Holy Spirit; as man, he became for the sake of that salvation obedient to his Father unto death, even death on a cross."[106] Christ's divine will is the will of the Holy Trinity, that is, common to the Father, Son, and Holy Spirit. Because of the mysterious hypostatic union, Christ's human will follows along and expresses the sovereignly divine will in a properly human way—in obedience.

Maximus' dyothelite Christology and his interpretation of the Gethsemane episode provides an immensely helpful framework within which to consider Barth's understanding of divine humility as intertrinitarian obedience. In *Church Dogmatics* 1.2, Barth makes a rare, perhaps lone, mention of dyothelite Christology. In an excursus explaining that Christ as *vere homo* means that Christ has "what we call man's inner nature" and could experience real temptation, he writes:

> From this may be seen how right was the attitude of those who in the so-called monothelite controversy of the seventh century upheld and eventually led to victory the doctrine that along with the true human nature of the God–Man there must likewise not be denied His true, human will, different from the will of God although never independent of it.[107]

Paul Dafydd Jones calls this Barth's "ringing endorsement of dyothelitism" made "with an intensity reminiscent of Maximus the Confessor." He goes on to note, however, that Barth "eschews talk about the will as a 'faculty' and prefers a more radical affirmation of the 'unity of act and being' that characterizes Christ's divine-human person."[108] Indeed, Barth's explicit affirmation of the real human agency of Christ is not in doubt. Dafydd Jones' contention, however, is that Barth carries on the heart of the patristic consensus within a revised theological ontology: "Barth aims to think *beyond* the dogmatic disputes of the early Christian writers, bringing to prominence a christological perspective of his own devising."[109] This christological perspective of Barth's own is his "actualism," the fact that Barth largely abandons the category of nature in favor of that of act.[110] The question to be asked, then, is whether it is possible to go on in the same way as the patristic trajectory within Barth's actualistic ontology. Barth's treatment of the Gethsemane episode serves to reveal his great distance from the Christology of Maximus and the Third Council and, in turn, a serious theological incoherence in his thought.

In an excursus designed to show that the passivity of Christ's suffering (his passion) is his supreme action, Barth turns to Christ's prayer in the garden. It is here, he says, that the judge does his work by submitting himself to judgment: "In this way he was obedient to God."[111] In keeping with his actualist ontology, Barth elaborates for nearly ten pages on the agony of Christ's prayer without making any distinction between Christ's two natures or his two wills. At the outset, and in keeping with his treatment of the obedience of the Son to the Father, he simply says in passing that what takes place here in Christ's temporal life directly indicates a "pause and trembling . . . in the bosom of God himself, in the relationship between the Father and the Son."[112] With that assumption operative, Barth goes on to make the case that Jesus' request that the cup pass from him is at once a genuine request of Christ's "own will" set in opposition to "the real will of God." To ward off the notion that Christ's will could have ultimately been for something different from that of God, Barth says that this was something Jesus "wished" but did not ultimately "set his will toward" because of the fact that it was not the will of God. In other words, Christ did not waver from his commitment to God's will, but simply prayed that God's will might be different. This is why Jesus says immediately "but not what I will, but what you will."[113] Thus this obedient submission, an anticipation of the passion, is itself a positive affirmation of God's will.

Seen against the background of Maximus' dyothelite Christology, Barth's treatment of Gethsemane brings out the ambiguous, and indeed problematic, nature of a Christology that dispenses with the category of nature. Without an explicit, operative understanding of the two natures, Barth can speak of Christ only at the level of a single subject, at the level of *hypostasis*. Without recourse to the two natures, Barth appears to speak of the Son's willing in terms of Christ's single person, rather than a unified action performed by both his two natures.

Just as the obedience of Christ to the Father mirrors the obedience of the eternal Son to the Father, in Barth's treatment of Gethsemane the temptation that Christ faces is described as a deliberative moment "in the bosom of God himself," a threat to the relation between the Father and the Son. Without distinguishing between the two natures, it seems Barth must see in Gethsemane a reflection, not only of obedience, but also of temptation and suffering that happens within the triune life. Ultimately, it seems that Barth would have to reckon as well with grief, sorrow, and even death within the being of God. Barth's deepest theological sensibilities keep him from saying too much here explicitly, but only in spite of self-consistency.[114]

As noted previously, Barth's revised doctrine of election argues that God does not merely determine a reality beyond his own being, but determines his own being to include (in the sense of being in christological union with) a reality beyond himself. The single divine-human subject is at the beginning of the ways of God in eternity. What is traditionally termed "the hypostatic union" of Jesus Christ is thus, for Barth, located in eternity. Barth writes: "The being of God is [Jesus Christ's] being, and similarly the being of man is originally [Jesus Christ's] being."[115] Indeed, the concept of "union" here becomes altogether dubious, since, as Cyril recognized, it makes little sense to speak of a "union" when there were never two separate things to begin with. Furthermore, the placement of the incarnate (or to-be-incarnate) Son in the doctrine of God—in eternity—requires Barth to posit the Son as already a volitional agent distinct from the Father. This makes a certain sort of sense on account of the fact that, in the Gospels, Jesus Christ possesses an agency distinct from, though in concert with, God's agency. And if the Gospels' account of Jesus Christ as a single divine-human subject is identical with the Son in eternity, then the Son has to possess a distinct agency from eternity. On this basis, Barth's theology assumes that the will is a feature of the hypostasis rather than the nature. Even in speaking of election, therefore, he will speak of the distinct willing of the Father, Son, and Holy Spirit: "In the beginning it was the choice of the Father himself to establish this covenant with man . . . it was the choice of the Son to be obedient to grace . . . it was the resolve of the Holy Spirit that the unity of God, of Father and Son should not be disturbed or rent by this covenant with man."[116] While Barth affirms the indissoluble unity of these acts of willing as "the harmony of the triune God," he does so because the Father, Son, and Spirit each will the same object from eternity.[117]

The way Barth conceives of Christ's will(s) inevitably leads to the introduction of multiple subjectivities in God. For, while Barth formally states an endorsement of dyothelitism, he has made theological decisions that require him to see the will as a feature of the hypostasis rather than the nature. Therefore, since Jesus Christ has only one hypostasis, then Jesus Christ has only one will. Furthermore, since the Father, Son, and Spirit are three hypostases, they would have three wills. Simply subscribing to some conception of three modes of willing will not mitigate this conclusion. For Barth's three "modes of being" are but his neologism for what the church has called the trinitarian hypostases. And these are three hypostases of one simple being that is identical in every way, excepting the relations of origin—an idea that Barth endorses clearly in his doctrine of the Trinity. In fact, Barth's entire reason for substituting "modes of being" for "persons" was to make clear in the doctrine of the Trinity "we are speaking not of three divine I's, but thrice of the one divine I."[118] However, after his doctrine of election places the humanity of Christ in some sense in the eternity of God, Barth has forfeited the conceptual space to think of the incarnation as an event in which God takes something truly alien to his own being. Jesus Christ, instead of being the personal, composite union of the divine nature with what is not God by nature, is the repetition in time of a simple divine-human subject that already exists from eternity. Because, however, it is the Son and not the Father or the Spirit that is this simple divine-human subject, Barth's doctrine of the Trinity takes a social turn in which hints of multiple subjectivities do emerge, anticipating the work of some influential theologians of the late twentieth century.

Jürgen Moltmann critiques Karl Barth's doctrine of the Trinity as it is found in the first volume of the *Church Dogmatics* as a "late triumph of modalism which the early church condemned." The argument is that Barth's assertion of God's single subjectivity entails that the three hypostases "be degraded to modes of being, or modes of subsistence, of the one identical subject."[119] Moltmann lays the blame for this move at the feet of Barth's idealist heritage, claiming that Barth reflects the structure of the individual, autonomous ("free") subject into God's trinitarian relations.[120] Moltmann is off the mark on two fronts. In the first place, his critique of Barth's doctrine of the Trinity as "Christian monotheism" is really a critique of what the early church fathers taught and what the ecumenical councils affirmed. Second, he fails to notice the way that Barth's doctrine of the Trinity changes dramatically not in spite of Barth's "reflection structure," but precisely because of it. Indeed, as Barth reflects the divine-human Jesus into the doctrine of God, he at least opens the door for something like Moltmann's claim of multiple subjectivities in God that are logically prior to their oneness of purpose. Wolfhart Pannenberg also walks through the door that Barth has opened, as he likewise seeks to attain a doctrine of the Trinity by reflecting the life of Jesus Christ into the doctrine of the Trinity without the discipline of divine simplicity, which he takes to be a tenet of natural rather than revealed theology.[121] Reflecting the distinction of the hypostases in the economy directly into the immanent life of God, he writes that the Father, Son, and Spirit "must be understood not merely as different modes of being of the one divine subject but as living realizations of separate centers of action."[122] Robert Jenson likewise argues for multiple agencies in God. He rejects the concept of being in favor of narrative identity and then states that "a story has more than one agent." And if God's narrative identity is not to depend on the agency of creatures, then there must be more than one agency in God's identity.[123] Barth himself never goes as far as Moltmann, Pannenberg, or Jenson. However, the way Barth's doctrine of election eschews the concept of nature, and the subsequent displacement of the will into the realm of the hypostasis, makes these interpretations possible.

Positing multiple subjectivities in God's triune life is in conflict with classic trinitarian doctrine and introduces a potential split between the persons of the Trinity. Indeed, in light of the crucifixion, this rift is necessarily actualized in some fashion. Moltmann will thus say that "Gethsemane and Golgotha tell the history of the passion which takes place between the Father and the Son."[124] Following this, Pannenberg says that the death of Jesus, because it is the death of the Son, calls into question the very deity of the Father.[125] And Jenson says that the Father abandons the Son at the cross, but the Son can be raised to new life because of his connection to the Father by the Spirit (the bond of love).[126] However, this not only creates a rift in the Trinity, but it also has knock-on effects for Christology as well. For if the will is located in the hypostasis, then Jesus is only one will, one center of action. In violating the sixth ecumenical council, this type of Christology does indeed call into question the genuine human accomplishment of Christ's life, death, and resurrection. This is evidenced by the fact that the extension of this implicitly monothelite logic in Moltmann, Pannenberg, and Jenson leads them to see the work of Christ as primarily an inter-trinitarian event between the Father and the Son, and only in some vague and secondary way a salvific happening between God and humanity. While none of these theologians (Barth especially) would explicitly endorse monothelitism, analysis shows that this is in fact implied by a doctrine of the Trinity that locates the will in the hypostases rather than the nature.

Maximus makes clear what is at stake doctrinally in either an explicit or an implicit monothelitism. He argues that this would mean that, as incarnate, God is implicated directly in creaturely desires and actions (such as eating and drinking), and thus that Christ's human willing and action is merely illusory, since everything must be attributed to the eternal person of the Son.[127] One of the underlying problems that grounds monothelitism is the false belief that the union is a subsistent thing, rather than a unique, personal relationship; Christ, Maximus says, is "nothing else apart from the natures from which and in which He exists."[128] He will later repeat this: "[T]he union is relational, and not a real object."[129] Thus, rather than take the union as a primary or simple reality, the union must be considered as the coming into a unique relationship of two distinct things, two natures. The hypostasis of the Son is always a hypostasis of the divine nature but only subsequently becomes the hypostasis of a human nature. That Christ's human nature is anhypostatic means that (1) the human nature is *not* originally the Son's being (contra Barth), and (2) the human nature never exists hypostatically apart from the union. The human nature of Jesus Christ stands in a relation of "ineffable union" in which the Son's divine nature remains unchanged by the incarnation.[130] This ineffable union is simply the relation of deification that exists between Christ's divine and human natures. In fact, it is by recourse to the notion of deification

as dynamic relation between that which deifies and that which is deified that Maximus is able to avoid both the error of separating the
divine and human natures, and the error of uniting them in
the manner of a single subsistent thing.[131]

Maximus does not pretend to give an account of the possibility
of this union that is deification—it is, after all, ineffable. It is as ineffable as God's relation to creation, and in fact is the telos of God's
relation to creation. What it does, however, is to establish the closest
possible relationship between the divine and human natures without
at all diminishing the integrity of either nature (the Cyrillian image
Maximus alludes to is that of iron heated by fire).[132] In fact, this conception of the union invites a reading of the gospels that is attentive to
the ongoing dynamism of the relation between Christ's two natures.
This is not a reading that allows Maximus to parcel out certain actions
and attribute them merely to the divine nature and others merely to
the human nature. Rather, every action, desire, and thought Christ
undertakes maintains its full human integrity, while being enabled
and empowered by the suffusing of the Son's divine nature and divine
will. For Maximus, then, Christ's shrinking at the passion in Gethsemane was a genuine, natural (i.e., non-sinful) human response to his
impending death but a fear that does not stop him from willing what
God wills with his human will, since his human will is deified.[133] Thus,
the obedience Jesus Christ offers is ultimately a voluntary obedience
of his human nature to his divine nature, since "neither obedience nor
disobedience are proper to the deity, for these things are appropriate
to those in an inferior position and under subjection."[134] It would make
no sense, Maximus says, to see Jesus as delighting to do the will of
the Father according to his divinity, since he has the same will as the
Father by the divine nature.[135] One does not delight to do one's own
will; one just does it. Thus, for Maximus, the salvific accomplishment
of Christ's obedience (obedience unto death) is due to the fact that,
through the hypostatic union that is deification, the man Jesus lives
his entire life in accordance with the divine will that he has as the Son.

In the end, the notion that Barth could successfully dispense with
the ontology of Chalcedonian Christology, and with Dyothelitism for
that matter, and yet uphold the central theological values thereof is
fraught. The kernel cannot ultimately be separated from the husk; this

effort to demythologize the confessions seems destined to fail. Barth not only eschews the linguistic terms ("nature" and "hypostasis") central to conciliar dogma, but attempts to replace them with a single, materially distinct concept ("history"). This replacement reaches its zenith in Barth's revised doctrine of election, as the mystery of the incarnation is pushed from Christmas Day into the depths of eternity, as the statement "The man Jesus Christ is God" is reversed to such an extent that the conclusion seems to be "God is the man Jesus Christ." This leads, in turn, to the equation of humility with obedience.

Conclusion: Correcting Barth on Divine Humility

This chapter began with an incisive line of questioning from Robert B. Price: "Why does Barth speak of humility and obedience as divine perfections when dogmatically it seems they must be personal properties of the Son?" Price goes on to wonder whether some unknown change has occurred in Barth's doctrine of divine attributes, or whether Barth's doctrine of the Trinity has undergone change through a reconciliation of the categories of "essence" and "person." While Price's casual musings are generally headed in the right direction, the changes that have led Barth to his equation of humility with obedience, and his positing of this humility-as-obedience within the Triune life of God, are complex. Nonetheless, a certain pathway of development has emerged from the preceding analysis and evaluation can be offered as follows:

In the first place, Barth employs a procedure of transcendentalist mirroring from temporal structures of revelation to God's eternal being. This is first seen in his trinitarian conception of the Word of God in the first volume of the *Church Dogmatics* and is transparently operative in the way Barth reads the humility and obedience of Christ into the trinitarian being of God. In one sense, this is how all theology based on revelation must proceed. The difference with Barth, however, is that this process of reflection is not set under the discipline of a doctrine of divine simplicity. The irony in this is that whereas divine simplicity was instrumental in the formulation of creedal statements about God's triunity, Barth dispenses with this axiom and starts instead with Triunity, effectively cutting off the theological branch on which he sits. Dispensing with the doctrine of divine simplicity opens the way for Barth to recast the divine being in terms of the category of "history," which does not seem to tolerate anything like the axiom of divine simplicity, in that the former, *per definitionem*, denotes the unity of parts, which the latter denies. If this is understood, it becomes plain to see how different Barth's "actualism" is from the statement of Aquinas that God is *actus purus et singularis*. The former serves to emphasize the essential historicality of God's being, while the latter is a statement designed precisely to deny historicality to God's being.

Second, when "history" has pride of place in the doctrine of God the door is opened for the history of the incarnate (or to-be-incarnate) Son of God to be attributed by Barth to the divine being—a door Barth walks through in revising his doctrine of election. Within the confines of a more traditional doctrine of God, this is a highly dubious undertaking in that it effectively abolishes the distinction between the categories of "nature" / "essence" and "person" / "hypostasis." Without the ability to attribute the earthly life of Jesus to God *hypostatically* but not *naturally*, Barth will reflect the structure of Jesus' earthly life (if not all its particulars) into the eternal being of God. The consequences of this are particularly acute when it comes to dealing with the obedience of Christ toward God. The voluntaristic act of obedience Christ offers to God, when reflected straightforwardly onto God's historical being, necessitates the introduction of multiple volitional agents within the divine being itself. This introduction of multiple volitional agents within the triune life requires, in turn, that the will itself be thought of as a feature of the persons or hypostases rather than the nature (for those theologians who are convinced that this distinction remains important). The downstream impact this has on Christology is that, despite his explicit affirmations of dyothelitism, the logic of Barth's thought appears to necessitate monothelitism, which does in fact undercut human volitional integrity in Christ's accomplishment of salvation. The primary focus of the achievement of the atonement is on what happens in God's own life and only secondarily an exchange that is effected between God and humanity.

The road to Barth's version of divine humility is long and winding, and a high dogmatic price is exacted along the journey. One must dispense with divine simplicity as classically conceived, which paves the way for a functional diminishment between the categories of nature and person(s). While this enables Barth to define God's being more strictly in terms of the "historicality" manifest in Jesus Christ, this, too, has its cost. His mode of reflecting Christ's life into the eternal life of God requires something like the introduction of multiple subjectivities into the doctrine of the Trinity, tending toward a social trinitarianism. It also means that Barth cannot consistently affirm the creedal statement of christological dyothelitism, which safeguards the integrity of Christ's human nature and its role in the accomplishment of human salvation effected by the person of the Son. It remains to be seen whether one could argue convincingly for inter-trinitarian humility-as-obedience without paying these prices. In any case, a wise man will want to count these costs carefully.

There are also important ethical outcomes to Barth's doctrine of divine humility. The fact that humility is attributed to the person of the Son (rather than to will of the divine nature or the will of the human nature) causes Barth to equate humility with obedience to a command. It makes humility into a form of subordination to the prior demand of another. But such subordination, while it may at times be appropriate to humility, does not suffice as "the virtue of virtues" (Basil); it is a deflated concept of humility. It does not square with the fact that the greatest acts of humility are those exercised not by subordinates, but by superiors. Barth's virtue of humility could be possessed and exercised with or without love. It would not be difficult to argue, from Barth's notion of humility-as-obedience, that this is a "monkish virtue" (Hume) or a "slave morality" (Nietzsche).

5

THE MYSTERY OF DIVINE ENERGY
Katherine Sonderegger

As Augustine wrestles with the juxtaposition of the being of God *in se* and the mercy of God *ad extra*, he brings humility into the doctrine of God in a way that has seldom been replicated until more modern times. His work on this front is, in the end, ambiguous. It is suggestive, but only suggestive. The treatment of Augustine in this book has attempted to take his suggestions as far as possible, but a cleft remains between "the name of being" and "the name of mercy." Perhaps this is as far as one can or should go; perhaps this is the point at which to cry "mystery" and sing out in praise. But it is slothful to do so without attempting to go further in the sense of discerning just what Scripture and, secondarily, the doctrinal tradition of the church will permit. After all, one must "love the LORD your God with all your heart, and with all your soul, and with all your mind." Karl Barth possesses just this daring zeal, as his theology attempts to understand more fully how the humility God evinced in the incarnation should inform an understanding of God's eternal being. Yet, as has been shown, his effort shows the weaknesses inherent when the concept of being is subsumed into that of divine act. Barth is dogged, provocative, thorough, and there is much to learn from him at every point. One thing that must be gleaned among the abundant sheaves of the *Church Dogmatics* is, as was argued, a cautionary tale for the Christian doctrine of God. The concern of this chapter is therefore to attempt to go on in the same way as Augustine; indeed, to go further than he goes—but not to go too far.

If Augustine's weakness is his failure to unite adequately the "moral" with the "perfect being," Barth errs by nearly entirely subordinating the latter to the former. In light of this, Katherine Sonderegger serves as a fitting dialogue partner. Sonderegger's doctrine of God is a self-conscious effort at a morally perfect being theology. "Deity is goodness itself," she says. "[A]ll the attributes of divine objectivity are ethical, through and through. For this reason alone, every property of deity is most properly called a perfection."[1] Divine being is morally perfect; God's moral character is perfect being. And it should come as no surprise to the reader that the concept of humility has a special role to play in this theological endeavor. The concept of humility will not be able to stand on its own—it is but a creaturely concept and is but one of the divine attributes—but it is nonetheless central to Sonderegger's project. To understand her account of this divine attribute, it will be necessary to understand her fundamental theological moves in the doctrine of God, and vice versa. This is no small task, as Sonderegger differs at key points with both the older theological tradition within which Augustine is prominently situated and some of the peculiar concerns of modern Anglo-European theology. The task of this chapter, then, is to excavate, mine, and question Sonderegger's doctrine of divine humility within the larger context of her doctrine of God.

This chapter analyzes Sonderegger's doctrine of divine humility along the following three lines. (1) First, we turn to her epistemology—her approach to the use of concepts within the doctrine of God. There are resonances between her "theological compatibilism" and the descriptive, bottom-up account of concepts provided by Kevin Hector. In fact, Sonderegger's doctrine of divine humility illumines and deepens such an approach, providing it with a dogmatic basis in the doctrine of God by locating the Spirit's entrance into the chain of recognition at the canonically foundational event of the divine naming at Horeb. This move opens the way for an account of divine humility that is not determined by the incarnation, but instead by the fundamental relation of God to the world—a relation that is itself God's own being. (2) The second main section examines the way Sonderegger formulates the attribute of divine omnipotence as holy humility. Central to this effort is the way she explicates God's power without making central either the concepts of cause or will, instead using the concept of energy. Divine humility in this register ethicizes the notion of God's perfect being, showing how God is intrinsically, ontologically moral both in himself and in his relation to the world. (3) The third section turns to the concept of mystery in Sonderegger's doctrine of divine humility, specifically analyzing her response to the counterfactual question of whether, if God is intrinsically humble, he could have done other-wise than create, redeem, and reconcile. Upon examination, she argues, this question is itself seen to be a communication of divine humility. Explicating and evaluating this doctrine of divine humility along these three lines will demonstrate that Sonderegger has presented a coher-ent and compelling way to move beyond the ambiguity presented by Augustine without succumbing to the problems inherent in Barth's radical Christocentrism.

THEOLOGICAL COMPATIBILISM AND GOD'S
REAL PRESENCE IN CONCEPTS

Sonderegger contends that the concept of oneness, or unicity, is foun-dational to the doctrine of God. "Oneness governs the divine perfec-tions: all in the doctrine of God must serve, set forth, and conform to the transcendent unity of God."[2] The oneness of God is the funda-mental claim of Scripture, both in the Old and New Testaments.[3] If divine oneness is truly a foundational, or basic, concept, then it cannot be argued for directly. Instead, it receives its warrant indirectly, prin-cipally from Scripture (though secondarily from theological tradition and the doctrine's philosophical coherence).[4] Since the foundation of the rest of the canon is the Torah, this is where one must begin.[5] And the foundational predicate of the Torah is that God is one (see Deut 6:4-5). Countering contemporary Anglo-American theologians (represented by Robert Jenson), Sonderegger states that it will not do to reject oneness as a metaphysical concept, a concept of the divine being itself, in favor of a oneness that is defined as narrative identity.[6]

Narrative is the formal pattern of Scripture, but this form is distinct from the content. The subject matter of Scripture is the revelation of God's being; therefore, "divine oneness, we must say, is a metaphysical predicate."[7]

As noted above, the oneness of God, or "divine unicity," is a foundational predicate in that it governs all the other attributes. To put this in other language, divine unicity functions as a grammatical rule in the doctrine of God. Divine unicity contrasts the being of God with every idolatrous creaturely conception. Sonderegger says that this oneness is not merely a conceptual negation, but rather is rooted in a sheer positivity of presence that overruns all concepts.[8] Even immaterial concepts have form—they *are* form in the Platonic sense—but divine oneness means that God is without all such form. In scholastic terms, God is in no genus, and neither is God himself a genus.[9] To speak then, as Aquinas does, of God as being itself is not to place God in a category shared in common with creatures, but rather to state that God is concrete or real, and that he is beyond all categories whatsoever.[10] "The fact that God is, that God is this very one, and known as such, overturns all thought, imagination, and concept."[11] To know God truly is to know him as the utterly unique and ineffable one, and this is genuine knowledge of his essence.

This particular notion of a genuine knowledge of God's essence—precisely in the concept of ineffable unicity—sets Sonderegger apart from Jean-Luc Marion. Marion, it will be recalled, is likewise committed to the ineffability of God and speaks similarly of the divine presence overrunning all concepts. Sonderegger's account of the burning bush even seems a striking example of what Marion would call a "saturated phenomenon." Yet Marion has a sensitive allergy to the notion that God could be a concrete being, an object of theological speech: "God can never serve as an object, especially not for theology, except in distinguished blasphemy."[12] Not so for Sonderegger, who argues that it is the objectivity of God's unicity that vouchsafes him and sets him apart from all idols. Marion, following Heidegger, still works within the Kantian framework whereby God is unknowable based on the epistemic function of the human mind. For these thinkers, the mind only knows what appears to it under the aegis of its spatio-temporal categories of thought, and any attempt to reason from this appearance to its cause in the "thing itself" is a misstep; in relation to God it is an idolatrous misstep.[13] By contrast, Sonderegger says that it is the insight of Thomas and other premodern theologians "that the utterly concrete reality of God . . . gives rise to epistemic and methodological problems, and not the other way around." Sonderegger is aware that she does not hereby offer a refutation of the Kantian "mind independence" framework, but rather resists it altogether, doing so on a dogmatic basis.[14] Because God *a se* is encountered in the world and words he has made, and is encountered as "superabundant light," the phenomenal-noumenal split can be rejected tout court.[15]

The differences between Sonderegger's approach to epistemology and that of an anti-metaphysical theologian like Marion are in one way inarbitrable; each has its own way of question begging at crucial points. The Kantian family of approaches assumes mind-independence, and Sonderegger ignores this phenomenal–noumenal split and starts with the positivity of divine revelation. An argument in favor of Sonderegger's approach, therefore, cannot take the form of a direct dialogue with anti-metaphysical theologians, but rather as a laying-out of a therapeutic account, a holistic picture of how concepts work. This is a "deflationary method"—a descriptive theological account. The criteria for evaluation here will therefore consist of theological consistency with the relevant doctrines and internal coherence as a descriptive epistemology. If such an approach sufficiently fulfils these criteria, it commends itself by virtue of its ability to say yes to the constructive endeavors of biblical exegesis and the formation of Christian doctrine, in contrast to the Kantian framework, which constantly interjects itself as an insoluble methodological problem.

Sonderegger's epistemology, her theological method, is an outworking of what she calls "theological compatibilism." This is essentially the conviction that God's being itself is not remote from but, rather, known within creaturely reality—"our earthly words and world and signs."[16] This is an epistemology that does not ground Christian doctrine but flows from it, as a description of an event that has taken place.[17] The paradigmatic event that reveals God's being and how it—God—relates to creation is, again, the burning bush of Exodus 3:1-8. By querying the formal architecture of this event Sonderegger concludes that God is fundamentally compatible with creaturely reality. "The bush burns with divine fire; yet the bush remains unconsumed. . . . *This* event and truth simply is the mystery of the cosmos itself. . . . *This* is the gospel. And every reflection upon epistemology and metaphysics must be in its turn gospel, rendered in formal analysis."

On the metaphysical front, Sonderegger speaks of the burning bush in terms that invoke the incarnation, saying that God himself has "descended down into a creature," disclosing his nature and his name forever.[18] In the scriptural text, Moses sees the burning bush but looks away so as not to look upon the Lord. The burning bush both is and is not the Lord. It is the Lord in creaturely form. This is not a paradox, Sonderegger is quick to add, because to conclude that this is a paradox is to work within a prior framework of what is and is not possible, and this, as a revelatory theophany, must define for us what is possible. "Proper theological method is neither paradox nor idolatry."[19] If this approach is granted, one need define God in terms of neither likeness with the creature nor unlikeness. God is the one who surpasses all concepts and categories, and yet he is, without contradiction, here as such in and with the creature.[20] What provides Sonderegger the ability to say this is an understanding of God's oneness in the mode of invisibility (her gloss on the traditional attribute of omnipresence). Because oneness here refers not to a numeric value, but rather to God's radical uniqueness such that he is neither in a genus nor is himself a genus, there can be no spatial dimension to God's presence. He can therefore be affirmed as wholly present to, and within, all of creation. Such transcendence-in-immanence is not alien to God's being, but proper to it. Therefore, no metaphysical or conceptual barrier can be erected such that God is seen to be either without or within the world. God can simply manifest himself immanently and in such a way that he does not thereby lose his utter transcendence. This is so because God's relation to creation simply is God's own being *a se.* There is no mediation, no distance, between God and creation.

In one sense, Sonderegger is a traditionalist with her emphasis on divine unicity as central to the doctrine of God, and yet there is a subtle profundity to how this concept functions here. It is instructive to see how her approach differs from that of, for example, Thomas Aquinas. When Aquinas treats the divine attributes at the head of the *Summa Theologica*, he speaks first of God's existence, then of divine simplicity.

God's existence is not self-evident but hidden, transcendent. And yet God's existence is made known through created realities—it is revealed, immanent. He proceeds to demonstrate (rather than prove) the manner in which God relates to the world. He reasons from the divine name (Exod 3:14) and shows that it takes at least five different types of creaturely relation to speak of the ineffable relation between God's being and creation: agency, cause, necessity, supremacy, and intelligence.[21] After existence, Thomas turns to the simplicity of God, the foundation of the *via negativa*. He begins to strip away false understandings of God's being. Though God's existence has been manifest, his being is shorn of all composition. No relation to creation can define God's being—including the five ways listed above. His essence simply *is* his existence.[22] Thomas speaks of God first as an existing being in relation to creation and then uses the concept of divine simplicity to a purgative effect. So Thomas' doctrine of God will proceed along two ways—by affirmation and by negation. Sonderegger, by starting with the canonically foundational event of Horeb and foregrounding the concept of oneness, has effectively dispensed with the procedure of balancing between positive and negative concepts. The nature of God's perfect being is such that to encounter him in the positivity of his revelation is at once to know him as the one who surpasses all knowledge.[23]

Sonderegger's "compatibilism" captures the insight that God transcends words and concepts not because he is distant from them, but precisely because in his very being he has taken up residence in them. The upshot of this is that there is no need to safeguard God's transcendence with a theory of predication that is either univocal or analogical. There is no need either for an actualistic doctrine of predication wherein we wait in hope that our inherently unsuitable words or concepts might be taken up in a moment of reference. God has already taken up certain concepts—drawn from scriptural words and events—and he may reliably be found there. But to find him there is to find him in his utter transcendence. Sonderegger refers to the philosophical dictum that "knowledge is not closed under entailment," meaning that to know something is not to know all that is entailed thereby. The divine name of Exodus 3:14 therefore genuinely communicates God's essence (contra Aquinas), but the entailments infinitely outstrip our knowledge of it. "We are never done with this invisibility and hiddenness, never done with this exceeding light, never far from this scorching fire. It is *communicated* to our hearts and to our intellects; yet never *identified* with them."[24]

It will be helpful here to return momentarily to the theological epistemology of Kevin Hector discussed in the first chapter of this work. Hector's approach is to understand concept use in terms of the norms implicit in the practices of everyday speech, and with this understanding in place, to make sense of theological speech along the same lines. His basic contention is that using a concept entails undertaking a commitment that is susceptible to normative assessment by one's linguistic community. If the use of a concept is successful, it becomes part of the normative trajectory by which other uses may be assessed.[25] On this front, Hector is in keeping with significant developments in twentieth-century philosophy that see concepts as, in some sense, open ended.[26] Concepts have necessary and sufficient conditions that are embedded in preceding usages, and yet, at least theoretically, they are not exhausted by such usages. To show how theological concepts function within this framework, Hector draws on Schleiermacher. Schleiermacher's notion of *Gefühl* posits an immediate, noninferential, relation between the knower and the thing known. The application of concept and language comes after the encounter with the object known—the knower gestures, speaks, names. As others in the linguistic community identify with the person's gesture, they may imitate this response in similar circumstances. Thus, *Gefühl*—a particular, immediate attunement to an object or circumstance—is itself communicated through the social practices (including concept use) of the community.[27] Into this account, Hector follows Schleiermacher in inserting Christ and "the Spirit of Christ." Christ establishes the social practices of the disciples that convey his own *Gefühl*, and this is passed on from them to others in a "chain of recognition" that "just is the normative Spirit of Christ."[28] This is not meant by Hector to diminish Scripture's role, but rather it is to say that Scripture has a special objective and authoritative role within this work of the Spirit.[29]

Sonderegger is critical of Schleiermacher's sense of *Gefühl*. This is a species of Kantianism, she says, inasmuch as it still sees God and the world as already given within the structure of the human mind or some other mystic faculty.[30] But this is not quite right, and one need not take on Schleiermacher's entire faculty psychology to appreciate and appropriate the function that *Gefühl* plays in his epistemology and, by extension, Hector's. The function of *Gefühl* is to indicate a mode of engagement with the world that is one of receptivity. "Knowing" and "doing" are fundamentally active in character, but the receptivity that is *Gefühl* must come first and give rise to the others. This is how Schleiermacher overcomes Kant—by declaring that the human knower is fundamentally receptive and does not impose itself or its concepts upon reality. Hector picks up on the fact that this is not at all an argument against Kant, but rather an appeal to the pragmatics of knowledge. The appeal to *Gefühl*, if stripped of its troubling partitive psychology, is of the same force as Sonderegger's claim that "we will not attempt to spell out just how God can be poured into our world and into our intellect in his own majestic perfections. Rather, we will report that he has, and lay out how we might interpret, receive, and praise just this mighty deed."[31]

When Hector speaks of the Spirit of Christ entering into the social and linguistic practices of the human community, there is a sort of affinity with Sonderegger's contention that God himself inhabits our words and concepts. However, one might read Hector as if to say that in doing this God is entering into an alien sphere. In fact, Hector's use of Barth's theory of predication affirms this interpretation. For Barth, God takes up ordinary concepts that have their own creaturely trajectory of meaning and applies them to his own being. Only retrospectively can it be seen how these concepts were fit for such an application.[32] Barth states that these concepts cannot denote God in themselves; they must be conscripted for this wholly new purpose.[33] Sonderegger counters Barth at precisely this point: "I say that there is indeed a fittingness, intrinsic to the creaturely word, that allows our language to reach out and lay hold of its divine object." The problem that Sonderegger notes with Barth's version of predication is the sense in which it always depends upon a fresh in-breaking of God upon creaturely reality, because the only real place where there is a two-sided contact between God and humanity is in Christ alone.[34] Hector's epistemology can use Barth's framework and ameliorate this concern to some extent in that it sees the initial event of divine predication as creating an ongoing, creaturely trajectory of concept use and not merely a punctiliar event that must be repeated over and over. In that this linguistic practice is in some sense the very Spirit of Christ, he makes common cause with Sonderegger. Yet this sits awkwardly with Barth's insistence that creaturely words cannot refer to God. Sonderegger's doctrine of God helps clear away this danger by positing a basic compatibility between divine and creaturely realities. Creaturely concepts are never alien to God; he inhabits them invisibly, transcendentally.

Sonderegger's theological compatibilism stems from a decisive relocation of divine humility. The doctrine of divine omnipresence shows that God's humility does not merely denote God's deeds *ad extra*, or even in the incarnation or crucifixion of Christ. Instead, "the Lord's humility begins with his hiddenness in the world he has made."[35] God in his very relation to creation—a relation that is his own being—is humble. This is not to say that God exists in ontological participation with created being; recall, God is not in a genus, neither is he a genus. Yet at the same time, God's "hiddenness in the world" undercuts the need to distinguish neatly between God's essence ("what God is") and God's action in and toward the world ("who God is").[36] Unnecessary here, too, is a division of the divine attributes into "communicable" and "incommunicable." In his sheer positivity, all the divine attributes communicate the being of God in a way that is both real and yet never fully grasped.[37]

Such a relocation of God's humility, broadened in this manner to the way God dwells with and in all of creation, does not entail a diminution of divine freedom. Abstracted from the context of her biblical exegesis, Sonderegger's compatibilist account of divine humility and its attendant epistemology could give the impression that God is publicly available, open to inspection apart from divine revelation. One can imagine a crude natural theology, but this is mistaken. Sonderegger knows full well that sensory experience and the laws of logic are strictly secular in nature; in and of themselves, the analysis of them can take us no further than their own operation.[38] However, operating from the perspective of faith, this hiddenness itself is a manifestation of the divine being. This is not some backdoor argument for God's existence, but rather an ex post facto statement predicated on the fact that the invisible God has manifest his being as the hidden, humble one in the concrete particularity of the events and words of holy Scripture.[39] While God is really, metaphysically present in and with creation, he is only known as such where he makes himself visible. Yet once the reality of God is made visible in the words, concepts, or records of events in Scripture, those things continue as authoritative, real manifestations of God's being—a continued and reliable site of his self-manifestation.

With this "compatibilist" account of God's humble presence in and with creation, Sonderegger has given legs to a theological epistemology rooted in the everyday sociolinguistic practices of the church—the people of God who are constituted as such by continuing the tradition of Scripture and sacrament. Whereas Hector's epistemology begins with a general account of social practices and proceeds to conceive of how knowledge of God might be made sense of within this framework, Sonderegger simply takes up a position within the canonical-ecclesial chain of recognition of God's presence among us. Where Hector's account alone may be susceptible to charges of ambiguity and the simple exchange of one philosophical paradigm for another, Sonderegger provides a far more potent therapy for lingering fears of metaphysics by developing an epistemology out of the doctrine of God and the fundamental God–world relation. This in turn allows a more robust account of what it means to know God. Hector's account, despite its attempt to do away with the notion of distance in epistemology, gives an account of concepts that has no clear way of explaining how these would refer to the being of God. With a robust doctrine of God's humble presence, Sonderegger can say: "We simply confess, with our small gratitude and joy, that God dwells with us, in our words, our very thoughts."[40] There is no danger here of confining theological knowledge to immanent sociolinguistic practices, since by virtue of divine humility these ordinary practices carry knowledge that is decidedly transcendent, ontological, and even, it must be said, metaphysical.

This section has laid out Sonderegger's theological epistemology. Though this epistemology is developed in her treatment of God's omnipresence, it is already suffused with a theology of divine humility. God's perfect being, she argues, is present as hidden and lowly in our world, words, and concepts. But what does it mean to say that God's perfect being is identical to this humility—and how best can it be expressed? Answering that question requires turning to Sonderegger's ethicized treatment of omnipotence.

HUMILITY AS DIVINE ENERGY: ETHICIZING OMNIPOTENCE

"Must God renounce power in order to be good?" Sonderegger asks. "Is holiness, or absolute power, only divine if it is tempered—or even overcome, superseded—by saving goodness? Is that, in truth, what humility entails?"[41] To this line of questioning, as we have seen, Barth and many contemporary theologians answer: yes. For Barth and those in his wake, the being of God, and thus his omnipotence, is here qualified, or even determined, by Christ's incarnation and cross. This strict christocentric chastening of the concept of power is commonly put forward as the only desirable alternative to a despotic God. Barth thus argues, when he begins his section on the perfection of omnipotence: "Power in itself is not merely neutral. Power in itself is evil. It is nothing less than freedom from restraint and suppression; revolt and domination. If power by itself were the omnipotence of God it would mean that God was evil, that he was the spirit of revolution and tyranny *par excellence.*"[42] Sonderegger sees the same modern bias against absolute power in the work of English kenoticist William Temple, who orders God's omnipotence to the telos of the atonement and thus defines power as the humble self-sacrifice of love.[43] This way of ethicizing power collapses it into goodness and allows power to express itself in one and only one way: self-sacrifice. It takes humility to be identical to goodness but defines them both as fundamentally weakness. As Sonderegger notes, this is "an oddly univocal and flattened sense of humility or divine goodness."[44] Another way must be sought that will affirm the intrinsic goodness of divine power, without subordinating it to divine love in this manner.

It will not do simply to return, without revision, to more traditional formulations of divine power. According to Sonderegger, there are deeply problematic implications embedded within these definitions of power. In the first place, these older accounts tend to treat omnipotence too abstractly, as a purely conceptual problem. The biblical witness, by contrast, "underscores to us that divine power is not tame, not ideal or commonplace, but rather dangerous."[45] Second, and more materially, the traditional accounts of God's power are fraught with problems stemming from the ambiguous relation between the categories of "will" and "cause." Augustine stands at the head of a venerable tradition that defines divine power as the power to do as one (God) wills. The problem with this, Sonderegger indicates, is that it introduces a power, the will, that stands over the "causal" power of God's being.[46] By contrast, in the theology of Thomas Aquinas, the category of cause is foregrounded in considering the meaning of omnipotence. While, for Aquinas, the implications of this are mitigated by using the category of cause equivocally, in modern theology a univocal use of cause is employed to explain divine power. Schleiermacher is the exemplar here. The problem that results from bringing cause into the doctrine of God in this manner is serious: "[T]he most general definition of cause—to bring something about—entangles the divine being, in its very power, with creation, or, *per impossibile*, with other gods."[47] Foregrounding will maintains God's freedom by introducing a power over God's being, while treating divine power as purely causal removes God's freedom altogether.[48] The former approach sees God's power as, at best, ethically neutral and in need of conditioning by something else in God. This is dogmatically problematic, since, *per definitionem*, the attributes of God are manifestations of God's simple, undivided essence. It also has the strange implication that God's power is only operative in his works *ad extra*. Meanwhile, taking cause as the primary definition of the divine being severely restricts divine power by making the omnipotent God coextensive with his effects.[49]

Sonderegger's solution to these quandaries is that "we must say that divine omnipotence, the Lord's holy humility, must be removed from the category of *cause* altogether."[50] The question, of course, is how to accomplish this. Sonderegger first, therefore, repeats the fundamental claim of her theological compatibilism; namely, that in Scripture we encounter God not merely in his works *ad extra*, but in his being *a se*.[51] God, as he is manifest in Scripture, is not inert or static, but dynamic. His being is intrinsically vital, powerful, and not merely so in his works.[52] Traditional theology describes the dynamic vitality that is God in the language of substance metaphysics—with terms like substance, being, and nature—in order to denote not only that God has power, but rather that God *is* power. While this use of substance terminology is justified in its fundamental intention, it must be understood aright.[53] God is not substance in the senses in which Aristotle used the term—neither as an individually subsisting thing, nor as a universal concept or "form." Instead, substance language in relation to God should be seen as denoting simply God's concrete objectivity.[54] Furthermore, there is a need, Sonderegger says, for a renewal of this conceptuality that captures the unique and dynamic nature of God's being, his objectivity.[55] There is a need for a way to articulate at once both the subjectivity and objectivity of the omnipotent God.

In the creaturely realm there is an inherent distinction that obtains between objectivity and subjectivity, between nature and intentional act. However, because of God's unicity (i.e., his metaphysical simplicity), such a distinction has no place in God.[56] The task of the doctrine of God is thus to seek most adequately to display God's subjectivity-in-objectivity and objectivity-in-subjectivity. Again, Sonderegger rejects the pedigreed attempts by the Augustinian tradition to find the unity of substance and agency in the analogues of the human mind or the human will. Such conceptuality, she notes, is predicated on a distinction between the capacity for thought and the content of thought. And again, such a distinction between potentiality and actuality cannot obtain when it comes to God. Thus, in order to capture both the objectivity and subjectivity of God *a se*, Sonderegger proposes to understand the attribute of divine omnipotence, or holy humility, in terms of the concept of "energy."[57]

Energy is a rough-and-ready analogy useful for holding together the objectivity and subjectivity of God's being, Sonderegger argues, because there is "an interplay here of quanta and objectivity, of dynamism and stability, in some way together, yet conceptually and metaphysically distinct."[58] However, in using any created reality to speak of God, an unlikeness still remains. In this case, energy is not actual, personal subjectivity. And neither does energy appear to be objective in the way other things are. Energy goes deeper even than atoms and can never be seen. In creaturely objects, energy is somehow always beneath what is concrete; objects are ultimately reducible to the more fundamental level of raw energy. Were energy to apply to God's being in this way, it would imply layers in God's being, such that a distinction

would have to be made between God's objectivity and his more fundamental essence. This, however, would be a denial of the utter unicity of
God.[59] Traditionally speaking, this would compromise the grammatical rule of divine simplicity—that God has no parts and is therefore
identical to the whole of his being. The concept must therefore be
purified—lifted up—in its theological elaboration.

Sonderegger follows the concept of energy along the *via eminen-
tiae*. She illustrates this approach by appealing to Thomas Aquinas'
account of creation.[60] There, once motion and temporality are removed
from the notion of creation as a temporal change in a thing from a
previous, raw state to another, crafted state, what remains is the bare
relation of God as creator to creation as thing made.[61] Sonderegger
applies a similar procedure to the concept of energy, stripping away
the notion of layers. Something like the resultant, purified concept
of energy, she says, is increasingly required by the indeterminacy of
the fundamental structures of created reality as they are observed by
post-Newtonian physics. Therefore, since this concept of energy illuminates the mystery of creaturely reality as coextensively, irreducibly
dynamic *and* concrete, it is intrinsically more useful for application
to God's being than other concepts. In thinking of energy as at once
both sheer dynamism and material objectivity, "we catch an echo
here through the Lord's own great condescension, of the Almighty's
own real relation, the subjectivity that is objective, both true, both
one . . . real difference; real identity."[62]

How does Sonderegger's purified concept of created energy serve
as an echo of "the Lord's great condescension"? How does this account
of God's being in terms of the concept of energy show divine omnipotence to be "holy humility"? In the first place, created energy, in its very
nature, is unbounded, shapeless, and foundational to all other reality.
Energy here occupies the same metaphysical space as prime matter for
Aristotle or fire for Heraclitus. And, as Augustine took prime matter
to be a sort of analogue to God's positive infinity, so Sonderegger does
with created energy.[63] In the second place, created energy, like prime
matter, actively gives rise somehow to the plenitude of concrete objects
in the world, without being confined to them. It is in the inseparability
of these two distinct aspects that created energy, for all its unlikeness,
provides a concept that points to God's omnipotence as at once both

(1) a free, powerful dynamism that underlies all creation and (2) a real, concrete presence in creation. "Almighty God is life, vitality, fire, utterly hidden in the dynamism in this world, poured out into the creaturely realm as its own power, objective, humble; yet never the creature, never contained and confined, always explosive, holy, personal."[64] The value of the concept of energy for the doctrine of God, again, is its ability to hold the subjectivity of God—his holiness—together in one with his objectivity—his humility. Omnipotence just is this holy humility; the Lord is graciously present in, with, and to creation as a burning fire.

In her doctrine of omnipotence, Sonderegger conceives of God's being as at once ethical and powerful, benevolent and searing, humble and holy. Again, God's is not a raw power tempered by goodness or humility. Rather, it is a power that is in itself ethically good, a humility that is almighty. This does away with the all-too-common error of pitting God's presentations in Scripture as a consuming fire against his redemptive acts of love.[65] Instead, here the encounter with the God who is at once holy, terrifying subjectivity and humble, objective presence results in an ordered, purposive movement for the creature from exile to return, death to resurrection.[66] The omnipotence of holy humility does truly slay but does so in order to make alive. This pattern, Sonderegger says, is the basic relation between the Creator and his creature, and as such Christian theology must be able to accept it and confirm the benevolence of this power.[67] Ultimately, such confirmation cannot be made with the detachment of an argument, but only by personal, subjective assent—an act of faith. This faith will confirm the goodness of the omnipotent God in that, even in the midst of dereliction, it knows him not to be a tyrant, but rather one who hears our lament. And this faith will also confirm God's goodness in that it believes even his fiery ways to be purposive and ordered toward a goal, and not random and cruel.[68] Thus a believing Job will say, in his blistering encounter with God, "Though he kill me, yet I will trust in him; but I will defend my ways to his face" (13:15). In this he foreshadows Christ's own prayer of faith in Gethsemane.

Now to draw together the main strands of this account of omnipotence as holy humility for the purpose of analysis. Here, the fundamental perfection of divine unicity serves a grammatical function, such that divine power is conceived of as strictly identical with the being of God. This is a novel insight not in itself, but rather in the entailments Sonderegger draws from it. For, if God's power is his being, then the paired concepts of "will" and "cause" are insufficient ways to conceptualize omnipotence. When the former is privileged, it introduces deliberation and even potentiality to God's omnipotence. When the latter has predominance, God's power is only actual in its creaturely effects and therefore requires creation. But Sonderegger posits an alternate concept for describing God's power, a single concept that can do the work of both "will" and "cause," while avoiding their serious errors: "energy." Energy, particularly as understood by post-Newtonian physics, is the dynamism that underlies and gives rise to all concrete reality without being exhausted or defined thereby. When shorn of creaturely notions of depth and emergence, this concept is said to echo how God's omnipotent being is both holy subjectivity and humble objectivity—"holy humility." The claim of holy humility is that God, as subjectivity, communicates himself to the creature objectively; God can really be with the creature, while retaining his freedom. This results for the creature in an encounter wherein God's gracious presence frees the creature from other lords, even if by fire. In this way, the power of God is intrinsically ethical; it is power itself, yes, but as such it is ordered to the *telos* of fellowship. God acts morally *ad extra* simply by communicating his own being *a se*.

The reader will recall that Augustine's nascent doctrine of divine humility was seen to be ambiguous. Augustine holds in tension God *in se* and God *pro nobis*, "the name of being" and "the name of mercy." The former represents the "what" of God's being, while the latter represents the "who" of God's personal, ethical character. Augustine uses the concept of being, which is chiefly a commitment to a version of divine simplicity and its entailments, to describe God's perfect nature. Meanwhile, "the name of mercy" denotes God's personal, ethical interactions with his creatures—culminating in the act of the incarnation. While the argument was made that some of Augustine's fundamental theological convictions push toward the unification of these two poles in a doctrine of God's humility, this is not a step that Augustine himself takes. Augustine raises the fundamental questions, but he does not help us to think through with any real precision what divine humility might mean as an attribute of God's simple being. In fact, in the end, a separation remains for Augustine between God's perfect being (the "what") and God's ethical character (the "who"). What, if anything, is to bridge this gap is unclear, though some conception of the divine will is the likeliest candidate. However, if an appeal to the will as a faculty of God's being is made, this would not only be theologically inconsistent—implying that God has parts—but it would also mean that the relation between God's being and God's ethical character is ultimately arbitrary. It would introduce potentiality into the divine being. This approach would also amount to the attribution of a gnomic will to the divine being and therefore result in a God who is not intrinsically moral.[69] If this route is taken, humility is ultimately not a perfection of God but merely something God does. By contrast, Sonderegger does not appeal to the will to bridge the gap between God *in se* and God *pro nobis*, and therefore does not generate these problems in her account. Instead, she attempts to show the natural co-inherence of God's perfect being and God's moral character, both in his relation to the world as well as in his eternal self-relating.

Thus far, it has been shown that Sonderegger defines humility in terms of God's relation to the creature, but it is important to see how she makes the claim that humility is an attribute of God *a se*. Sonderegger says that God's being is itself a personal relation. This is an insight from the scholastic tradition. As noted above, when Aquinas speaks of God in a causal relation to creation, the concept of cause is stripped of motion and temporality, such that all that can be affirmed is a bare relation. If one understands that there can be no ontological medium between God and creation, then this is a relation that is simply God himself. God's own being is his relation to the world. If God is truly himself as personal relation to the world, Sonderegger reasons, then he must also somehow be personal relation in himself. This is not only a logical deduction, it is what the doctrine of the Trinity teaches: "[T]he transcendental relation, the concrete foundation of this personal God to creation and to creatures, cannot refer to another God than the immanent Trinity. . . . Rather, this personal *relatio* to another echoes and is suffused by the modes of God's very life, his processions."[70] Sonderegger, like Barth before her, knows that humility must be rooted somehow in God's immanent trinitarian life; there must be a transcendental reality to this attribute manifest in God's dealings toward the creature. The ways in which Barth and Sonderegger understand this transcendental foundation, however, differ sharply.

For Barth, the relation between God and creation is manifest in a relation of command and obedience between God the Father and the divine-human Jesus Christ. This relation, in turn, is transcendentally rooted in the eternal relation of command and obedience between the Father and the *Logos incarnandus* (with the Spirit as the mutual affirmation between the two). Barth radically foregrounds the concept of the divine will in this way by relocating predestination to the heart of the doctrine of God. With his unique account of predestination, Barth avoids the troubling implication of introducing potentiality into the doctrine of God by making God's decision to be humbly present to creation (via the incarnation) a feature of the divine being itself. But this seems to send Barth's theology careening into the same difficulty that faces those which foreground the concept of cause. It is conceptually difficult for Barth to affirm with consistency that God is who and what he is apart from his relation to creation—a few scattered references to the importance of a doctrine of the immanent Trinity notwithstanding. For Barth, humility is first and foremost a relation between the Father and the Son. By contrast, Sonderegger understands the relation between God and creation on the basis of the sheer, overrunning subjectivity-in-objectivity of the divine being exemplified in the burning bush. The fundamental relation of God to creation here is one not of will or cause, but of presence. This is no inertly objective presence but that of a dynamic and personal energy. Sonderegger shares the conviction that the manifestation of God's being in his relation to creation must be transcendentally grounded. She too, therefore, appeals to the doctrine of the Trinity. However, disciplined by the foundational perfection of divine unicity, she posits a voluntaristic relation not of two (or three) "persons," but rather of the one divine being in the tried-and-true terms of an eternal, generative self-relation: "As personal relation, the Lord *brings forth*; he begets and inspires."[71] This being does not have a will as a faculty, but rather is inherently, ontologically intentional.[72]

A previous chapter argued that Barth's particular christocentric actualism ensnares him in two intertwined difficulties: that of introducing two (or three) volitional centers into the trinitarian being of God and that of operating with what is functionally a monothelite Christology. Sonderegger's account not only does not demand these positions from her, but it also funds a significantly different definition of humility than Barth is able to offer. For, no matter how harmoniously Barth takes the obedient, eternal submission of the Son to the Father to be, this relation within the being of God is, in the end, an ethical zero-sum game. The Father commands, the Son obeys; there is an above and a below. If one stripped away from this the troubling notion of multiple centers of willing in the divine life, then one would have to deny that there is any meaningful "above" and "below" in God after all and instead speak with more theological precision and say that God *simpliciter* commands and that God *simpliciter* obeys his own command. In the end, this would be a doctrine of self-mastery rather than one of humility, and it would lose all meaningful connection with the human Jesus' relation to the Father that gives rise to it in the first place. For her part, Sonderegger offers an account of divine humility that does not depend on a contrast between "above" and "below." Here, submission of an inferior to a superior is not a necessary condition for God's humility. There is no need here for humility to be grounded within the trinitarian relations in the problematic way that Barth employs. Instead, "holy humility" is the personally generative and inspiring energy that simply is the divine being—Father, Son, and Spirit. God is holy humility both in his "personal" relation to himself and, in a second way, in his personal relation to creation.

As shown, Sonderegger makes progress with the doctrine of divine humility that is only nascent in Augustine's thought and that is taken too far, and is too deeply flawed, in Barth. Equating humility and omnipotence avoids from the very outset the notion that humility must be somehow a contradiction of the divine being. Treating humility under this heading keeps Sonderegger from assuming an ethically dubious definition of humility, such as weakness or subjection to the will of another. Her version of humility is not the restriction of power, but the sheer exercise of it. That said, the success of Sonderegger's account of divine humility vis-à-vis those of Augustine and Barth depends almost entirely on the legitimacy of her making foundational the concept of energy in explicating divine omnipotence and the concurrent resituating of the concepts of cause and will. Sonderegger herself does not justify this move explicitly. As such, the introduction of the concept of energy risks appearing at best all too convenient, and at worst arbitrary. It is helpful to pause, therefore, and consider the reasons that one might give for this important conceptual move.

In terms of scriptural warrant, the concept of power is closely associated with that of energy and equated with God the Holy Spirit. After all, it is the Spirit whose power in creation is pronounced as he broods generatively over the primordial waters of chaos (Gen 1:2). It is the Spirit, or divine breath, that energizes the dust that becomes humanity (Gen 2:7). The Spirit comes upon craftsmen, judges, prophets, and kings, empowering them to carry out the works of the Lord. "The Holy Spirit" is "the power of the Most High" that overshadows Mary and carries out an act of new creation in her womb (Luke 1:35). The Spirit leads Christ into the wilderness and grants him power over the tempter (Matt 4:1ff). Along these lines, then, the apostle Paul concludes that the Spirit is the power behind Jesus' resurrection and the subsequent new life that the Christian experiences (Rom 8:11). The Spirit is the implied power, or source of "energy," that sustains Paul in his apostolic ministry (Col 1:29). Paul's prayer is that those who receive his gospel will experience the Spirit as their own inner power (Eph 3:16). Of course, Jesus names the Spirit that will come upon the disciples at Pentecost "power from on high" (δύναμιν, Luke 24:49; see also Acts 1:8). It is clear, then, that even a cursory survey of scriptural texts shows that (1) the Spirit that is God is fundamentally regarded as "power," and (2) that the notion of "power" is virtually synonymous with a vivifying and energizing presence in creation and in the church. It perhaps tells us something important that theologians (not to mention the mass of Christians) almost invariably alternate between describing the Spirit with personal pronouns and as something akin to a force at work in the world. In any case, a strong biblical case can be made for taking the concept of energy as foundational for understanding divine power and pushing that of cause and will to a more subsidiary role.

Giving pride of place to the concept of energy might also be justified on the basis of its ability to yield better theological outcomes in the doctrine of God than the concepts of cause and will. Energy is more closely related to power than these concepts, and so does not carry with it some of their more difficult implications. To speak of divine power in terms of causation is already to introduce a necessary relation between God as cause and his effects. This must be taken either as a relation between God and the world or a relation between God and his own being. The former would posit creation as absolutely necessary for divine omnipotence, compromising divine aseity; the latter would make God *causa sui*, placing God within the realm of becoming. Likewise, to conceive of omnipotence in terms of will has its own problematic, seemingly unavoidable implications. The notion of will has deep connotations of either a faculty of decision or a concrete act of decision. Here, implications of deliberation seem unavoidable, as does a notion of potentiality that logically precedes actuality. Therefore, to make either of these two concepts, cause or will, foundational to divine power requires that they be purified to such an extent that they are eviscerated; one must remove what is most central to their ordinary meanings. By contrast, the concept of energy has a rough-and-ready applicability that is not lost in the process of purification. It is already virtually synonymous with power. The concept of energy that Sonderegger takes from modern science can accommodate relations of causation without making them necessary. And there is nothing inherently deliberative about energy. Add to this the fact that since energy is, creaturely speaking, properly basic, neither does it imply potentiality that precedes actuality. Thus energy, as Sonderegger makes use of it, is a conceptual structure that goes at least some way toward solving some seemingly intractable problems within the doctrine of God.

Though Sonderegger herself says no such thing, the concept of energy in her doctrine of divine humility also commends itself for its potential to overcome an important theological rift that has divided the West from East for nearly a millennium. The reader will have recognized that the concept of energy is not new to the doctrine of God; it has its own contested history in Christian theology. Since at least Gregory of Palamas in the fourteenth century, Orthodox theologians have formalized a real distinction between God's essence and God's manifold energies. The essence is the incommunicable, unknowable being of God; the energies are uncreated communications of God to his creatures. This is the dogmatic distinction that was deemed necessary to underwrite a soteriology centered around theosis.[73] The Western tradition has rejected this distinction because of its implications for divine unity, rightly noting the problematic nature of introducing any real distinction in God's essence. (After all, even the real distinction of the trinitarian hypostases is not a real distinction in the divine essence, since the Son and the Spirit are the entirety of the divine essence.) The two traditions have thus generally remained at odds on this fundamental point—the East taking soteriology as in some sense basic, and the West insisting as a starting point that divine unity means there can be no real distinction in God other than the hypostases. The soteriological concern of the former requires amendment to the doctrine of God in ways that seem problematic, and the other's understanding of God's being keeps it from adequately making sense of the scriptural statement that human beings "may become participants of the divine nature" (2 Pet 1:4). In relation to this context of debate, Sonderegger's doctrine of divine humility presents a possible rapprochement. Her understanding of the divine essence in terms of energy does not posit the real distinction that is generally problematic to the Latin doctrine of God. However, by understanding God's essence itself as personal energy—holy humility—there is real participation in the divine nature here. Doubtless, alarm bells in the East will sound because this implies that theosis is participation in the divine essence. However, because Sonderegger's understanding of divine unicity as God's being beyond all genus conceives of God's relation to creation as sheer infinite positivity of humble presence—blinding light, if one will—there is no need for fear that this real participation in God divinizes the creature or confines God to the realm of his creation. Participation in the divine essence is compatible with, and in fact grounds, the most radical transcendence and unknowability.

Seeking a way to illustrate how holy humility describes God's being as a purposive, personal energy without falling back upon the faulty notions of cause and will, Sonderegger appeals to Schleiermacher against Schleiermacher. Though he conceives the fundamental relation between God and the world in terms of absolute cause, when it comes to describing the way Christ redeems the world, Schleiermacher sees Christ charismatically radiating his own life outward with irresistible attraction.[74] Sonderegger claims that this is the way to understand how the personal relation that is the eternal divine being—the Holy Trinity—brings into existence a world that is not God. "We might say that God's personal nature draws the world into being, and immediately occupies the realm between Creator and creature."[75] The goal here is to describe God's being, and therefore God's relation to the world, as personal through and through. This notion of charismatic energy is put forward as an advancement over the two concepts of cause and agency that, respectively, tend toward either the idea that creation and redemption are necessary or that they are ultimately arbitrary. By disavowing both of these troubled notions, Sonderegger achieves, not a resolution, but rather a dramatic intensification, of the question, "Could God have intended only the divine end, and not the creaturely?"[76] How Sonderegger's doctrine of divine humility responds to this species of counterfactual question is the focus of the next section.

MYSTERY, COUNTERFACTUALS, AND THE RELOCATION OF THE DIVINE WILL

By speaking of God's being as his own humble relation to creation—by dispensing with the divine will as a faculty standing beyond God's being and his works—Sonderegger might be taken to imply that God's works *ad extra* (and creation itself) are necessary entailments of God's eternal life. Yet at the same time, her insistence that God's entire being is "intentional, personal, and living" intends to preserve God's freedom within all these dealings. The difficulty of the modal questions of whether God could have done anything other than what he has done or could have been different than he is are intensified. As Sonderegger tells it, the asking of these sorts of questions is not merely the raising of conceptual problems to be solved. Sonderegger takes the dilemma by the horns and posits that "such counterfactual questions are the communication to us, his proud creatures, of the sublime humility of the holy God. I think, that is, that these are *moral* questions, ethical struggles, that pour down upon us from the Father of Lights."[77] To ask the counterfactual question is to experiment intellectually and morally with one's own annihilation and that of all creation. Asking this type of question is a moral endeavor because it is personal, existentially involving to the core. And such an exercise, she argues, is not speculation to be avoided, but rather the proper creaturely echo of the self-giving humility of God.[78] The modal questions analogously replicate the moral question that God faces—and answers—from eternity. The counterfactual questions, Sonderegger says, bring Christian theology face-to-face with "the *necessity* of the divine nature itself."[79] Put another way, they bring the questioner into contact with what is meant by the term 'necessity' in relation to God's being. There is one way the counterfactual questions are surely false—when they amount to divine self-contradiction. If the question is whether God could be other than he actually is, then, reductio ad absurdum, the counterfactual situation cannot exist. Taking a classic puzzle case, Sonderegger affirms with the scholastics that God cannot create a rock too heavy for him to lift, since to do so would be to contradict his own essential deity, which is omnipotence. Yet in the very next breath she says that there is a second way these questions can be asked in which they must be affirmed as true. They are true insomuch as they point to the mystery of God's morally perfect being as divine humility as revealed in the incarnation. "They are true—metaphysically true—because the disposition to incarnation is true and real, the saving and necessary truth of the divine nature." The counterfactuals (or some of them anyways) are true—they are possibilities—inasmuch as they are actualities of the divine being that are made known (though not established) in Christ.[80] Though it appears at first blush that her statements are sheer paradox, what Sonderegger is attempting here is to recast the notion of divine necessity in a decidedly moral register: "[T]he necessity here is of the species of the *personal*."[81] No state of affairs compels God to be and act as he does in moving eternally toward creation and incarnation, other than the moral metaphysics, if one will, of his own divine humility. In sum, God's morally perfect being—his holy humility—is the absolute necessity from which the contingent necessities of creation, blessing, and salvation flow.

It is instructive to set Sonderegger's approach to these counterfactual questions over against that of John Webster. Webster summarizes the thrust of nearly the entire theological tradition with reference to the mystery of these counterfactual questions when he writes, "[T]he hinge between the inner works of God and his economic activity is the divine will."[82] Webster is careful to issue the important caveat that the divine will, or divine decision, is not deliberative or discursive. All the same, such a statement inevitably posits the divine will as an interval between God *in se* and *pro nobis*. But as a matter of fact, this interval has to be wiped away nearly instantly. The reference to decision, Webster writes, denotes a purposiveness that is "eternal, antecedent, wholly spontaneous and unconditioned by any consequent, 'before the foundation of the world' (Eph 1:5), arising solely from God. . . . This is because God's will is inseparable from his goodness and wisdom, and so is the gift of life."[83] Understood correctly, then, that which mediates between God's inner life and his economic life is simply God's own being. For her part, rather than posit the concepts of will and decision merely to render them virtually unrecognizable the next moment, Sonderegger appeals instead to the divine attribute of humility as a moral "disposition" God has toward his outer works of creation and redemption. This moral attribute is theological bedrock; it is the deepest mystery at which theological thought may arrive and where it must halt in praise. To put this difference in the simplest possible terms, Sonderegger answers the question of why God does as he does in the economy not by asserting that he simply chose to do so, but by saying that his moral–metaphysical character is such that he is eternally predisposed to do so. God is humble.

The placement of the divine will as a hinge between God's inner life and God's economic life pushes back the counterfactual questions; it cannot answer them. Such a move purports to shield the divine being from these difficult questions, but the issue immediately becomes: "[C]ould God's will, his decision, have been radically different?" To answer in the affirmative would be to deny that what God wills *ad extra* is rooted in his eternal, essential being. To answer in the negative would be to make his works *ad extra* necessary in an absolute sense. What both of these failed solutions share is a continued reliance on the divine will conceived as a middle factor between God's essence and God's act. To the dilemma posed by these two solutions, Sonderegger offers the alternative of divine humility. The cogency of this approach depends, in turn, on whether she can successfully displace the will from its mediating function in the doctrine of God.

It is Augustine who, Sonderegger says, explicitly articulates the notion that divine power is that of sheer will, distinct from the divine nature. But it is also Augustine in whom she finds implicit the resources for reconceptualizing the divine will in the doctrine of God. In Augustine's later struggles with Pelagianism, and his formulation of the doctrine of sin, he came to the insight that, even in the case of human beings, the will does not stand over against the nature but rather is intimately bound up within the nature. In fact, it is the heretic, Pelagius, who sees the will as a modal faculty, capable of deciding between possibilities. Sonderegger writes, "[I]t is Pelagius, not Augustine, who can neatly sever the act from the power to act, effective will from nature, the constitution from the will that resides in it."[84] As Augustine polemicizes against the logical outworking of Pelagianism, he comes to see that the will is an impenetrable mystery. Arguing theologically—from Scripture rather than abstraction—Augustine concludes that it is the whole of human nature that is corrupted by sin, including the intentionality denoted by the so-called faculty of the will. As Sonderegger maintains, "[T]he will, if we continue to call it that, is diffused through the whole person; our will just is our whole person, our human nature, in the state of desire. . . . Freedom—but slavery too—are states of human nature, and they both can be found in the midst of necessity and constraint."[85] Arguing *a minore ad maius*, Sonderegger claims that we should see the intentional—the so-called will—not as a faculty of God's being, but as a divine perfection. "To be a person, we might say, is to intend an end; and God is personal mystery, we dare to say, in just this sense."[86] Here, she claims, is the double-sided mystery that must be confessed: the nature of God intends the personal trinitarian relations, and the nature of God echoes this in intending personal relations with that which is not God.[87] The divine will is as much mystery as the being of God, because the divine will simply *is* the being of God. And the divine will is not an abstract power, but is simply the personal, moral intentionality denoted by the concept of divine humility.

Sonderegger's doctrine of divine humility, with its reconceptualization of the notion of divine will, addresses the same counterfactual questions that impel Barth's revised doctrine of election in the

Church Dogmatics. Barth is concerned to rid the doctrine of God of any interval between God's eternal being and his works *ad extra*. He, too, attempts to achieve this by relocating the divine will. Rather than having the will serve a mediatorial role between God's self-contained life and his movement toward creaturely reality, Barth places God's will to create and redeem in the doctrine of God proper. While this closes the gap between the immanent and economic life in God, it also makes it difficult to state with any consistency that creation and incarnation are not absolutely necessary—that they are not themselves necessary conditions for God's necessary being. In fact, Barth's theology invites the interpretation that God determines his own being by his eternal decision. Barth subordinates the concept of being to that of God's act and understands God's eternal act as a decision for creation and redemption. By contrast, Sonderegger conceives of God's being as the primordial reality, with something like logical priority to that of act. However, by way of divine humility she defines God's being itself as intrinsically moral in that it is predisposed as intentionality toward a reality other than itself. This predisposition, or intentionality, of humility is rooted in God's own being *in se* as the divine Father begets the divine Son, and together the Father and Son spirate the divine Spirit. Then, as a necessity contingent upon this self-giving, the divine humility moves outward in creation and redemption. Divine humility is the way that Sonderegger defines the relation in God between the "necessary and the possible, the infinite and the finite."[88] She can thus affirm, in decidedly Barthian language, that "even in the farthest reaches of the divine reality . . . God in his humility and truth has taken on our nature, our conditions, and our frame."[89] Yet by referring to an eternal moral disposition rather than a voluntary act of decision, Sonderegger affirms all this without the possible entailment that God somehow constitutes his own being through his work *ad extra*. No, she says, God's work *ad extra* flows as a contingent necessity from the absolute necessity of his morally perfect being.

The question of how to conceive of the divine will in theology is ultimately a question as to the proper location of mystery. When the will, however carefully conceived, serves as a "hinge" between God's inner life and his works, it functions as an explanation of the way God has his being from eternity. But for the divine will, there can be no explanation—it is simply mystery, the given reality that is its own explanation. The problem with locating mystery in the divine will in this manner, as has been shown, is that it either (1) makes arbitrary (in the truest sense of the word) the way God enacts his life economically or, more radically, (2) leads to the conclusion that somehow God constitutes his own being by an eternal act of will. In the former, the economic life of God has no necessary connection to the eternal being of God; in the latter, God's works *ad extra* have the same status of absolute necessity as God's eternal being. Locating mystery in the divine will in this sense appears to be, therefore, inherently problematic. What Sonderegger accomplishes by making intentionality (the concrete intentionality of humility) a perfection of God's being is to eschew any explanation for who and what God is other than God himself. The counterfactual questions of whether God could have been otherwise, in the end, result simply in praise before this mystery—the mystery that this is the being of God from all eternity. Sonderegger reasserts the mystery of God's being as having a primacy over that of divine act. Because this being is conceived of as intrinsically intentional—morally formed through and through—this allows her to close the gap between the immanent and economic life of God, but without collapsing the former into the latter. The mystery of holy humility, rather than the mystery of the divine will (however carefully conceived), allows Sonderegger to affirm what Barth and so many other twentieth-century theologians seek, but without exposing her doctrine of God to the conceptual dangers that seem to haunt their accounts.

Perhaps the best way to illuminate Sonderegger's account of the concrete intentionality of divine humility as the bedrock mystery in the doctrine of God, is to situate it vis-à-vis Anselm's *Cur Deus Homo*. The counterfactual question that motivates Anselm therein is, "by what logic or necessity did God become man, and by his death . . . restore life to the world" when he, per his omnipotence, could have done otherwise?[90] Anselm says that a proper solution to this question will be cogent not because of its power to explain the being of God, but rather because of its "usefulness and the beauty of its logic."[91] As Anselm proceeds to lay out the *ratio* of redemption, the thrust of this complex argument is that the incarnation has a "fittingness" (*convenientia*) with God's being. The metaphysics of God's perfect being entail God's moral stature as infinitely honorable. When God takes it upon himself to create, he necessarily brings the creature into a moral relationship in which infinite honor is due.[92] Sin is the failure to render this honor to God, and it is not only a moral deficiency in the creature, but a metaphysical threat to God's perfect being.[93] Thus God is, it seems, faced with a moral-metaphysical dilemma. If he acts to undo the creature's existence in punishment, justice is upheld but his honor is not, as his purpose for the creature fails. Likewise, if he overlooks the threat posed to him by the creature, mercy is shown but God does not receive due honor. Thus it follows necessarily that salvation must be accomplished by God himself taking the nature of a human being; God the Son, Jesus Christ, fulfils the original purposes for his creature not by punishing, nor by overlooking, but by saving. He saves by becoming a human in order to offer to God—on behalf of all human beings—the total honor owing to his perfect being.[94] Why did God become man? Because, Anselm says, it was required by God's perfect being. But this is not necessity in the normal sense of external compulsion. Rather, this is an act of "free will," which is to say it has the necessity of grace—a necessity contingent upon, and only upon, God's perfection.[95] This internal compulsion of grace described in *Cur Deus Homo* is not only God's redemptive intentionality but also, going one step deeper, the intentionality he has to put his own honor, his own perfect being, on the line in the first place. This internal compulsion denoted by Anselm, the intentionality of grace that simply is the divine being—this is the bedrock theological mystery. This is the point at which all predication in the doctrine of God leads. This is what Sonderegger appears to refer to when she advances an account of humility as a divine perfection. It is in this way that the counterfactual question communicates God's perfection.

Sonderegger sees the counterfactual question—"could God have done other than he has done in creating and redeeming the world?"—as itself a communication of the perfection of God's humility. If theology is attentive to the fact that this is the question of all questions in the doctrine of God; and if theology understands that the divine will is never a neutral mediating factor but rather the concrete intentionality of God's own being; then it follows that God's being, perfect from eternity, must be said to have this internal and intrinsic disposition to share life. God is humble. This humility is an attribute of his being that denotes this mysterious and foundational disposition. Humility as an attribute of God's eternal existence is absolutely necessary and is the absolute necessity upon which creation and redemption are contingent. To put it in terms that border on the absurd but are nonetheless helpful: there is no possible world in which God is not humble, just as, *per definitionem*, there is no possible world in which God does not exist. While the world itself is not necessary, there is no possible world in which there is no world. God's absolute necessity is morally, personally ordered toward, and granting life to, the contingent world. As Sonderegger writes: a God who does not share his life with creatures "is not God, and never has been nor will be, the LORD of life. Since this is personal necessity, neither coercive nor substantial, it is not logically contradictory to assign such counter-factual possibility to the LORD."[96] To arrive at this point, where one sees to the insoluble mystery is "not a sign of our *failure* in knowledge, but our *success*. It is because we *know* truly and properly . . . that God is mystery."[97]

Conclusion: Divine Humility without Christocentrism

The opening volume of Sonderegger's *Systematic Theology* provides a full-orbed account of divine humility. In one sense, she takes what is ambiguous in Augustine's gestures toward divine humility, makes it explicit, and develops it conceptually. Seen from another angle, her account responds to some of the deepest problems that arise in Barth's doctrine of God and that come to full fruition when he turns to incorporate humility into the doctrine of God. Sonderegger advances in this arena by way of a revised and clarified theological metaphysics. We have laid out three facets of this approach.

First, her doctrine of God stands under the discipline of divine unicity. This is closely associated with the classical attribute of divine simplicity with the important difference that, where simplicity can be interpreted as a negation of creaturely categories, unicity denotes God's sheer positive presence. This divine unicity undergirds a compatibilist epistemology wherein God transcends theological concepts by virtue of his taking up residence in the world—his omnipresence.

Thus she can thus say that reference to the immanent-transcendent God happens reliably in the seemingly mundane sociolinguistic practices that the Christian community engages in—the multitudinous practices that center around the biblical word and sacraments. This theological compatibilism, she claims, does away with both the angst of occasionalism and the fear that God could be collapsed into creaturely categories.

Second, what allows God to stand in this positive, compatibilist relation to his creation is his divine power, his omnipotence. God's omnipotent being is neither the power of cause nor that of will; these concepts as such create problems in the doctrine of God. Were God absolute cause, Sonderegger argues, his relation to creation would itself be absolutely necessary; he would be metaphysically dependent upon his effects. On the other hand, were God's power rooted in his ability to do whatever he wills, his power itself would be abstracted, severed from his goodness—a theological incoherence from the perspective of divine unicity and a severe problem for faith. As a way forward, Sonderegger conceives of God's power under the rubric of energy. Energy, when purified from the notion of depth, shows in some way how God's holy subjectivity and his humble objectivity coinhere. As subjectivity-in-objectivity (and vice versa), this energy is not impersonal but personal—it is the moral energy that is humility, life radiating outward in givenness toward another. This is a novel use of the concept of energy in the doctrine of God, but one that seems justified by Scripture as well as by its explanatory potential.

Finally, the energy that is divine humility does not solve the counterfactual question of whether or not God could have done otherwise than create and redeem. Instead, it brings theology to the proper point of divine mystery. The counterfactual questions are only intensified here, and for Sonderegger this is exactly as it should be. Why has God become man? Why does God's eternal being from eternity enact the world that he does, a world in which he creates, takes up residence, and ultimately redeems the world? Simply because God is himself morally and metaphysically disposed toward this telos. God is humble. The import and the cogency of this formulation requires a displacement of the divine will as a mediating faculty between God *in se* and God *pro nobis*, and a reconceptualization of the notion of intentionality as a divine attribute identical to God's being. The morally intentional being of God in its totality is the absolute necessity from which creation and redemption flow as contingent necessities.

As stated previously, following Basil Studer, the ambiguity posed by Augustine's thought centers on the question of whether Christian theology ought to be primarily theocentric or primarily christocentric. Barth's legacy is a decidedly, and even radically, christocentric answer to this question. Such an approach is concerned about the errors that might follow from defining the being of God apart from the economic work of God that culminates in the incarnation. But radical Christocentrism has its own problems, and it is not the only option. In fact, Sonderegger's doctrine of God, with divine humility as a defining feature, puts the lie to this overemphasis in contemporary theology. Her doctrine of God is theocentric and christotelic. The doctrine of God maintains its integrity over against Christology proper, and yet at the same time the incarnation flows from the being of God with the necessity of Anselm's "fittingness." She maintains a distinction between the immanent life of God and his economic enactment of that life and does so without risking the conceptual danger of an unknown God lurking behind divine revelation. Reading John 1:18, she writes: "It's all there in that one verse, isn't it? . . . God's uniqueness and formlessness, his majestic life as dynamic light, his deep hiddenness and humility—is it not captured in a few words?"[98] "No one has ever seen God"; yes, he is invisible, transcendent mystery. And yet, "the only begotten has made him known"—communicated to creation the attributes of God's morally perfect being. Christ is epistemologically determinative, but ontologically the divine perfections must rule. "The doctrine of divine attributes must be the sum and summit of theology, and all we do hereafter must be nothing more than an outworking of this doctrine, a return to it so that everything—really everything—is bathed in its light."[99]

CONCLUSION

In his essay "The Holiness and Love of God," John Webster argues for the need to conceive the divine attributes as an exposition of the particular identity of God the Holy Trinity, as opposed to basing them on a general concept of deity. The doctrine of God's attributes, Webster contends, "is to ask not *what* God is but *who* God is."[1] He is critical of efforts in contemporary analytic philosophy to conceive of God along the lines of maximally perfect being, but also of attempts to ground the divine attributes in a phenomenological analysis of, for example, love. For their vast differences, these two approaches to the doctrine of God repeat the same error inasmuch as "they determine the *essentia dei* by first determining the content of a predicate . . . and then applying the result to God."[2] Webster's suggestion, by contrast, is that an account of the divine attributes should not be "the projection of a category on to God," but rather "a repetition of the name of God . . . a conceptual expansion of that name which does not add to it or go beyond it but simply utters it as it has already been uttered, returning to that name as something which cannot be enhanced, mastered or resolved into anything other than itself."[3] In this treatment of divine humility, I have attempted to contribute to this ongoing work of theological utterance—not by saying something fundamentally new about God, but instead by reaching into the storehouses of Christian thought to bring out something old, something that itself is an echo of the divine Word.

Since the Enlightenment, theology has often had the terms for its utterances dictated to it by philosophy. Hume's empiricism leads to Kant's idealism, and a general skepticism over the meaning and legitimacy of metaphysical claims ensues. This generates particularly acute problems for the doctrine of God, and one way of viewing the story of modern theology is that of a quest to cope with, or overcome, this epistemological crisis. Various options present themselves. These include locating utterances about God in the operations of reason (e.g., Hegel), finding a human affective faculty more basic than reason that will anchor statements about God (e.g., Schleiermacher), or denying all inherent connection between the infinite and the finite and focusing instead on a purely subjective encounter and a personal decision (e.g., Kierkegaard). In the two former alternatives, the subjectivity of God—his transcendence, freedom, and aseity—are called severely into question. In the latter option, the objectivity of God—his real presence in and to the world—becomes dubious. Within the framework of the autonomy of reason, it becomes difficult, if not impossible, to utter the name of God in any sense that is in continuity with the biblical and theological tradition.

I began, in the first chapter of this book, with Martin Heidegger's critique of ontotheology and his corresponding metaphysics of *Dasein*. Heidegger is arguably the culmination of Enlightenment philosophy, bringing together in his thought the implications of the autonomy of human reason, offering a comprehensive account of the rational, affective, and even religious and ethical impulses of human life. Heidegger locates objectivity within the subject and transcendence in the subject's immanent wholeness as it approaches death. Whether implicitly or explicitly, Heidegger has exerted influence over important strands of contemporary theology. Thinkers like Jürgen Moltmann, Robert W. Jenson, Colin Gunton, John Caputo, and Jean-Luc Marion have all, in their own unique ways, assumed with Heidegger that there is something inherently wrong with so-called substance-metaphysics and have therefore sought to reconceive Christian doctrine in other terms. I argued that the problem with these approaches is that, when seen in terms of its own historical context, analyzed along the lines of a MacIntyrean "conflict of traditions," Heidegger's influential critique is questionable even in relation to its own Enlightenment tradition, and certainly not compelling for the rival tradition of inquiry that is Christian theology. Efforts, like that of Marion, to conceive of God without the metaphysical concept of "being" and somehow to conceptualize God along purely subjective lines with moral concepts like that of "love" are destined to fail. They are dubious in relation to their own Christian tradition and are category errors within the Enlightenment tradition as well.

Nonetheless, these efforts in contemporary theology do raise a legitimate and important question: how is it that the so-called metaphysical attributes of divine objectivity—being—relate to the moral attributes of divine subjectivity in the doctrine of God? Answering this question—bringing the moral and metaphysical together (or bringing them back together) requires a fresh account of human knowing in relation to God. Here, Kevin Hector was helpful in providing a descriptive account of how concepts—even that of being—are not projected onto realities, but given from without in a subjective, moral encounter with objects in the world. What and who God is *in se* is known and conceived of in the encounter with what God does *pro nobis*. God's perfect being is known in a moral, personal encounter—the doctrine of God must take the form of a "morally perfect being theology," I argued. The name of God is re-uttered, echoed in the human community of the church. The fact that God is this way—that he exists in precisely this way, as "morally perfect being," as subjectivity-in-objectivity and objectivity-in-subjectivity is, I argued, a divine attribute in and of itself. This attribute, I contended, is what certain theologians (namely St. Augustine, Karl Barth, and, more recently, Katherine Sonderegger) have sought to denote with the concept of humility.

The concept of humility is not commonly regarded as an attribute of God, has a range of semantic meanings (some of which appear to be antithetical to deity), and has been called into question as potentially ethically injurious in modern thought. Therefore, in chapter 2, I took the opportunity to sort through this polythetic concept. I began with a set of analytic definitions and proceeded to trace the historical developments in the concept of humility through the lens of these definitions. What emerged was that humility conceived of as lowliness-as-such was a severely deflated notion of humility. Within the early Christian tradition, I showed, humility was an expansion upon the Aristotelian virtue of magnanimity. Humility gave to the concept of magnanimity greater concretion, lifting it up and sanctifying it in light of Christ. Humility is true greatness, inasmuch as it is the use of one's strength for the sake of the true *polis*. It is a greatness that cannot be defined in zero-sum terms over against the greatness of others; it is a greatness that increases as it is lifts others up. Where lowliness, poverty, and suffering are included in humility, they are such as the means to an end of exalting others and not as an essential feature of humility. It is this rich notion of humility, defined as it is within the social vision of the city of God, that is eligible for application not only to Christ as man, but to Christ as God.

In chapter 3 I turned more decisively toward understanding how the concept of humility might be applied to God, and for this my interlocutor was Augustine. I showed that while Augustine applies the concept of humility to God explicitly, he is not transparent about what he means by this use. The task of that chapter, then, was to understand the underlying theological impetuses for this move, and the huge role that humility plays in his thought in general. I argued that Augustine confronts a recurring theological tension between God *in se* and God *pro nobis*, and that the concept of divine humility emerges from this tension. To make this argument, I looked at Augustine's treatment of three touchstone passages of Scripture: Exodus 3:14-15, John 5:19-30, and Philippians 2:6-7. I argued that the interpretation of these passages leads to the conclusions—or at least the suggestions—that, for Augustine, humility (1) is that which links together God's "name of being" and his "name of mercy"; (2) is a manifestation of the unified agency of the being of God per se (and not merely something predicated of the Son); and (3) denotes the manner in which the immutable God is present in and to his mutable creation. This gesturing toward divine humility remained only highly suggestive, created by the generative tension that is at the heart of Augustine's thought.

For Karl Barth, there is no ambiguity about divine humility, but rather a direct and bold assertion that God is humble and that this humility consists of eternal, inter-trinitarian obedience. Barth himself recognizes the stunning novelty of this formulation, and in chapter 4 I showed the theological procedures that led Barth to this point. I argued, first, that Barth employs a unique version of transcendentalism in his theology, wherein the structure of the economic works mirror the immanent being of God without qualification outside the event of revelation itself. God is act through and through. Second, I contended that Barth's "actualist" ontology is fundamentally voluntaristic in nature; the act that is God is an act of decision. I argued that these procedures issue in Barth's conception of divine humility as intertrinitarian obedience, and that there are significant doctrinal problems with this formulation. Command and obedience require two volitional centers in God, and indeed, I showed that Barth posits something like multiple volitional centers. Barth attempts to keep this novelty within the bounds of theological orthodoxy by way of understanding these in terms of the trinitarian relations, with each volitional center seen as what I called a "mode of willing." As I showed, this creates problems of its own. In taking the will to be a feature of the hypostases, rather than the divine essence, a monothelite Christology is the only logically consistent outcome. Thus, Barth's assertion of divine humility—itself the logical outcome of his central theological procedures—leads him unwittingly into conflict both with his own christological thought and that of the Christian theological tradition.

In chapter 5, I turned to Katherine Sonderegger. I showed how Sonderegger rejects some of the fundamental tenets of Barthian thought. She is deliberately not christocentric but begins her doctrine of God with the canonically foundational event of revelation in the Old Testament—the burning bush and the giving of the divine name in Exodus 3. An analysis of this event results in what she calls "theological compatibilism"—a descriptive epistemology wherein God's self-existence is manifest in and to creaturely reality and yet remains transcendent by virtue of his nature as all-surpassing light. This compatibilist, dwelling-with of God to his creation is what Sonderegger calls "humility." God's humble relation to creation, she argues, is neither one of cause, nor one of will, but rather one of sheer presence. This is not an inert presence, but a powerful (indeed, omnipotent) presence that is rightly understood in terms of "energy." This understanding of God as humble—present to creation in the fullness of omnipotent energy—heightens the question of whether God could have done or been otherwise. The counterfactual question is only intensified here and, Sonderegger says, this brings human thought into participation in divine humility. I showed that this could be understood in terms of Anselm's notion of "fittingness," in which God's being *pro nobis* is contingent upon, and only upon, God's being *a se*. The benefit of Sonderegger's approach, I argued, was its ability to create an intrinsic link—a link of necessity—between God's being and God's works.

One of the more interesting and potentially significant moves in the doctrine of divine humility as it was offered by Sonderegger, and endorsed in this book, was the resituating of the concept of the divine will. Appeals to the will as a sort of hinge between God's being and God's works are of ancient pedigree. Nonetheless, this is inherently problematic insomuch as divine simplicity demands that God's will is identical to God's being, and a good doctrine of omniscience precludes deliberation in God's life. The resituating of the divine will as, effectively, the inherent and eternal intentionality of the divine nature more faithfully encapsulates these insights. However, one question that emerges from this situation is, what will become of the doctrine of election? It seems that a significant revision of this important (especially to Protestant theology) doctrine will be required. I would be remiss to offer an endorsement of divine humility without mentioning this monumental task that is entailed therewith. It is beyond the scope of this conclusion to address this task with anything approaching adequacy, but it seems that this would likely take the form of a reformulation of Barth's already-revised doctrine of election. The emphasis here would be on God's intentionality to be with the creature and the way that this, in turn, determines the creature's being. Whether this would constitute a doctrinal advance, or whether there are other possibilities, will require further exploration and is beyond the scope of this book.

It was evident in the treatment of Sonderegger's conception of holy humility as a reformulation of divine omnipotence that humility here was not mere lowliness, but rather God's presence in strength for the sake of his creation. This presence was seen to be an "energy," a holy fire that both kills and makes alive. The moral shape of this humility incorporates both God's wrath and God's love, putting them in an ordered relation of crucifixion leading to resurrection. As such this was a significant advance upon the notions of divine humility in Augustine and Barth. For Augustine, humility was the concept that resulted from the generative tension of God's "name of being" and "name of mercy";

for Sonderegger, humility brings the omnipotent being of God and his mercy together in a dynamic and inseparable way. In contrast to Barth, humility is not taken by Sonderegger to equate straightforwardly with obedience or predicated only of the second person of the Trinity. Instead, humility here is a more expansive concept that was in keeping with the notion of humility as magnanimity.

This book on divine humility, while advancing a "morally perfect being theology," did not engage questions of moral theology or theological ethics surrounding humility. This is because to do so would have been to depart from questions about the being of God and engage in questions about the being of humanity. Nevertheless, properly conceived, these two areas of theological discourse cannot remain forever separate and indeed must ultimately move toward some form of fruitful and properly ordered integration. Theology (proper) can never itself be ethics, but ethics can indeed be theology when human behavior is considered as response to, and participation in, the being of God. In light of divine humility, therefore, what might be said, by way of anticipation, about human humility?

In the first place, the structure of humility is an active orientation toward the good of another. Oliver O'Donovan notes a "sovereignty of love" in the biblical writings (e.g., 1 Cor 13) and therefore in moral theology. This means, he says, that community is the *telos* of God, and of human behavior as it responds to God. Human humility must be defined in the light of this goal. Thus, commenting on the *carmen Christi*, O'Donovan describes humility in the following manner:

> What is the content of "humility," and how are we to "think of each other" in order to practice it? In a phrase that has been peculiarly vulnerable to zero-sum interpretations, Paul requires us to think of others as "above" ourselves. The translation "better than," favored in the English translation tradition, yields no sense. What could it mean to think of others (*all* others, not just some, and all the time!) as "better than" ourselves? The inevitable implication was drawn by fourteenth-century Platonist poet Bianco da Siena: it meant a permanent disposition of self-denigration and self-hatred. In Littledale's popular English translation, "true lowliness of heart . . . o'er its own shortcomings weeps with loathing." "Loathing" is not only repellent, but irrelevant to the apostle's sense. We may sometimes

have shortcomings to weep over, sometimes successes to rejoice in, but humility can be exercised in both those conditions and not only in the first of them. It is a virtue of restraint and deference, a discipline of allowing space for others to take practical initiatives.[4]

O'Donovan is correct in his assertion that humility is not to be defined as "loathing" per se and can in fact involve rejoicing in one's successes. Furthermore, the humility of God in creation and redemption was exercised to allow space for the meaningful action of other human persons. O'Donovan's description of humility as self-restraint and deference is apt under good conditions—when the parties involved are engaged in good-faith efforts to create community. However, O'Donovan's language about humility is still too passive, especially when it comes to situations that are oppressive or unjust. Divine humility shows that humility can be decidedly active—a subversive force.

One way of imagining the active, subversive nature of humility is represented in a pivotal sermon by Dr. Martin Luther King Jr. Taking Jesus' instruction to his disciples to "be wise as serpents and innocent as doves" (Matt 10:16), King commends the synthesis of "a tough mind and a tender heart." The tough-minded person is fundamentally a shrewd realist and a principled resister of those things that stand in the way of the harmonious community envisioned in the kingdom of God. But this tough-mindedness is not enough because, by itself, it will lead to bitterness—a bitterness leading either to resignation or to violence. One must thus also be not only tough-minded but tenderhearted and compassionate, ordering one's response to the enemy by the goal of transformation and reconciliation. The combination of these two forces—fierce protest ordered by active love—amounts to a "nonviolent resistance . . . [that] avoids the complacency and do-nothingness of the soft-minded and the violence and bitterness of the hardhearted."[5] With this, I argue, King gestures toward what I have denoted as humility, albeit without using the term. To be humble under the conditions of sin is to resist actively—though without violence—those things that restrict the moral agency of oneself and others. This is something that is ultimately rooted in the very nature of God: "The greatness of our God lies in the fact that he is both tough-minded and tenderhearted . . . our God combines in his nature a creative synthesis of love and justice."[6]

David Kelsey argues that the act of theological interpretation is the attempt to employ a "single synoptic, imaginative judgment" to capture the essence of Christianity—the nature of God and the nature of humanity in God. While Kelsey speaks, in context, of the interpretation of Scripture, his insight expresses well the core task of this study in systematic theology. Its goal has been to locate, or construct, a single conceptual apparatus that "tries to catch up what Christianity is basically all about."[7] Humility, I have contended, is a viable way to do just this. Humility captures the eternal disposition of God toward the sharing of his life with creatures in love and justice—humility is divine. And, though this second part has only been anticipated, humility is the way human beings participate in the being of the humble God—by active moral engagement for the good of others. "God opposes the proud, but gives grace to the humble" (1 Pet 5:5).

NOTES

INTRODUCTION

1 John B. Webster, *God without Measure: Working Papers in Christian Theology*, vol. 1, *God and the Works of God* (London: Bloomsbury, 2016), 27.

2 Webster, *God without Measure*, 1:27–28.

1. MORALLY PERFECT BEING THEOLOGY

1 Matthew Levering, *Scripture and Metaphysics: Aquinas and the Renewal of Trinitarian Theology* (Oxford: Blackwell, 2004), 15.

2 Alasdair MacIntyre, *Whose Justice? Which Rationality?* (Notre Dame, Ind.: University of Notre Dame Press, 2008), 8, 359.

3 Alasdair MacIntyre, "Epistemological Crises, Narrative, and the Philosophy of Science," *Why Narrative? Readings in Narrative Theology*, ed. Stanley Hauerwas and L. Gregory Jones (Grand Rapids: Eerdmans, 1989), 146–47.

4 MacIntyre, *Whose Justice?* 364–65.

5 MacIntyre, "Epistemological Crises," 147.

6 MacIntyre, *Whose Justice?* 365.

7 MacIntyre, *Whose Justice?* 362.

8 Godzieba, "Ontotheology to Excess: Imagining God without Being," *Theological Studies* 56 (1995): 6.

9 MacIntyre, *Whose Justice?* 166–67.
10 Iain Thomson, "Ontotheology? Understanding Heidegger's *Destruktion* of Metaphysics," *International Journal of Philosophical Studies* 8, no. 3 (2000): 298.
11 Immanuel Kant, *Critique of Pure Reason*, trans. Paul Guyer and Allen W. Wood (Cambridge: University of Cambridge Press, 1998), A632/B660.
12 Kant, *Critique of Pure Reason*, A638/B666–A640/B668.
13 Kant, *Prolegomena to Any Future Metaphysics: And the Letter to Markus Herz, February 1772*, trans. James W. Ellington, 2nd ed. (Indianapolis, Ind.: Hackett, 2001), 363.
14 Kant, *Critique of Pure Reason*, A640/B668–A642–B670. Kant will ground the existence of God not in pure reason, but in practical or moral reason.
15 Ludwig Feuerbach, *The Essence of Christianity*, trans. George Eliot (New York: Harper & Row, 1957), 35.
16 Brian D. Ingraffia, *Postmodern Theory and Biblical Theology* (New York: Cambridge University Press, 1995), 4–6.
17 Kant, *Critique of Pure Reason*, Bxxx.
18 Martin Heidegger, *Kant and the Problem of Metaphysics*, 5th ed., trans. Richard Taft (Bloomington: Indiana University Press, 1997), 141. In context, the quotation applies only to Kant.
19 Thomson, "Ontotheology?" 300. Thomson's article is immensely helpful in reconstructing Heidegger's deconstruction of Western philosophy.
20 Thomson, "Ontotheology?" 302.
21 Thomson, "Ontotheology?" 304.
22 Thomson, "Ontotheology?" 304–5.
23 Thomson, "Ontotheology?" 306.
24 Thomson, "Ontotheology?" 307.
25 Thomson, "Ontotheology?" 309.
26 Thomson, "Ontotheology?" 310.
27 Thomson, "Ontotheology?" 312.
28 Thomson, "Ontotheology?" 314.
29 Thomson, "Ontotheology?" 318–19.
30 Richard Taft, "Translator's Introduction to the Fourth Edition," in Heidegger, *Kant and the Problem of Metaphysics*, xii.
31 Heidegger, *Kant and the Problem of Metaphysics*, 4.
32 Heidegger, *Kant and the Problem of Metaphysics*, 11.

33 Heidegger, *Kant and the Problem of Metaphysics*, 15–17.
34 Heidegger, *Kant and the Problem of Metaphysics*, 19–20.
35 Heidegger, *Kant and the Problem of Metaphysics*, 23.
36 Kant, *Critique of Pure Reason*, A15/B29; Heidegger, *Kant and the Problem of Metaphysics*, 25–26.
37 Heidegger, *Kant and the Problem of Metaphysics*, 35–36.
38 Heidegger, *Kant and the Problem of Metaphysics*, 40–41.
39 Kant, *Critique of Pure Reason*, A77/B103; Heidegger, *Kant and the Problem of Metaphysics*, 44.
40 Heidegger, *Kant and the Problem of Metaphysics*, 51.
41 Heidegger, *Kant and the Problem of Metaphysics*, 59.
42 Heidegger, *Kant and the Problem of Metaphysics*, 71.
43 Heidegger, *Kant and the Problem of Metaphysics*, 73–74.
44 Heidegger, *Kant and the Problem of Metaphysics*, 75.
45 Heidegger, *Kant and the Problem of Metaphysics*, 84.
46 Heidegger, *Kant and the Problem of Metaphysics*, 87–88.
47 Heidegger, *Kant and the Problem of Metaphysics*, 140.
48 Heidegger, *Kant and the Problem of Metaphysics*, 141.
49 Heidegger, *Kant and the Problem of Metaphysics*, 141.
50 Heidegger, *Kant and the Problem of Metaphysics*, 88; see also 3–4.
51 Martin Heidegger, *Being and Time*, trans. John Macquarrie and Edward Robinson (San Francisco: Harper & Row, 1962), 227 (emphasis in original).
52 Heidegger, *Being and Time*, 195.
53 Heidegger, *Being and Time*, 228.
54 Heidegger, *Being and Time*, 229.
55 Heidegger, *Being and Time*, 230.
56 Heidegger, *Being and Time*, 231–32.
57 Heidegger, *Being and Time*, 234.
58 Heidegger, *Being and Time*, 235.
59 Heidegger, *Being and Time*, 236.
60 Heidegger, *Being and Time*, 285. "[T]o master this task successfully, we must presuppose that precisely what we are seeking in this investigation—the meaning of Being in general—is something which we have already found and are quite familiar."
61 Heidegger, *Being and Time*, 279.
62 Heidegger, *Being and Time*, 279 (emphasis in original).
63 Heidegger, *Being and Time*, 294.
64 Heidegger, *Being and Time*, 303.

65 Heidegger, *Being and Time*, 309.

66 Heidegger, *Being and Time*, 307. "[Death] is the possibility of the impossibility of every way of comporting oneself towards anything, of every way of existing. . . . Being-towards-death, as anticipation of possibility, is what first *makes* this possibility *possible*, and sets it free as possibility."

67 Heidegger, *Being and Time*, 374 (emphasis in original).

68 Heidegger, *Being and Time*, 375 (emphasis in original).

69 Jean-Luc Marion, *God without Being*, trans. Thomas A. Carlson (Chicago: Chicago University Press, 1991), 2.

70 Marion, *God without Being*, 3.

71 Marion, *God without Being*, 3.

72 Marion, *God without Being*, 16.

73 Marion, *God without Being*, 18.

74 Marion, *God without Being*, 20.

75 Marion, *God without Being*, 23–24.

76 Marion, *God without Being*, 28–29.

77 Marion, *God without Being*, 29–32.

78 Marion, *God without Being*, 34.

79 Marion, *God without Being*, 46.

80 Marion, *God without Being*, 47.

81 Marion, *God without Being*, 47–48.

82 Marion, *God without Being*, 65–67.

83 Marion, *God without Being*, 68.

84 Marion, *God without Being*, 70.

85 Marion, *God without Being*, 72.

86 Marion, *God without Being*, 80–81.

87 Marion, *God without Being*, 83–86.

88 Marion, *God without Being*, 86.

89 Marion, *God without Being*, 88–89.

90 Marion, *God without Being*, 89.

91 Marion, *God without Being*, 95.

92 Marion, *God without Being*, 96.

93 Marion, *God without Being*, 97.

94 Marion, *God without Being*, 100.

95 Marion, *God without Being*, 100.

96 Marion, *God without Being*, 101.

97 Marion, *God without Being*, 101.

98 Marion, *God without Being*, 101–3.

99 Marion, *God without Being*, 105–6.
100 Marion, *God without Being*, 107.
101 Marion, *God without Being*, 106.
102 Marion, *God without Being*, 106.
103 Jean-Luc Marion, "'They recognized him; and he became invisible to them,'" *Modern Theology* 18, no. 2 (2002): 145–52.
104 Kevin W. Hector, *Theology without Metaphysics: God, Language, and the Spirit of Recognition* (Cambridge: Cambridge University Press, 2011), 9.
105 Hector, *Theology without Metaphysics*, 27.
106 Hector, *Theology without Metaphysics*, 32.
107 Hector, *Theology without Metaphysics*, 34.
108 Hector, *Theology without Metaphysics*, 35–37.
109 Hector, *Theology without Metaphysics*, 47.
110 Hector, *Theology without Metaphysics*, 45.
111 Hector, *Theology without Metaphysics*, 52–53.
112 Hector, *Theology without Metaphysics*, 52–53.
113 Hector, *Theology without Metaphysics*, 56.
114 Hector, *Theology without Metaphysics*, 61–62.
115 Hector, *Theology without Metaphysics*, 67.
116 Hector, *Theology without Metaphysics*, 69.
117 Hector, *Theology without Metaphysics*, 73.
118 Hector, *Theology without Metaphysics*, 81.
119 Hector, *Theology without Metaphysics*, 83–84.
120 Hector, *Theology without Metaphysics*, 91.
121 Hector, *Theology without Metaphysics*, 92.
122 Hector, *Theology without Metaphysics*, 93.
123 Hector, *Theology without Metaphysics*, 105–6.
124 Hector, *Theology without Metaphysics*, 108–9.
125 Hector, *Theology without Metaphysics*, 124.
126 Karl Barth, *Church Dogmatics*, vol. 2.1, *Doctrine of God*, ed. G. W. Bromiley and T. F. Torrance (Edinburgh, UK: T&T Clark, 1957), 204–54.
127 Hector, *Theology without Metaphysics*, 130–31; Barth, *Church Dogmatics*, 2.1:227.
128 Barth, *Church Dogmatics*, 2.1:229–30.
129 Hector, *Theology without Metaphysics*, 159–60.
130 Hector, *Theology without Metaphysics*, 168.
131 Hector, *Theology without Metaphysics*, 162.
132 Hector, *Theology without Metaphysics*, 172–76.
133 Hector, *Theology without Metaphysics*, 202–03.

134 Hector, *Theology without Metaphysics*, 211.
135 Hector, *Theology without Metaphysics*, 213–14.
136 Hector, *Theology without Metaphysics*, 217.
137 Hector, *Theology without Metaphysics*, 219.
138 Hector, *Theology without Metaphysics*, 228.
139 Hector, *Theology without Metaphysics*, 230.
140 Hector, *Theology without Metaphysics*, 232–33.
141 Hector, *Theology without Metaphysics*, 236.
142 Friedrich Schleiermacher, *The Christian Faith*, ed. H. R. Mackintosh and J. S. Stewart (London: T&T Clark, 1999), 10–11.
143 Schleiermacher, *The Christian Faith*, 194. Schleiermacher says in his subsection heading: "All attributes which we ascribe to God are to be taken as denoting not something special in God, but only something special in the manner in which the feeling of absolute dependence is to be related to him."
144 Schleiermacher, *The Christian Faith*, 739.
145 Augustine, *The Trinity: De Trinitate*, trans. Edmund Hill, O.P. (Hyde Park, N.Y.: New City, 2007), 1.1.
146 Augustine, *The Trinity* 1.2.
147 This is not to deny any Neoplatonic influence, but rather to sideline this question, avoiding the genetic fallacy, and to examine the theological function of the concept of being in Augustine's work.
148 Barth, *Church Dogmatics*, 2.1:259 (emphasis added).
149 Barth, *Church Dogmatics*, 2.1:260.
150 Barth, *Church Dogmatics*, 2.1:272.
151 Brian Leftow, "Why Perfect Being Theology?" *International Journal of the Philosophy of Religion* 69, no. 2 (2011): 104–5.
152 Leftow, "Why Perfect Being Theology?" 108 (emphasis added).
153 Leftow, "Why Perfect Being Theology?" 108.
154 Leftow, "Why Perfect Being Theology?" 108.
155 Leftow, "Why Perfect Being Theology?" 109.
156 Leftow, "Why Perfect Being Theology?" 107. Curiously, as he makes his case for S-PBT, Leftow does not engage with Exodus 3:17 and its divine name YHWH, the *locus classicus* for Jewish and Christian understandings of the divine nature.
157 Isaak August Dorner, *Divine Immutability: A Critical Reconsideration*, trans. Robert R. Williams (Minneapolis: Fortress, 1994), 82–86.
158 Dorner, *Divine Immutability*, 89.
159 Dorner, *Divine Immutability*, 92.

160 Dorner, *Divine Immutability*, 95.
161 Dorner, *Divine Immutability*, 98.
162 Dorner, *Divine Immutability*, 98.
163 Dorner, *Divine Immutability*, 110–11. "Deism has only the world, just as substance pantheism or acosmism has only God."
164 Schleiermacher, *The Christian Faith*, 203–6, 231–32.
165 Dorner, *Divine Immutability*, 127.
166 Dorner, *Divine Immutability*, 99.
167 Dorner, *Divine Immutability*, 135.
168 Barth, *Church Dogmatics*, 2.1:493.
169 Matthias Gockel, "On the Way from Schleiermacher to Barth: A Critical Reappraisal of Isaak Dorner's Essay on Divine Immutability," *Scottish Journal of Theology* 53, no. 4 (2000): 490–510.

2. Definitions of Humility

1 James Kellenberger, "Humility," *American Philosophical Quarterly* 47, no. 4 (2010): 321–22.
2 Kellenberger, "Humility," 324; J. L. Austin, *Sense and Sensibilia* (New York: Oxford University Press, 1964), 70–71.
3 Kellenberger, "Humility," 328–29.
4 Kellenberger, "Humility," 331.
5 Kellenberger, "Humility," 333.
6 J. L. A. Garcia, "Being Unimpressed with Ourselves: Reconceiving Humility," *Philosophia* 34, no. 4 (2006): 419.
7 Garcia, "Being Unimpressed with Ourselves," 419–20; Julia Driver, *Virtues of Ignorance* (New York: Cambridge University Press, 1996), 16–41; Owen Flanagan, *Self-Expressions: Mind, Morals, and the Meaning of Life* (New York: Oxford University Press, 1996), 171–80; Norvin Richard, "Is Humility a Virtue?" *American Philosophical Quarterly* 25, no. 3 (1988): 253–59; Richard Roberts and Jay Wood, *Intellectual Virtues: An Essay in Regulative Epistemology* (New York: Oxford University Press, 2007).
8 Garcia, "Being Unimpressed with Ourselves," 420; Roberts and Wood, *Intellectual Virtues,* 257–79.
9 Garcia, "Being Unimpressed with Ourselves," 417.
10 Garcia, "Being Unimpressed with Ourselves," 421–22.
11 Garcia, "Being Unimpressed with Ourselves," 422. It should be noted that it is not accurate to classify Aquinas' account of humility as

outwardly directed, since he says explicitly that what makes humility a virtue is not the external action but "the inward choice of the mind." See Thomas Aquinas, *Summa Theologica*, rev. ed., trans. Fathers of the English Dominican Province (Cincinatti: Benziger Brothers, 1947) 161.1–2.

12 Alasdair MacIntyre, *After Virtue: A Study in Moral Theory*, 3rd ed. (London: Bloomsbury, 2007), 159.

13 MacIntyre, *After Virtue*, 159 (emphasis in original).

14 McIntyre, *After Virtue*, 176.

15 Aristotle, *Nicomachean Ethics*, trans. Martin Oswald (London: Pearson, 1962) 1.1.

16 Aristotle, *Nicomachean Ethics* 1.2.

17 Aristotle, *Nicomachean Ethics* 1.4.

18 MacIntyre, *After Virtue*, 148.

19 Aristotle, *Nicomachean Ethics* 1.7.

20 Aristotle, *Nicomachean Ethics* 1.7.

21 Aristotle, *Nicomachean Ethics* 2.5. See also MacIntyre, *After Virtue*, 148.

22 Aristotle, *Nicomachean Ethics* 2.6.

23 Aristotle, *Nicomachean Ethics* 4.3.

24 Aristotle, *Nicomachean Ethics* 4.3.

25 MacIntyre, *After Virtue*, 116.

26 See Jane Foulcher, "Reclaiming Humility: Four Studies in the Monastic Tradition" (Ph.D. diss., Charles Sturt University, 2011), 15–16.

27 Aristotle, *Nicomachean Ethics* 4.3.

28 Aristotle, *Nicomachean Ethics* 4.4.

29 Aristotle, *Nicomachean Ethics* 4.4.

30 Jane Foulcher comments specifically on the "social embeddedness" of his concept of magnanimity: "Aristotle is fundamentally concerned with the arena of honour in his discussion of magnanimity. In Aristotle's world, this self-appraisal cannot be separated from the *polis*. And . . . it cannot be separated from *fortuna* and from one's place in the scheme of life. Foulcher, "Reclaiming Humility," 17.

31 Christopher Cordner, "Aristotelian Virtue and Its Limitations," *Philosophy* 69 (1994): 293–94.

32 Cordner, "Aristotelian Virtue and Its Limitations," 297–98.

33 Cordner, "Aristotelian Virtue and Its Limitations," 309.

34 Foulcher, "Reclaiming Humility," 20.

35 David Hume, *A Treatise of Human Nature*, 2nd ed., ed. P. H. Nidditch (Oxford: Clarendon, 1978), 2.3.3, p. 415.

36 Hume, *A Treatise of Human Nature*, 2.1.1, pp. 276–77.

37 Hume, *A Treatise of Human Nature*, 2.1.2, pp. 277–78.

38 Hume, *A Treatise of Human Nature*, 2.1.2, pp. 277–78.

39 Hume, *A Treatise of Human Nature*, 2.1.2, p. 279.

40 Hume, *A Treatise of Human Nature*, 2.1.3, pp. 280–82.

41 Hume, *A Treatise of Human Nature*, 2.1.4, pp. 282–84.

42 Hume, *A Treatise of Human Nature*, 2.1.5, p. 286.

43 David Hume, *Enquiries concerning Human Understanding and Concerning the Principles of Morals*, 3rd ed., ed. P. H. Nidditch (Oxford: Clarendon, 1975), 9.1, p. 270.

44 Hume, *Enquiries concerning Human Understanding* 8.1, p. 265.

45 Friedrich Nietzsche, *Beyond Good and Evil*, in *Basic Writings of Nietzsche*, trans. Walter Kaufmann (New York: Modern Library, 2000), 201.

46 Nietzsche, *Beyond Good and Evil*, 202.

47 Nietzsche, *Beyond Good and Evil*, 195.

48 Nietzsche, *Genealogy of Morals*, in *Basic Writings of Nietzsche*, 1–2.

49 Nietzsche, *Genealogy of Morals*, 7.

50 Nietzsche, *Genealogy of Morals*, 9.

51 Nietzsche, *Genealogy of Morals*, 13.

52 Nietzsche, *Genealogy of Morals*, 13.

53 Nietzsche, *Genealogy of Morals*, 14.

54 Nietzsche, *Beyond Good and Evil*, 62. "[A] smaller, almost ridiculous type, a herd animal, something eager to please, sickly, and mediocre has been bred, the European of today."

55 See MacIntyre, *After Virtue*, 136.

56 Nietzsche, *Beyond Good and Evil*, 259.

57 Reinhold Niebuhr, *Beyond Tragedy: Essays on the Christian Interpretation of History* (New York: Scribner, 1965), 197–98.

58 Reinhold Niebuhr, *The Nature and Destiny of Man: A Christian Interpretation* (Louisville, Ky.: Westminster John Knox, 1996), 188–89.

59 Anders Nygren, *Agape and Eros*, trans. Philip S. Watson (London: SPCK, 1957), 722–33. Nygren's concern, of course, is to show the failure of the attempted Augustinian synthesis of *eros* and *agape*, and to reassert (with Luther) the sufficiency of divine *agape*.

60 Valerie Saiving Goldstein, "The Human Situation: A Feminine View," *Journal of Religion* 40, no. 2 (1960): 101–2.

61 Goldstein, "The Human Situation," 103–5.

62 Goldstein, "The Human Situation," 107.

63 Goldstein, "The Human Situation," 107.

64 Goldstein, "The Human Situation," 108.

65 Goldstein, "The Human Situation," 109.

66 Goldstein, "The Human Situation," 110–11.

67 Daphne Hampson, *Theology and Feminism* (Oxford: Basil Blackwell, 1990), 155. Quoted in Sarah Coakley, "Kenosis and Subversion: On the Repression of 'Vulnerability' in Christian Feminist Writing," in *Powers and Submissions: Spirituality, Philosophy and Gender* (Oxford: Blackwell, 2002), 3.

68 Kellenberger, "Humility," 328–29.

69 MacIntyre, *After Virtue*, 204.

70 MacIntyre, *After Virtue*, 218.

71 MacIntyre, *After Virtue*, 235.

72 Augustine, *Confessions*, trans. Maria Boulding, O.S.B., 2nd ed. (Hyde Park, N.Y.: New City, 2012) 8.6.15.

73 Athanasius, *The Life of St. Anthony*, trans. Mary Emily Keenan, S.C.N., in *Early Christian Biographies* (Washington, D.C.: Catholic University of America Press, 1952) 14.

74 Athanasius, *Life of St. Anthony* preface.

75 Athanasius, *Life of St. Anthony* 1.

76 E.g., Athanasius, *Life of St. Anthony* 4.

77 Athanasius, *Life of St. Anthony* 12.

78 Athanasius, *Life of St. Anthony* 30.

79 Athanasius, *Life of St. Anthony* 46.

80 Athanasius, *Life of St. Anthony* 74.

81 Peter Brown, "The Rise of the Holy Man," *Journal of Roman Studies* 61 (1971): 100.

82 Brown, "The Rise of the Holy Man," 91–92.

83 Brown, "The Rise of the Holy Man," 93.

84 Barsaniphius, "Letter 100," in *Barsaniphius and John: Letters*, vol. 1, trans. John Chryssavgis (Washington D.C.: Catholic University of America Press, 2006), 122–23.

85 Augustine, *Letters 100–155*, trans. Roland Teske, S.J., in *The Works of St. Augustine II/2*, ed. Boniface Ramsey (Hyde Park, N.Y.: New City, 2003), 202.

86 Augustine, *Letters 100–155* 208–9.
87 Augustine, *Letters 100–155* 210–11.
88 Augustine, *The City of God: De civitate Dei (Books 1–10)*, trans. William Babcock (Hyde Park, N.Y.: New City, 2012), preface.
89 Augustine, *The City of God* 1.31.
90 Augustine, *The City of God* 2.6.
91 Augustine, *The City of God* 2.8.
92 Augustine, *The City of God* 2.13.
93 Augustine, *The City of God* 2.13.
94 Augustine, *The City of God* 2.14.
95 Augustine, *The City of God* 2.18.
96 Augustine, *The City of God* 3.15.
97 Augustine, *The City of God* 3.17.
98 Augustine, *The City of God* 4.6.
99 Augustine, *The City of God* 4.14.
100 Augustine, *The City of God* 5.13.
101 Augustine, *The City of God* 5.14.
102 Augustine, *The City of God* 5.20.
103 Augustine, *The City of God* 5.25.
104 Augustine, *The City of God* 5.23.
105 Augustine, *The City of God* 7.34–35.
106 Augustine, *The City of God* 7.31–33.
107 Augustine, *The City of God* 9.20.
108 Augustine, *The City of God: De civitate Dei (Books 11–22)*, trans. William Babcock (Hyde Park, N.Y.: New City, 2013), 14.14.
109 Augustine, *The City of God* 14.14–15.
110 See Saint Basil of Caesarea, *An Ascetical Discourse and Exhortation on the Renunciation of the World and Spiritual Perfection*, in *Saint Basil: Ascetical Works*, trans. M. Monica Wagner, C.S.C., ed. Roy Joseph Deferrari (Washington, D.C.: Catholic University of America Press, 1962), 17–18.
111 Basil, *An Ascetical Discourse* 18.
112 Basil, *An Ascetical Discourse* 18–26.
113 Basil, *An Ascetical Discourse* 29.
114 Basil, *An Ascetical Discourse* 30.
115 Basil, *An Ascetical Discourse* 21.
116 Basil, *An Ascetical Discourse* 121.

117 Saint Basil of Caesarea, *Morals*, in *Saint Basil: Ascetical Works* 177. See also Saint Basil of Caesarea, *The Long Rules*, in *Saint Basil: Ascetical Works* 30.
118 Basil, *The Long Rules* 10.
119 Basil, *The Long Rules* 43.
120 Basil, *Morals* 210.
121 Basil, *The Long Rules* 35.
122 Basil, *Morals* 213.
123 Basil, *The Long Rules* 7.
124 Basil, *The Long Rules* 21.
125 It is certain that Augustine knew the writings of Basil via Rufinus. It is therefore possible that Augustine's definition of humility was inspired by reading Basil's writings, but this would be nothing more than conjecture. See Joseph T. Lienhard, S.J., "Augustine of Hippo, Basil of Caesarea, and Gregory Nazianzen," in *Orthodox Readings of Augustine*, ed. George Demacopoulos and Aristotle Papanikolaou (New York: St. Vladimir's Seminary Press, 2008), 81–99.
126 Saint Benedict Abbot of Monte Cassino, *The Rule of St. Benedict in English with Notes*, ed. Timothy Fry (Collegeville, Minn.: Liturgical, 1981) 7.7.
127 Benedict, *The Rule* 5.1.
128 Benedict, *The Rule* 7.31–32.
129 Benedict, *The Rule* 7.34.
130 Benedict, *The Rule* 7.35.
131 Benedict, *The Rule* 7.49.
132 Benedict, *The Rule* 7.51.
133 Benedict, *The Rule* 7.55.
134 Benedict, *The Rule* 7.56–61.
135 Benedict, *The Rule* 7.62–63.
136 Benedict, *The Rule* 7.67–70.
137 Benedict, *The Rule* 73.1–9.
138 Basil, *The Long Rules* 47.
139 Benedict, *The Rule* prologue 1.
140 Aquinas, *Summa Theologica* 2a.55.1.
141 Aquinas, *Summa Theologica* 2a.56.1.
142 Aquinas, *Summa Theologica* 2a.56.3.
143 Aquinas, *Summa Theologica* 2a.62.1.
144 Aquinas, *Summa Theologica* 2b.141.3–4.
145 Aquinas, *Summa Theologica* 2b.141.8.

146 Aquinas, *Summa Theologica* 2b.143.1.

147 Aquinas, *Summa Theologica* 2b.143.1 (emphasis added).

148 See, for example, Shawn Floyd, "Can Humility Be a Deliberative Virtue?" in *The Schooled Heart: Moral Formation in Higher Education*, ed. Douglas Henry and Michael Beaty (Waco, Tex.: Baylor University Press, 2007), 155–70; Michael Foley, "Thomas Aquinas' Novel Modesty," *History of Political Thought* 25, no. 3 (2004): 402–23; Michael Keating, "The Strange Case of the Self-Dwarfing Man: Modernity, Magnanimity, and Thomas Aquinas," *Logos: A Journal of Catholic Thought and Culture* 10, no. 4 (2007): 55–76; Mary Keys, "Aquinas and the Challenge of Aristotelian Magnanimity," *History of Political Thought* 24, no. 1 (2003): 37–65; Catherine Hudak Klancer, "How Opposites (Should) Attract: Humility as a Virtue for the Strong," *Heythrop Journal* 53, no. 4 (2012): 662–77; Joseph Lawrence Tadie, "Between Humilities: A Retrieval of Saint Thomas Aquinas on the Virtue of Humility" (Ph.D. diss., Boston College, 2006).

149 Sheryl Overmyer, "Exalting the Meek Virtue of Humility," *Heythrop Journal* 56, no. 4 (2015): 651.

150 Overmyer, "Exalting the Meek Virtue of Humility," 652.

151 Overmyer, "Exalting the Meek Virtue of Humility," 654.

152 Overmyer, "Exalting the Meek Virtue of Humility," 655.

153 Aquinas, *Summa Theologica* 2b.161.1.

154 Aquinas, *Summa Theologica* 2b.161.1.

155 Aquinas, *Summa Theologica* 2b.161.2.

156 Aquinas, *Summa Theologica* 2b.161.5.

157 Aquinas, *Summa Theologica* 2b.161.5.

158 Aquinas, *Summa Theologica* 2b.161.1.

159 Aquinas, *Summa Theologica* 2b.161.3.

160 Aquinas, *Summa Theologica* 2b.161.5; 2b.162.5.

161 Aquinas, *Summa Theologica* 2b.161.1.

162 See Overmyer, "Exalting the Meek Virtue of Humility," 657–60.

163 Aquinas, *Expositio in Symbolum Apostolorum: reportatio Reginaldi de Piperno* 6.3, Corpus Thomisticum, http://www.corpusthomisticum.org/csv.html (accessed December 1, 2018).

164 Aquinas, *Summa Theologica* 1.6.

165 Aquinas, *Summa Theologica* 2a.23.6.

166 Augustine, *City of God* 14.28.

167 Augustine, *Homilies on the First Epistle of John (Tractatus in Epistolam Joannis ad Parthos)*, trans. Boniface Ramsey (Hyde Park, N.Y.: New City, 2008) 7.2.

168 George Herbert, "The Church-Porch," in *The English Poems of George Herbert*, ed. Helen Wilcox (Cambridge: Cambridge University Press, 2007), 59.

169 Jane Austen, *Pride and Prejudice* (New York: Oxford University Press, 2008), chap. 10.

170 Austen, *Pride and Prejudice,* chap. 15.

171 Austen, *Pride and Prejudice*, chap. 58.

172 David Bentley Hart, *The Beauty of the Infinite: The Aesthetics of Christian Truth* (Grand Rapids: Eerdmans, 2003), 124.

3. Scripture's Suggestive Tensions

1 Basil Studer, *The Grace of Christ and the Grace of God in Augustine of Hippo: Christocentrism or Theocentrism?* trans. Matthew J. O'Connell (Collegeville, Minn.: Liturgical, 1997), 4.

2 Studer, *The Grace of Christ and the Grace of God*, 153.

3 Studer, *The Grace of Christ and the Grace of God*, 74.

4 Augustine, *Sermons 1–19*, trans. Edmund Hill, O.P., in *The Works of St. Augustine III/1*, ed. Boniface Ramsey (Hyde Park, N.Y.: New City, 2009), 6.1.

5 Augustine, *Sermons* 6.2.

6 Augustine, *Sermons* 6.3.

7 Augustine, *Sermons* 6.4.

8 Augustine, *Sermons* 6.5.

9 Augustine, *Expositions of the Psalms*, vol. 5, *Psalms 99–120*, trans. Maria Boulding, O.S.B., in *The Works of St. Augustine III/19*, ed. Boniface Ramsey (Hyde Park, N.Y.: New City, 2003), 101.14.

10 Augustine, *Expositions of the Psalms* 101.14.

11 Augustine, *Expositions of the Psalms*, vol. 6, *Psalms 121–150*, trans. Maria Boulding, O.S.B., in *The Works of St. Augustine III/20*, ed. Boniface Ramsey (Hyde Park, N.Y.: New City, 2004), 121.1–3.

12 Augustine, *Expositions of the Psalms* 121.5

13 Augustine, *Expositions of the Psalms* 121.8.

14 Augustine, *Expositions of the Psalms* 121.12. "God himself is the fullness of delights and our all-sufficient riches. He is Being-Itself, in which the city participates; in this will our abundance consist. But

how can this be? Through charity, which is to say, through the city's strength. But who has charity, brothers and sisters? The person who in this life is not self-seeking."

15 Augustine, *Expositions of the Psalms* 134.3.

16 Augustine, *Expositions of the Psalms* 134.3. "He is being, as he is also goodness, the good of all good things."

17 Augustine, *Expositions of the Psalms* 134.6.

18 Augustine, *Expositions of the Psalms* 134.6.

19 Augustine, *Expositions of the Psalms* 134.6.

20 Augustine, *Expositions of the Psalms* 134.6–7.

21 Augustine, *Expositions of the Psalms* 134.8.

22 See Augustine, *The Trinity* 1.2.

23 Augustine, *The Trinity* 5.2.3.

24 Augustine, *The Trinity* 5.6.

25 See Lewis Ayres, *Augustine and the Trinity* (New York: Cambridge University Press, 2010), 222. Ayres says, "[I]t is the basic statement of divine simplicity that grounds Augustine's discussion" concerning the nature of God. It is, in effect, a rule governing the other things Augustine says of God.

26 Augustine, *Sermons* 8.7 (emphasis added).

27 Augustine, *Sermons* 8.7.

28 Ayres, *Augustine and the Trinity*, 249.

29 I will treat only tractates 18, 19, and 23, which seem to have been given over consecutive days.

30 Augustine, *Homilies on the Gospel of John (1–40)*, trans. Edmund Hill, O.P. (Hyde Park, N.Y.: New City, 2009) 18.3.

31 Augustine, *Homilies on the Gospel of John* 18.4. Augustine's shorthand charge of paganism is that the Arian interpretation creates two gods.

32 Augustine, *Homilies on the Gospel of John* 18.4 (emphasis added).

33 Augustine, *Homilies on the Gospel of John* 18.6.

34 This is not to endorse the idea that Augustine has an underdeveloped pneumatology. It is enough to note that the Johannine passage under examination only directly concerns the relation between Father and Son.

35 Augustine, *Homilies on the Gospel of John* 18.6.

36 Augustine, *Homilies on the Gospel of John* 18.9.

37 Augustine, *Homilies on the Gospel of John* 18.10.

38 Augustine, *Homilies on the Gospel of John* 18.11.

39 Augustine, *Homilies on the Gospel of John* 19.1.

40 Augustine, *Homilies on the Gospel of John* 19.4.

204 // NOTES TO PAGES 91–100

41 Augustine, *Homilies on the Gospel of John* 19.6–10.

42 Augustine, *Homilies on the Gospel of John* 19.11.

43 Augustine, *Homilies on the Gospel of John* 19.13. Augustine says "that he is Father, he is because of the Son," and "his being Son is because of the Father."

44 Ayres, *Augustine and the Trinity*, 230.

45 Robert W. Jenson, *Systematic Theology*, vol. 1, *The Triune God* (New York: Oxford University Press, 1997), 113n166.

46 Augustine, *The Trinity* 1.8; Peter Lombard, *The Sentences, Book 3: On the Incarnation of the Word*, translated by Giulio Silano (Toronto, On.: PIMS, 2008), 3.1.2; Jenson, *Systematic Theology*, 1:111–12nn150, 153.

47 Jenson, *Systematic Theology*, 1:112.

48 Ayres, *Augustine and the Trinity*, 146–47.

49 Augustine, *De diversis quaestionibus octoginta tribus*, in *Responses to Miscellaneous Questions*, trans. Boniface Ramsey (Hyde Park, New City, 2008), 69.1.

50 Augustine, *De diversis quaestionibus octoginta tribus* 69.5, 69.1.

51 Michael J. Gorman, *Inhabiting the Cruciform God: Kenosis, Justification, and Theosis in Paul's Narrative Soteriology* (Grand Rapids: Eerdmans, 2009), 20–22.

52 Gorman, *Inhabiting the Cruciform God*, 20.

53 Gorman, *Inhabiting the Cruciform God*, 22–25.

54 Gorman, *Inhabiting the Cruciform God*, 36.

55 Gorman, *Inhabiting the Cruciform God*, 35.

56 "The Definition of Chalcedon," trans. Albert C. Outler, in *Creeds of the Churches: A Reader in Christian Doctrine from the Bible to the Present*, 3rd ed., ed. John H. Leith (Louisville, Ky.: Westminster John Knox, 1982), 36.

57 Gorman, *Inhabiting the Cruciform God*, 36n92.

58 Augustine, *The City of God* 9.15.

59 Augustine, *The City of God* 9.13.

60 Augustine, *The City of God* 9.13.

61 The question then becomes, how would one lose this blessedness? And further, how do we know that redeemed humans will not similarly lose this blessedness and thus be immortally miserable?

62 Augustine, *The Trinity* 9.14–15.

63 See Paul Jacobs, "Pneumatische Realpräsenz bei Calvin," *Revue d'Histoire et de Philosophie Religieuse* 44 (1964): 391–92.

64 Augustine, *The Trinity* 1.7.14.

65 Augustine, *The Trinity* 1.7.14.
66 Paul Ricoeur, *Oneself as Another,* trans. Kathleen Blamey (Chicago: University of Chicago Press, 1995), 2–4. See also Kevin Vanhoozer, *Remythologizing Theology: Divine Action, Passion, and Authorship* (New York: Cambridge University Press, 2012), 208.
67 Augustine, *The Trinity* 1.7.14.
68 Dominic Keech, *The Anti-Pelagian Christology of Augustine of Hippo, 396–430* (New York: Oxford University Press, 2012), 179.
69 Keech, *The Anti-Pelagian Christology of Augustine of Hippo,* 188.
70 Augustine, *The Trinity* 1.8.15. Though he is also clear that he does not regard this minority view as heretical.
71 Augustine, *The Trinity* 1.8.15.
72 Augustine, *The Trinity* 69.3.
73 Augustine, *The Trinity* 1.8.16.
74 Augustine, *De diversis quaestionibus octoginta tribus* 69.4.
75 Augustine, *The Trinity* 1.8.16; *De diversis quaestionibus octoginta tribus* 69.4–5.
76 Augustine, *The Trinity* 1.8.18. See also *De diversis quaestionibus octoginta tribus* 69.5: "For our blessedness is in direct proportion to our enjoyment of God in contemplation."
77 Augustine, *The Trinity* 1.10.21.
78 Augustine, *The Trinity* 13.19.24.
79 Augustine, *De diversis quaestionibus octoginta tribus* 69.10.
80 Augustine, *The Trinity* 13.10.13.
81 Augustine, *The Trinity* 13.14.18.
82 Augustine, *The City of God* 1, preface.
83 Augustine, *The City of God* 2.7.
84 Augustine, *The City of God* 4.30.
85 Augustine, *The City of God* 7.33, 14.13.
86 Augustine, *The City of God* 4.1.12.
87 Augustine, *The City of God* 13.17.22.
88 Augustine, *De fide et symbolo,* in *On Christian Belief,* trans. Edmund Hill, O.P. (Hyde Park, N.Y.: New City, 2005) 3.6.
89 Augustine, *De fide et symbolo* 4.6.
90 Augustine, *De fide et symbolo* 5.11.
91 Augustine, *The City of God* 9.20.
92 Augustine, *Confessions* 1.11.17.
93 Augustine, *De diversis quaestionibus octoginta tribus* 80.2.
94 Augustine, *Enchiridion,* in *On Christian Belief* 28.108.

95 Augustine, *Letters 210–270 and Divjak 1*–29**, trans. Roland Teske, S.J. (Hyde Park, N.Y.: New City, 2005), 232; Augustine, *Sermons 184–229z*, trans. Edmund Hill, O.P. (Hyde Park, N.Y.: New City, 1993) 188.3.

96 John C. Cavadini, "Pride (*Superbia*)," in *Augustine through the Ages: An Encyclopedia*, ed. Allan D. Fitzgerald, O.S.A. (Grand Rapids: Eerdmans, 1999), 682.

97 Augustine, *The Trinity* 7.3.5.

98 Augustine, *Homilies on the Gospel of John* 51.3.2.

99 Augustine, *Homilies on the Gospel of John* 55.7.

100 Augustine, *Homilies on the First Epistle of John* 3.1.

4. Divine Humility as an "Offensive Fact"

1 Barth, *Church Dogmatics*, 4.1:193.

2 Robert B. Price, *Letters of the Divine Word: The Perfections of God in Karl Barth's Church Dogmatics* (London: T&T Clark, 2011), 195–96.

3 Barth, *Church Dogmatics*, 4.1:157–210.

4 G. C. Berkouwer, *The Triumph of Grace in the Theology of Karl Barth: A Scriptural Examination and Assessment*, trans. Harry R. Boer (Grand Rapids: Eerdmans, 1956), 133.

5 Berkouwer, *The Triumph of Grace*, 304.

6 Berkouwer, *The Triumph of Grace*, 307.

7 Berkouwer, *The Triumph of Grace*, 308–10.

8 Berkouwer, *The Triumph of Grace*, 306–7.

9 Darren O. Sumner, *Karl Barth and the Incarnation: Christology and the Humility of God* (London: T&T Clark, 2014), 12–13.

10 Paul Dafydd Jones, *The Humanity of Christ: Christology in Karl Barth's Church Dogmatics* (London: T&T Clark, 2008), 214–15.

11 Jones, *The Humanity of Christ*, 212.

12 Kevin Giles, "Barth and Subordinationism," *Scottish Journal of Theology* 64, no. 3 (2011), 341.

13 Giles, "Barth and Subordinationism," 346.

14 Paul Molnar, "The Obedience of the Son in the Theology of Karl Barth and of Thomas F. Torrance," *Scottish Journal of Theology* 67, no. 1 (2014), 63.

15 R. D. Williams, "Barth on the Triune God," in *Karl Barth—Studies of his Theological Methods*, ed. S. W. Sykes (Oxford: Clarendon, 1979), 175.

16 Barth, *Church Dogmatics*, 4.1:157.

17 Barth, *Church Dogmatics*, 4.1:159.
18 Barth, *Church Dogmatics*, 4.1:158.
19 Barth, *Church Dogmatics*, 4.1:160–61.
20 Barth, *Church Dogmatics*, 4.1:163.
21 Barth, *Church Dogmatics*, 4.1:163.
22 Barth, *Church Dogmatics*, 4.1:163–64. See also Paul Dafydd Jones, "Obedience, Trinity, and Election: Thinking with and beyond the *Church Dogmatics*," in *Trinity and Election in Contemporary Theology* (Grand Rapids: Eerdmans, 2011), 143. Jones writes: "One might well say that, for Barth, humility and obedience serve as categorical summaries of Christ's life."
23 Barth, *Church Dogmatics*, 4.1:164.
24 Barth, *Church Dogmatics*, 4.1:172–75.
25 Barth, *Church Dogmatics*, 4.1:176–77.
26 Barth, *Church Dogmatics*, 4.4:108.
27 Barth, *Church Dogmatics*, 4.1:177.
28 Barth, *Church Dogmatics*, 4.1:177.
29 Barth, *Church Dogmatics*, 4.1:179–80.
30 Barth, *Church Dogmatics*, 4.1:183.
31 Barth, *Church Dogmatics*, 4.1:183.
32 Barth, *Church Dogmatics*, 4.1:184.
33 Barth, *Church Dogmatics*, 4.1:184.
34 Barth, *Church Dogmatics*, 4.1:185.
35 Barth, *Church Dogmatics*, 4.1:186.
36 Barth, *Church Dogmatics*, 4.1:188.
37 Barth, *Church Dogmatics*, 4.1:188.
38 Barth, *Church Dogmatics*, 4.1:192.
39 Barth, *Church Dogmatics*, 4.1:193.
40 Barth, *Church Dogmatics*, 4.1:195.
41 Barth, *Church Dogmatics*, 4.1:195.
42 Barth, *Church Dogmatics*, 4.1:195.
43 Barth, *Church Dogmatics*, 4.1:199–201.
44 Barth, *Church Dogmatics*, 4.1:200–201.
45 Barth, *Church Dogmatics*, 4.1:202–3.
46 Barth, *Church Dogmatics*, 4.1:203.
47 Barth, *Church Dogmatics*, 4.1:209.
48 Barth, *Church Dogmatics*, 4.1:209.
49 See, again, Williams, "Barth on the Triune God," 175.
50 Barth, *Church Dogmatics*, 4.1:177.

51 Barth, *Church Dogmatics*, 4.1:177.
52 Barth, *Church Dogmatics*, 1.1:132.
53 Barth, *Church Dogmatics*, 1.1:132.
54 Barth, *Church Dogmatics*, 1.1:133–34.
55 Barth, *Church Dogmatics*, 1.1:136.
56 Barth, *Church Dogmatics*, 1.1:137–38.
57 Barth, *Church Dogmatics*, 1.1:139–40.
58 Barth, *Church Dogmatics*, 1.1:140.
59 Barth, *Church Dogmatics*, 1.1:140.
60 Barth, *Church Dogmatics*, 1.1:147–48.
61 Barth, *Church Dogmatics*, 1.1:149.
62 Barth, *Church Dogmatics*, 1.1:153.
63 Barth, *Church Dogmatics*, 1.1:156–57.
64 Barth, *Church Dogmatics*, 1.1:160–61.
65 Barth, *Church Dogmatics*, 1.1:162.
66 Barth, *Church Dogmatics*, 1.1:165.
67 Barth, *Church Dogmatics*, 1.1:166.
68 Barth, *Church Dogmatics*, 1.1:174.
69 Barth, *Church Dogmatics*, 1.1:175.
70 Barth, *Church Dogmatics*, 1.1:182.
71 Barth, *Church Dogmatics*, 1.1:307–8.
72 Dietrich Bonhoeffer, *Act and Being: Transcendental Philosophy and Ontology in Systematic Theology*, trans. H. Martin Rumscheidt; ed. Wayne Whitson Floyd Jr. (Minneapolis: Fortress, 2009), 83.
73 Augustine, *The Trinity* 8.1.
74 Augustine, *The Trinity* 8.2.3.
75 Augustine, *The Trinity* 8.3.4.
76 Augustine, *The Trinity* 8.6.9.
77 Augustine, *The Trinity* 8.1.2.
78 Augustine, *The Trinity* 15.21.
79 Roland J. Teske, "Properties of God and the Predicaments in *De Trinitate V*," *Modern Schoolman* 59, no. 1 (1981): 14.
80 Augustine, *The Trinity* 1.4–13.
81 Barth, *Church Dogmatics*, 1.1:348.
82 Barth, *Church Dogmatics*, 1.1:348.
83 Barth, *Church Dogmatics*, 1.1:350.
84 Stephen R. Holmes, *The Holy Trinity: Understanding God's Life* (Milton Keynes, UK: Paternoster, 2012), 97–120.

85 Bruce L. McCormack, "Karl Barth's Historicized Christology: Just How 'Chalcedonian' Is It?" in *Orthodox and Modern: Studies in the Theology of Karl Barth* (Grand Rapids: Eerdmans, 2008), 222.

86 McCormack, "Karl Barth's Historicized Christology," 223: "If, in Jesus Christ, God has elected to become human, then the human history of Jesus Christ is constitutive of the being and existence of God in the second of God's modes to the extent that the being and existence of the Second Person of the Trinity cannot be rightly thought of in absence of this human history."

87 McCormack, "Karl Barth's Historicized Christology," 228.

88 Barth, *Church Dogmatics*, 4.1:51.

89 McCormack, "Karl Barth's Historicized Christology," 220.

90 Barth, *Church Dogmatics*, 4.1:52.

91 See Demetrios Bathrellos, *The Byzantine Christ: Person, Nature, and Will in the Christology of Maximus the Confessor* (New York: Oxford University Press, 2004), 19.

92 See Bathrellos, *The Byzantine Christ*, 11.

93 Cyril of Alexandria, *On the Unity of Christ*, trans. John Anthony McGuckin (New York: St. Vladimir's Seminary Press, 2015), 77.

94 "The Definition of Chalcedon," 35–36.

95 Cyril, *On the Unity of Christ*, 94.

96 Cyril, *On the Unity of Christ*, 77.

97 The Monophysites found the basis for this interpretation in some of Cyril's unguarded statements, such as: "We say that there is one Son, and that he has one nature . . ." (Cyril, *On the Unity of Christ*, 77).

98 Bathrellos, *The Byzantine Christ*, 100.

99 Bathrellos, *The Byzantine Christ*, 104.

100 Bathrellos, *The Byzantine Christ*, 111.

101 Maximus, *The Disputation with Pyrrhus of Our Father among the Saints Maximus the Confessor*, trans. Joseph P. Farrell (Waymart, Pa.: St. Tikhon's Monastery Press, 2015), 289D–292A.

102 Maximus, *Opusculum 6: Two Hundred Chapters on Theology*, trans. Luis Joshua Salés (Yonkers, N.Y.: St. Vladimir's Seminary Press, 2015), 65A–65C.

103 Maximus, *Opusculum 6 68B–68C*.

104 Maximus, *Opusculum 6 68C*.

105 Maxiums, *Opusculum 6 68C*.

106 Maximus, *Opusculum 6 68D*.

107 Barth, *Church Dogmatics*, 1.2:158.

108 Dafydd Jones, *The Humanity of Christ*, 41.
109 Dafydd Jones, *The Humanity of Christ*, 49.
110 Dafydd Jones, *The Humanity of Christ*, 247.
111 Barth, *Church Dogmatics*, 4.1:259.
112 Barth, *Church Dogmatics*, 4.1:265.
113 Barth, *Church Dogmatics*, 4.1, pp. 269–70.
114 By contrast, Cyril's insistence on the hypostatic unity of Christ's two natures does not prevent him from making use of this distinction to denote what is proper to the divine nature and what is proper to the human nature. In commenting on the Gethsemane prayer he affirms that we are "to attribute the suffering to him and to no other, insofar as he appeared as a man, even if he remained impassible insofar as he is understood as God" (Cyril, *On the Unity of Christ*, 126).
115 Barth, *Church Dogmatics*, 2.1:94.
116 Barth, *Church Dogmatics*, 2.1:101.
117 Barth, *Church Dogmatics*, 2.1:105.
118 Barth, *Church Dogmatics*, 1.1:351.
119 Jürgen Moltmann, *The Trinity and the Kingdom*, trans. Margaret Kohl (Minneapolis: Fortress, 1993), 139.
120 Moltmann, *The Trinity and the Kingdom*, 142.
121 Wolfhart Pannenberg, *Systematic Theology*, vol. 1, trans. Geoffrey W. Bromiley (Grand Rapids: Eerdmans, 1991), 288.
122 Pannenberg, *Systematic Theology*, 1:319.
123 Jenson, *Systematic Theology*, 1:75.
124 Moltmann, *The Trinity and the Kingdom*, 76.
125 Pannenberg, *Systematic Theology*, 1:329.
126 Jenson, *Systematic Theology*, 1:191.
127 Maximus, *Disputation with Pyrrhus* 7.
128 Maximus, *Disputation with Pyrrhus* 13.
129 Maximus, *Disputation with Pyrrhus* 181.
130 Maximus, *Disputation with Pyrrhus* 31.
131 Maximus, *Disputation with Pyrrhus* 116.
132 Maximus, *Disputation with Pyrrhus* 116.
133 Maximus, *Disputation with Pyrrhus* 33.
134 Maximus, *Disputation with Pyrrhus* 136.
135 Maximus, *Disputation with Pyrrhus* 137.

5. The Mystery of Divine Energy

1 Katherine Sonderegger, *Systematic Theology*, vol. 1, *The Doctrine of God* (Minneapolis: Fortress, 2015), xiii. In this and subsequent citations of Sonderegger's work, her idiosyncratic capitalizations have been suppressed in favor of a more conventional approach.

2 Sonderegger, *Systematic Theology*, 1:xiv.

3 Sonderegger, *Systematic Theology*, 1:3–4.

4 Sonderegger, *Systematic Theology*, 1:9.

5 Sonderegger, *Systematic Theology*, 1:12.

6 Sonderegger, *Systematic Theology*, 1:6–8.

7 Sonderegger, *Systematic Theology*, 1:15.

8 Sonderegger, *Systematic Theology*, 1:24.

9 Sonderegger, *Systematic Theology*, 1:25–26.

10 Sonderegger, *Systematic Theology*, 1:26.

11 Sonderegger, *Systematic Theology*, 1:26.

12 Marion, *God without Being*, 139.

13 Marion, *God without Being*, 35: "In thinking 'God' as *causa sui*, metaphysics gives itself a concept of 'God' that at once marks the indisputable experience of him and his equally incontestable limitation."

14 Sonderegger, *Systematic Theology*, 1:40–41.

15 Sonderegger, *Systematic Theology*, 1:42.

16 Sonderegger, *Systematic Theology*, 1:77.

17 Sonderegger, *Systematic Theology*, 1:80.

18 Sonderegger, *Systematic Theology*, 1:81.

19 Sonderegger, *Systematic Theology*, 1:82.

20 Sonderegger, *Systematic Theology*, 1:83.

21 Aquinas, *Summa Theologica* 1.2.3.

22 Aquinas, *Summa Theologica* 1.3.4.

23 Sonderegger, *Systematic Theology*, 1:85: "We need not seek the aseity of God by abstracting everything earthy from around his dwelling: not so does *negation* in divine predication find and lay hold of and describe the true God."

24 Sonderegger, *Systematic Theology*, 1:87–88.

25 Hector, *Theology without Metaphysics*, 54.

26 See Morris Weitz, *The Opening Mind: A Philosophical Study of Humanistic Concepts* (Chicago: University of Chicago Press, 1977), 25–49.

27 Hector, *Theology without Metaphysics*, 80–81.

28 Hector, *Theology without Metaphysics*, 91.

29 Hector, *Theology without Metaphysics*, 233n35.
30 Sonderegger, *Systematic Theology*, 1:118.
31 Sonderegger, *Systematic Theology*, 1:127.
32 Hector, *Theology without Metaphysics*, 133.
33 Barth, *Church Dogmatics*, 2.1:231.
34 Sonderegger, *Systematic Theology*, 1:104–5.
35 Sonderegger, *Systematic Theology*, 1:143.
36 Sonderegger, *Systematic Theology*, 1:111.
37 Sonderegger, *Systematic Theology*, 1:114.
38 Sonderegger, *Systematic Theology*, 1:62–63.
39 Sonderegger, *Systematic Theology*, 1:66.
40 Sonderegger, *Systematic Theology*, 1:86.
41 Sonderegger, *Systematic Theology*, 1:155.
42 Barth, *Church Dogmatics* 2.1:524.
43 Sonderegger, *Systematic Theology*, 1:158–59.
44 Sonderegger, *Systematic Theology*, 1:161–62.
45 Sonderegger, *Systematic Theology*, 1:175.
46 Sonderegger, *Systematic Theology*, 1:176.
47 Sonderegger, *Systematic Theology*, 1:178.
48 Sonderegger, *Systematic Theology*, 1:180–81.
49 Sonderegger, *Systematic Theology*, 1:183.
50 Sonderegger, *Systematic Theology*, 1:177.
51 Sonderegger, *Systematic Theology*, 1:185.
52 Sonderegger, *Systematic Theology*, 1:186.
53 Sonderegger, *Systematic Theology*, 1:188.
54 Sonderegger, *Systematic Theology*, 1:191.
55 Sonderegger, *Systematic Theology*, 1:189.
56 Sonderegger, *Systematic Theology*, 1:194–95.
57 Sonderegger, *Systematic Theology*, 1:200–201.
58 Sonderegger, *Systematic Theology*, 1:203.
59 Sonderegger, *Systematic Theology*, 1:205.
60 Sonderegger, *Systematic Theology*, 1:205–6.
61 See Aquinas, *Summa Theologica* 1.45.2.
62 Sonderegger, *Systematic Theology*, 1:206–7.
63 Sonderegger, *Systematic Theology*, 1:208.
64 Sonderegger, *Systematic Theology*, 1:209.
65 Sonderegger, *Systematic Theology*, 1:228.
66 Sonderegger, *Systematic Theology*, 1:234.
67 Sonderegger, *Systematic Theology*, 1:242–43.

68 Sonderegger, *Systematic Theology*, 1:245–46.

69 Sonderegger, *Systematic Theology*, 1:251–52.

70 Sonderegger, *Systematic Theology*, 1:268.

71 Sonderegger, *Systematic Theology*, 1:268.

72 Sonderegger, *Systematic Theology*, 1:315–17.

73 John Meyendorff summarizes: "If God were absolutely transcendent, but also could be 'experienced' and 'seen' as an uncreated and real presence, one had to speak of a totally transcendent divine 'essence' and of uncreated, but revealed 'energies.'" Meyendorff, introduction to *Gregory Palamas: The Triads* (Pahwah, N.J.: Paulist, 1983), 7.

74 Sonderegger, *Systematic Theology*, 1:262–63.

75 Sonderegger, *Systematic Theology*, 1:268.

76 Sonderegger, *Systematic Theology*, 1:318.

77 Sonderegger, *Systematic Theology*, 1:319.

78 Sonderegger, *Systematic Theology*, 1:320.

79 Sonderegger, *Systematic Theology*, 1:320.

80 Sonderegger, *Systematic Theology*, 1:321–22.

81 Sonderegger, *Systematic Theology*, 1:323.

82 Webster, *God without Measure*, 52.

83 Webster, *God without Measure*, 1:52.

84 Sonderegger, *Systematic Theology*, 1:313.

85 Sonderegger, *Systematic Theology*, 1:315.

86 Sonderegger, *Systematic Theology*, 1:316–17.

87 Sonderegger, *Systematic Theology*, 1:318.

88 Sonderegger, *Systematic Theology*, 1:322.

89 Sonderegger, *Systematic Theology*, 1:324.

90 Anselm, *Why God Became Man*, trans. Janet Fairweather, in *Anselm of Canterbury: The Major Works*, ed. Brian Davies and G. R. Evans (New York: Oxford University Press, 1998), 1.1.

91 Anselm, *Why God Became Man* 1.1.

92 Anselm, *Why God Became Man* 1.13.

93 Anselm, *Why God Became Man* 1.15.

94 Anselm, *Why God Became Man* 1.25.

95 Anselm, *Why God Became Man* 2.5.

96 Sonderegger, *Systematic Theology*, 1:326.

97 Sonderegger, *Systematic Theology*, 1:24.

98 Sonderegger, *Systematic Theology*, 1:390–91.

99 Sonderegger, *Systematic Theology*, 1:394–95.

Conclusion

1 John Webster, *Confessing God: Essays in Christian Dogmatics*, vol. 2 (London: Bloomsbury, 2005), 111–12.
2 Webster, *Confessing God*, 2:113.
3 Webster, *Confessing God*, 2:114.
4 Oliver O'Donovan, *Entering into Rest: Ethics as Theology*, vol. 3 (Grand Rapids: Eerdmans, 2017), 20–21.
5 Martin Luther King Jr., *Strength to Love* (Minneapolis: Fortress, 2010), 8.
6 King, *Strength to Love*, 8–9.
7 David H. Kelsey, *The Uses of Scripture in Recent Theology* (Philadelphia: Fortress, 1975), 159.

BIBLIOGRAPHY

Anselm. *Why God Became Man*. Translated by Janet Fairweather. In *Anselm of Canterbury: The Major Works*. Edited by Brian Davies and G. R. Evans, 260–356. New York: Oxford University Press, 1998.

Aquinas, Thomas. *Summa Theologica*. Revised ed. Translated by the Fathers of the English Dominican Province. Cincinatti: Benziger Brothers, 1947.

Aristotle. *Nicomachean Ethics*. Translated by Martin Oswald. London: Pearson, 1962.

Athanasius. *The Life of St. Anthony*. Translated by Mary Emily Keenan, S.C.N. In *Early Christian Biographies*. Edited by Roy J. Deferrari, 125–216. Washington, D.C.: Catholic University of America Press, 1952.

Augustine. *The City of God: De civitate Dei (Books 1–10)*. Translated by William Babcock. In *The Works of St. Augustine I/6*. Edited by Boniface Ramsey. Hyde Park, N.Y.: New City, 2012.

———. *The City of God: De civitate Dei (Books 11–22)*. Translated by William Babcock. In *The Works of St. Augustine I/7*. Edited by Boniface Ramsey. Hyde Park, N.Y.: New City, 2013.

———. *Confessions*. Translated by Maria Boulding, O.S.B. 2nd ed. In *The Works of St. Augustine I/1*. Edited by Boniface Ramsey. Hyde Park, N.Y.: New City, 2012.

———. *Expositions of the Psalms*. Vol. 5, *Psalms 99–120*. Translated by Maria Boulding, O.S.B. In *The Works of St. Augustine III/19*. Edited by Boniface Ramsey. Hyde Park, N.Y.: New City, 2003.

———. *Expositions of the Psalms*. Vol. 6, *Psalms 121–150*. Translated by Maria Boulding, O.S.B. In *The Works of St. Augustine III/20*. Edited by Boniface Ramsey. Hyde Park, N.Y.: New City, 2004.

———. *Homilies on the First Epistle of John (Tractatus in Epistolam Joannis ad Parthos)*. Translated by Boniface Ramsey. In *The Works of St. Augustine III/14*. Edited by Boniface Ramsey. Hyde Park, N.Y.: New City, 2008.

———. *Homilies on the Gospel of John (1–40)*. Translated by Edmund Hill, O.P. *The Works of St. Augustine III/12*. Edited by Boniface Ramsey. Hyde Park, N.Y.: New City, 2009.

———. *Letters 100–155*. Translated by Roland Teske, S.J. *The Works of St. Augustine II/2*. Edited by Boniface Ramsey. Hyde Park, N.Y.: New City, 2003.

———. *Letters 210–270 and Divjak 1*–29**. Translated by Roland Teske, S.J. Hyde Park, N.Y.: New City, 2005.

———. *On Christian Belief*. Translated by Edmund Hill, O.P., Ray Kearney, Michael G. Campbell, and Bruce Harbert. In *The Works of St. Augustine I/8*. Edited by Boniface Ramsey. Hyde Park, N.Y.: New City, 2005.

———. *Responses to Miscellaneous Questions*. Translated by Boniface Ramsey. In *The Works of St. Augustine I/12*. Edited by Boniface Ramsey. Hyde Park, N.Y.: New City, 2008.

———. *Sermons 1–19*. Translated by Edmund Hill, O.P. In *The Works of St. Augustine III/1*. Edited by Boniface Ramsey. Hyde Park, N.Y.: New City, 2009.

———. *Sermons 184–229z*. Translated by Edmund Hill, O.P. Hyde Park, N.Y.: New City, 1993.

———. *The Trinity: De Trinitate*. Translated by Edmund Hill, O.P. In *The Works of St. Augustine I/5*. Edited by Boniface Ramsey. Hyde Park, N.Y.: New City, 1991.

Austen, Jane. *Pride and Prejudice*. New York: Oxford University Press, 2008.

Austin, J. L. *Sense and Sensibilia*. New York: Oxford University Press, 1964.

Ayres, Lewis. *Augustine and the Trinity*. Cambridge: Cambridge University Press, 2010.

Barsaniphius. "Letter 100." In *Barsaniphius and John: Letters*. Vol. 1. Translated by John Chryssaygis, 122–23. Washington, D.C.: Catholic University of America Press, 2006.

Barth, Karl. *Church Dogmatics*. Edited by G. W. Bromiley and T. F. Torrance. Edinburgh: T&T Clark, 1956–75.

Basil of Caesarea. *Saint Basil: Ascetical Works*. Translated by Monica Wagner, C.S.C. Edited by Roy Joseph Deferrari. Washington, D.C.: Catholic University of America Press, 1962.

Bathrellos, Demetrios. *The Byzantine Christ: Person, Nature, and Will in the Christology of Maximus the Confessor*. New York: Oxford University Press, 2004.

Benedict. *The Rule of St. Benedict in English with Notes*. Edited by Timothy Fry. Collegeville, Minn.: Liturgical, 1981.

Berkouwer, G. C. *The Triumph of Grace in the Theology of Karl Barth: A Scriptural Examination and Assessment*. Translated by Harry R. Boer. London: Paternoster, 1956.

Bonhoeffer, Dietrich. *Act and Being: Transcendental Philosophy and Ontology in Systematic Theology*. Dietrich Bonhoeffer Works 2. Edited by Wayne Whitson Floyd Jr. Translated by H. Martin Rumscheidt. Minneapolis: Fortress, 2009.

Brown, Peter. "The Rise of the Holy Man." *Journal of Roman Studies* 61 (1971): 80–101.

Cavadini, John C. "Pride (*Superbia*)." In *Augustine through the Ages: An Encyclopedia*. Edited by Allan D. Fitzgerald, O.S.A., 296–97. Grand Rapids: Eerdmans, 1999.

Coakley, Sarah. *Powers and Submissions: Spirituality, Philosophy and Gender*. Oxford: Blackwell, 2002.

Cordner, Christopher. "Aristotelian Virtue and Its Limitations." *Philosophy* 69 (1994): 291–316.

Crisp, Oliver D. "*Ad* Hector." *Journal of Analytic Theology* 1, no. 1 (2013): 133–39.

Cyril of Alexandria. *On the Unity of Christ*. Translated by John Anthony McGuckin. New York: St. Vladimir's Seminary Press, 2015.

"The Definition of Chalcedon." Translated by Albert C. Outler. In *Creeds of the Churches: A Reader in Christian Doctrine from the Bible to the Present*. 3rd ed. Edited by John H. Leith. Louisville, Ky.: Westminster John Knox, 1982.

Dorner, Isaak August. *Divine Immutability: A Critical Reconsideration*. Translated by Robert W. Williams. Minneapolis: Fortress, 1994.

Driver, Julia. *Virtues of Ignorance.* New York: Cambridge University Press, 1996.

Feuerbach, Ludwig. *The Essence of Christianity.* Translated by George Eliot. New York: Harper & Row, 1957.

Flanagan, Owen. *Self-Expressions: Mind, Morals, and the Meaning of Life.* New York: Oxford University Press, 1996.

Floyd, Shawn. "Can Humility Be a Deliberative Virtue?" In *The Schooled Heart: Moral Formation in Higher Education.* Edited by Douglas Henry and Michael Beaty, 155–70. Waco, Tex.: Baylor University Press, 2007.

Foley, Michael. "Thomas Aquinas' Novel Modesty." *History of Political Thought* 25, no. 3 (2004): 402–23.

Foulcher, Jane. "Reclaiming Humility: Four Studies in the Monastic Tradition." Ph.D. diss., Charles Sturt University, 2011.

Garcia, J. L. A. "Being Unimpressed with Ourselves: Reconceiving Humility." *Philosophia* 34, no. 4 (2006): 417–35.

Giles, Kevin. "Barth and Subordinationism." *Scottish Journal of Theology* 64, no. 3 (2011): 327–46.

Gockel, Matthias. "On the Way from Schleiermacher to Barth: A Critical Reappraisal of Isaak Dorner's Essay on Divine Immutability." *Scottish Journal of Theology* 53, no. 4 (2000): 490–510.

Godzieba, Anthony J. "Ontotheology to Excess: Imagining God without Being." *Theological Studies* 56 (1995): 3–20.

Goldstein, Valerie Saiving. "The Human Situation: A Feminine View." *Journal of Religion* 40, no. 2 (1960): 100–12.

Gorman, Michael J. *Inhabiting the Cruciform God: Kenosis, Justification, and Theosis in Paul's Narrative Soteriology.* Grand Rapids: Eerdmans, 2009.

Hampson, Daphne. *Theology and Feminism.* Oxford: Wiley-Blackwell, 1991.

Hart, David Bentley. *The Beauty of the Infinite: The Aesthetics of Christian Truth.* Grand Rapids: Eerdmans, 2003.

Hector, Kevin W. "Responses to *JAT*'s Symposium on *Theology without Metaphysics.*" *Journal of Analytic Theology* 1 (2013): 140–47.

———. *Theology without Metaphysics: God, Language, and the Spirit of Recognition.* Cambridge: Cambridge University Press, 2011.

Heidegger, Martin. *Being and Time.* Translated by John Macquarrie and Edward Robinson. San Francisco: Harper & Row, 1962.

———. *Kant and the Problem of Metaphysics.* 5th ed. Translated by Richard Taft. 5th ed. Bloomington: Indiana University Press, 1997.

Herbert, George. *The English Poems of George Herbert*. Edited by Helen Wilcox. Cambridge: Cambridge University Press, 2007.

Holmes, Stephen R. *The Holy Trinity: Understanding God's Life*. Milton Keynes, UK: Paternoster, 2012.

Hume, David. *Enquiries concerning Human Understanding and Concerning the Principles of Morals*. 3rd ed. Edited by P. H. Nidditch. Oxford: Clarendon, 1975.

———. *A Treatise of Human Nature*. 2nd ed. Edited by P. H. Nidditch. Oxford: Clarendon, 1978.

Ingraffia, Brian D. *Postmodern Theory and Biblical Theology*. Cambridge: Cambridge University Press, 1995.

Jacobs, Paul. "Pneumatische Realpräsenz bei Calvin." *Revue d'Historie et de Philosophie Religieuse* 44 (1964): 389–401.

Jenson, Robert W. *Systematic Theology*. Vol. 1, *The Triune God*. New York: Oxford University Press, 1997.

Jones, Paul Dafydd. *The Humanity of Christ: Christology in Karl Barth's Church Dogmatics*. London: Bloomsbury, 2008.

———. "Obedience, Trinity, and Election: Thinking with and beyond the *Church Dogmatics*." In *Trinity and Election in Contemporary Theology*. Edited by Michael T. Dempsey, 138–61. Grand Rapids: Eerdmans, 2011.

Kant, Immanuel. *Critique of Pure Reason*. Translated by Paul Guyer and Allen W. Wood. Cambridge: University of Cambridge Press, 1998.

———. *Prolegomena to Any Future Metaphysics: And the Letter to Markus Herz, February 1772*. Translated by James W. Ellington. 2nd ed. Indianapolis, Ind.: Hackett, 2001.

Keating, Michael. "The Strange Case of the Self-Dwarfing Man: Modernity, Magnanimity, and Thomas Aquinas." *Logos: A Journal of Catholic Thought and Culture* 10, no. 4 (2007): 55–76.

Keech, Dominic. *The Anti-Pelagian Christology of Augustine of Hippo, 396–430*. New York: Oxford University Press, 2012.

Kellenberger, James. "Humility." *American Philosophical Quarterly* 47, no. 4 (2010): 321–36.

Kelsey, David H. *The Uses of Scripture in Recent Theology*. Philadelphia: Fortress, 1975.

Keys, Mary. "Aquinas and the Challenge of Aristotelian Magnanimity." *History of Political Thought* 24, no. 1 (2003): 37–65.

King, Martin Luther, Jr. *Strength to Love*. Minneapolis: Fortress, 2010.

Klancer, Catherine Hudak. "How Opposites (Should) Attract: Humility as a Virtue for the Strong." *Heythrop Journal* 53, no. 4 (2012): 662–77.

Leftow, Brian. "Why Perfect Being Theology?" *International Journal of the Philosophy of Religion* 69, no. 2 (2011): 103–18.

Levering, Matthew. *Scripture and Metaphysics: Aquinas and the Renewal of Trinitarian Theology.* Challenges in Contemporary Theology. Oxford: Wiley-Blackwell, 2004.

Lienhard, Joseph T., S.J. "Augustine of Hippo, Basil of Caesarea, and Gregory of Nazianzus." In *Orthodox Readings of Augustine.* Edited by George Demacopoulos and Aristotle Papanikolaou, 81–100. New York: St. Vladimir's Seminary Press, 2008.

Lombard, Peter. *The Sentences, Book 3: On the Incarnation of the Word.* Translated by Giulio Silano. Toronto, On.: PIMS, 2008.

MacIntyre, Alasdair. *After Virtue: A Study in Moral Theory.* 3rd ed. London: Bloomsbury, 2007.

————. "Epistemological Crises, Narrative, and the Philosophy of Science." In *Why Narrative? Readings in Narrative Theology.* Edited by Stanley Hauerwas and L. Gregory Jones, 138–57. Grand Rapids: Eerdmans, 1989.

————. *Whose Justice? Which Rationality?* Notre Dame, Ind.: University of Notre Dame Press, 2008.

Marion, Jean-Luc. *God without Being.* Translated by Thomas A. Carlson. Chicago: University of Chicago Press, 1991.

————. "'They recognized him; and he became invisible to them.'" *Modern Theology* 18, no. 2 (2002): 145–52.

Maximus. *The Disputation with Pyrrhus of Our Father among the Saints Maximus the Confessor.* Translated by Joseph P. Farrell. Waymart, Pa.: St. Tikhon's Monastery Press, 2015.

————. *Opusculum 6: Two Hundred Chapters on Theology.* Translated by Luis Joshua Salés. Yonkers, N.Y.: St. Vladimir's Seminary Press, 2015.

McCormack, Bruce L. "Karl Barth's Historicized Christology: Just How 'Chalcedonian' Is It?" In *Orthodox and Modern: Studies in the Theology of Karl Barth.* Edited by Bruce L. McCormack, 201–34. Grand Rapids: Eerdmans, 2008.

Meyendorff, John. Introduction to *Gregory Palamas: The Triads.* Translated by Nicholas Gendle, 1–23. Pahwah, N.J.: Paulist, 1983.

Molnar, Paul D. "The Obedience of the Son in the Theology of Karl Barth and of Thomas F. Torrance." *Scottish Journal of Theology* 67, no. 1 (2014): 50–69.

Moltmann, Jürgen. *The Trinity and the Kingdom.* Translated by Margaret Kohl. Minneapolis: Fortress, 1993.

Niebuhr, Reinhold. *Beyond Tragedy: Essays on the Christian Interpretation of History.* New York: Scribner, 1965.

———. *The Nature and Destiny of Man: A Christian Interpretation.* Louisville, Ky.: Westminster John Knox, 1996.

Nietzsche, Friedrich. *Basic Writings of Nietzsche.* Translated by Walter Kaufmann. New York: Modern Library, 2000.

Nygren, Anders. *Agape and Eros.* Translated by Philip S. Watson. London: SPCK, 1957.

O'Donovan, Oliver. *Entering into Rest: Ethics as Theology.* Vol. 3. Grand Rapids: Eerdmans, 2017.

Overmyer, Sheryl. "Exalting the Meek Virtue of Humility." *Heythrop Journal* 56, no. 4 (2015): 650–62.

Pannenberg, Wolfhart. *Systematic Theology.* Vol. 1. Translated by Geoffrey W. Bromiley. Grand Rapids: Eerdmans, 1991.

Price, Robert B. *Letters of the Divine Word: The Perfections of God in Karl Barth's Church Dogmatics.* T&T Clark Studies in Systematic Theology 9. London: T&T Clark, 2011.

Richard, Norvin. "Is Humility a Virtue?" *American Philosophical Quarterly* 25, no. 3 (1988): 253–59.

Ricoeur, Paul. *Oneself as Another.* Translated by Kathleen Blamey. Chicago: University of Chicago Press, 1995.

Roberts, Richard, and Jay Wood. *Intellectual Virtues: An Essay in Regulative Epistemology.* New York: Oxford University Press, 2007.

Schleiermacher, Friedrich D. E. *The Christian Faith.* Edited by H. R. Mackintosh and J. S. Stewart. London: Continuum, 1999.

Sonderegger, Katherine. *Systematic Theology.* Vol. 1, *The Doctrine of God.* Minneapolis: Fortress, 2015.

Studer, Basil. *The Grace of Christ and the Grace of God in Augustine of Hippo: Christocentrism or Theocentrism?* Translated by Matthew J. O'Connell. Collegeville, Minn.: Liturgical, 1997.

Sumner, Darren O. *Karl Barth and the Incarnation: Christology and the Humility of God.* London: Bloomsbury, 2014.

222 // BIBLIOGRAPHY

Tadie, Joseph Lawrence. "Between Humilities: A Retrieval of Saint Thomas Aquinas on the Virtue of Humility." Ph.D. diss., Boston College, 2006.

Teske, Roland J. "Properties of God and the Predicaments in *De Trinitate V.*" *Modern Schoolman* 59, no. 1 (1981): 1–19.

Thomson, Iain. "Ontotheology? Understanding Heidegger's *Destruktion* of Metaphysics." *International Journal of Philosophical Studies* 8, no. 3 (2000): 297–327.

Vanhoozer, Kevin J. *Remythologizing Theology: Divine Action, Passion, and Authorship.* Cambridge Studies in Christian Doctrine. Cambridge: Cambridge University Press, 2010.

Webster, John B. *Confessing God: Essays in Christian Dogmatics.* Vol. 2. London: Bloomsbury, 2005.

———. *God without Measure: Working Papers in Christian Theology: God and the Works of God.* London: Bloomsbury, 2016.

Weitz, Morris. *The Opening Mind: A Philosophical Study of Humanistic Concepts.* Chicago: University of Chicago Press, 1977.

Williams, Rowan. "Barth on the Triune God." In *Karl Barth: Studies of His Theological Method.* Edited by S. W. Sykes, 147–93. Oxford: Clarendon, 1979.

INDEX OF NAMES AND SUBJECTS